THE CHURCH
COMES HOME

ROBERT & JULIA BANKS

THE CHURCH

COMES HOME

A New Base for Community and Mission

AN ALBATROSS BOOK

© Robert and Julia Banks 1986

Published in Australia and New Zealand by
Albatross Books Pty Ltd
PO Box 320, Sutherland
NSW 2232, Australia
in the United States of America by
Albatross Books
PO Box 131, Claremont
CA 91711, USA
and in the United Kingdom by
Lion Publishing
Peter's Way, Sandy Lane West
Littlemore, Oxford OX4 5HG, England

First edition 1986, published as *The Home Church*
Revised edition 1989, published as *The Church Comes Home*

National Library of Australia
Cataloguing-in-Publication data

    Banks, Roberts, 1939-
    The Church Comes Home

    Simultaneously published: Littlemore, Oxford:
    Lion Publishing

    ISBN 0 86760 023 3 (Albatross)
    ISBN 0 7459 1185 4 (Lion)

    1. House churches I. Banks, Julia, 1940-
    II. Title

    262'.001

Cover photo: Roger Hanlon
Typeset by Rochester Communications Group, Sydney
Printed by Singapore National Printers

Companions to this volume:

R. Banks, *Paul's Idea of Community: The Earliest Home Churches in their Historical Setting*, Sydney: Anzea, 1979

R. Banks, *Going to Church in the First Century: An Eyewitness Account*, Sydney: Hexagon, 1985
(study guides available)

*To the first generation
of children who have grown up
in a home church setting*

Contents

Preface

WE HAVE WAITED MANY YEARS to write this book and even now put pen to paper with some reluctance. It draws primarily on our experience of home church life over the last sixteen years, as well as on what we have learned from assisting congregations to develop home churches themselves. We do not make any claims to knowing everything about the home church way of meeting. The book's shortcomings are all too obvious to us. We look forward to learning more from the comment and discussion that the book will undoubtedly stimulate.

A word of explanation is needed about our use of the term 'home church'. In the light of related terms, it would be easy to misunderstand what we have in mind.

The term 'home church' should not be confused with what is commonly referred to as 'the house church movement'. This latter expression has several meanings, none of which accurately describe what we mean. In England and Canada, 'the house church movement' refers to those charismatic groups which have seceded from the mainstream churches, setting up separate denominational networks. Though most of these groups began in houses, the importance of the home as the key venue for church has largely disappeared. Such groups usually see themselves in opposition to the traditional denominations. Large Sunday morning gatherings now dominate their activities and they have largely written off the institutional church as a context for renewal. Only one network of charismatic congregations appears to have retained a strong emphasis upon the home and pursued a more ecumenical approach to other Christians.

The term 'house church' is also beginning to be used in mainline church circles for any Christian meeting held in a home. This is an unhelpful way of talking. Meetings in a home for Bible study, prayer and the exercise of gifts are not 'church' in the full sense. Nor are meetings in a home for evangelism, fellowship and pastoral care. Generally, these meetings exclude children. They do not include all elements of what happens in 'church'. Those who attend them do not value them as highly as Sunday 'worship'. In the few cases where the home is a focus for 'church' in the fullest sense, it is regarded as a temporary expedient to be replaced as soon as possible by a proper building.

When we use the term 'home church', we are referring to small groups of people operating as a genuine extended Christian family, gathering for church in homes in a congregational, inter-denominational or non-denominational setting. Where 'home churches' exist in a congregational setting, these forms of gathering are fundamental to the framework of a typical local church, not merely an introductory step towards something else. Where they exist outside a denominational setting, they are part of a missionary endeavour to retain or reclaim Christians already lost by the mainline churches, or to reach non-Christians not being touched by them. While this form of home church life has its criticisms of mainline churches, it does not have a sectarian mentality. Rather it endeavours to encourage and help mainline churches to develop home churches themselves.

Writing this book has been a complex but rewarding effort. Although we are responsible for its form, and it is our names that appear on the cover, it is in fact the product of many hands. As in a home church meeting itself, the book is the result of a corporate effort. To the individual members of home churches and home churches as a whole who contributed to it, we extend our thanks. Independent, inter-denominational and congregationally-based home churches in both Australia and New Zealand gave both time and energy to supplying us with information and help.

Nevertheless, the final account is very much our interpretation. In this book we do not speak for all who belong to home churches. We have no right to do so. Many members of home churches would put things differently to the way we have here. We have simply tried to provide one coherent portrait of home church life.

We also wish to express our gratitude to Ruth and Clive Monty, Doris and Charles Rowland, and Jan and Ken Goodlet who generously cleared time to read and correct an earlier draft of the book and offer valuable insights and advice. John Waterhouse of Albatross Books Pty Ltd also gave patient and detailed attention to our initial draft. The book is immeasurably better for their efforts.

We also wish to thank the editors of the following publications for permission to include extracts from earlier articles or papers on the subject: 'A Foretaste of Christ's Kingdom', *On Being*, Vol.8, No.11, 1981, pp.58-62; 'The Early Church as a Caring Community and its Implications for Social Work Today', *Interchange*, No.30, 1982, pp.32-46 (reprinted in *Evangelical Review of Theology*, Vol.7, No.2, 1983, pp.310-327); 'Small is Beautiful : The Relevance of Paul's Idea of Community for the Local Church Today', *Theological Renewal*, Vol.22, 1982, pp.4-18 (reprinted in *Zadok Papers*, 1983, Series 2).

Robert and Julia Banks
September 1985
Canberra

P.S. We have felt it necessary to alter the names, places and events described by members of home churches in this book. In doing this, we have not changed the essential character of the incidents described. But we wanted to protect the individuals and groups concerned, especially in view of their openness and candour.

Introduction

ALL OVER THE WORLD the church has started to come home. It has been away for a long, long time. Only now and again in the course of its wanderings has it returned to the humble quarters from which it began. But now people of God in many countries have decided it is time for it to do so.

Some of them have turned their faces in this direction because they were weary or in great personal need. Others have come because they felt lost, lost in an impersonal institution or disenchanted by its preoccupation with self-preservation. There are those who have been hurt in the church and by it, and those whose instincts tell them there must be something more to church than they experience at present. A few commenced the journey because they stumbled across a signpost in their guidebook – the Bible – and this gave them a new orientation.

In some places political conditions were so intolerable, or the physical and social needs so great, that there was literally nowhere else to go. But all these, whatever their motivation or their starting point, are treading towards the one place: home – where the church began and where, at one level of its operation, it was always intended to be.

Although it is not counted amongst them, this gradual but universal homecoming of the church is one of the most significant social, as well as religious, movements of our time. Unlike the migrations of refugees or emigrants, it is a journeying *towards* home rather than a flight from it, though like them it does involve bidding farewell to familiar institutions and some measure of physical relocation. The church also has its refugees and emigrants, some living in exile, others moving from one denomination to another in search of something more.

Among many of these people there is a desire to regroup themselves in homes, either within the congregation or outside it, in order to engage more effectively in community and mission. Whether timidly or resolutely, uncertainly or confidently, all these know that they must leave behind some of the securities, comforts and landmarks of their previous church experience. Something is stirring within them; they are troubled by a divine disquiet; an edge of desperation has entered into their soul.

As in other respects today, this desperation is felt most keenly in the countries of the Two-thirds World, rather than in the West. There the issues are sharper, the problems more severe, the stakes higher. In Latin American countries in particular the church has begun to come home on a mass scale. Though many of its leaders initially supported this, now they feel threatened, as control more and more passes out of their hands into the hands of the people themselves.

In many communist lands, the church has only been able to survive by taking domestic form. In some countries, state authorities continue to regard such cells as subversive and do everything in their power to eradicate them. In others, they would like to see the recognised church co-opt and ultimately weaken them.

In the West, the number of Christians coming home to church is far fewer. Tranquillised by the satisfaction of their basic physical and political needs, and the possibilities offered them in an economically and ecclesiastically more open society, most have not allowed their deep psychic, social and religious needs to come sufficiently to the surface. Content to remain in whatever material and institutional far-country they have chosen for themselves, they have not yet heard the call of home insistently echoing about them.

But they surely cannot remain deaf to its voice for long. Nothing is more certain than the growth of unemployment and of an underclass in the West in the midst of greater work opportunities and affluence for the lucky ones. Nothing is more certain than the increasing centralisation of political, bureaucratic and technological power — and a consequent sense of powerlessness and insignificance among people at large. Nothing is more certain than the inability of large educational or ecclesiastical organisations to meet the needs or foster the capacities of those whom they serve. Nothing is more certain than the deepening crisis in personal identity, breakdown in family relationships, and trivialisation of friendship that we see all about us. The heart is going out of modern society and all the desperate attempts to regain it through psychological techniques, mystical exercises, discussion groups and social rearrangements are only compensating for what is happening or, in some cases, actually enlarging the vacuum.

Along with their neighbours, Christians in the West are going to feel their deprivation in these areas more and more keenly. Neither charismatic experiences nor the small group movements are enough in themselves to overcome it. The privatisation of the experience renders it incapable of genuinely transforming the way the church operates or creatively impinging on society at large — at least not in the way envisaged by John V. Taylor in his imaginative and powerful evocation of the wide-ranging activity of the 'go-between God'.[1] As C.M. Olsen notes:

> Although small groups have been utilised as a church renewal scheme, they have rarely been legitimised as a full expression of the church. They have been conceived as an adjunct for the personal growth of the participants... Meanwhile the 'real' church gathers in the sanctuary at eleven every Sunday... the small group is relegated to serving as a means to a larger end... In this role [it] cannot become anything but a halfway house.[2]

---

1 J.V. Taylor, *The Go-Between God*, London: SCM, 1972

2 C.M. Olsen, *The Base Church: Creating Community Through Multiple Forms*, Atlanta: Forum House, 1973, p.16

This is why in some places the heart only beats faintly in the church, providing too little warmth to meet the needs of those within it. For home is where the heart is, as the old saying goes, and the church is still some distance away. Its various experiments with small groups, house fellowships, pastoral clusters, charismatic cells and the like have pointed in the right direction, but have not been wholehearted enough to take the church as far as it needs to go. All represent a stage on the way, but all stop short of the full return God longs for. He waits for these experiments to be taken further. He is willing to go out and meet those who attempt this, conducting them the remaining steps of the way. He aches for this to happen, for at heart God is a family person. He loves to have his children around him in familial surroundings. He knows that they are most at home there and that there they can be most at home with him.

Only when the church comes home to him in this way does it have a chance of becoming the home of a heartless world, the source of its comfort and the stimulus for its change. To a significant extent, the future of the world – the quality of its lifestyle, relationships and structures – lies dormant within the genuinely communal groups that are being formed now. What we do in this area – or do not do, as the case may be – will be decisive for the world in which our children live.

1

The inside story:

Some word pictures of home churches

HOME CHURCHES ARE BETTER experienced than merely explained. When they are explained, people either assume they know what you are talking about when they probably do not, or are puzzled and ask fairly early in the conversation, 'But what goes on in a home church anyway?'

Those who assume they understand what a home church is are generally equating it with a cell or a house group. People read their own meaning into terms like 'informal', 'commitment', 'relationships', 'learning', 'concern', 'love', 'sharing' and 'fellowship' even after prolonged explanations. This is best demonstrated by a real-life story. There were two friends, one of whom attended a home church and the other a small group in a congregation. Understanding the difference between the two was a problem until both of them saw a dramatised version of the booklet entitled *Going to Church in the First Century*. The person in the small group then honestly responded: 'Despite all the conversations and the talks I have heard, I have never been able to understand the difference between what you do when you meet with your home church and what we do in our small group. But now, having watched this version of what early Christians did when they met together in a home, I can *see* the difference.'

Those who are puzzled by the home church idea probably find it hard to relate the word 'church' to anything but a building and what happens inside it on a Sunday morning: they have genuine difficulty in seeing a meeting 'in a home' as anything more than a small-scale version of a service in a church building. Some years ago, for example, our home church received an invitation to appear in the television series, *The Sunburnt Soul*. After several weeks' discussion over such matters as whether the intrusion of TV cameras would inhibit us and uncertainty as to how the sequence would be edited and presented, we agreed to go ahead. As it happened, the television crew did not act as a restraint upon our meeting: if anything, we were less inhibited than usual. The editing and presentation of the sequence were handled with considerable care: there was obviously a genuine desire on the producer's part to do justice to the meeting. However, because his understanding of 'church' was governed largely by the traditional associations of the word, he selected out of the meeting those moments which had the greatest affinity with a typical church service. He did this well, but it meant that such features as the quality of relationships between the members, the infectious joy present in the gathering and the recognition of the presence of God in even the most ordinary things (for example, washing up together) did not come very strongly into the picture. He filmed them, but ultimately did not *see* them.

The only way to fully appreciate the difference between a home church gathering and the meeting of a small group or the holding of a worship service is to attend one. Indeed, one needs to attend several times, for in the beginning there is the tendency to see or not see what one is looking for rather than what is actually there.

How then can we, through the medium of print, convey something of what it is like to belong to a home church? We can only succeed by using word pictures: drawing on first-hand accounts which attempt to visualise what happens and sense the spirit that is present. If some repetition is involved, this is quite deliberate. It is important to 'see' more than once and from more than one angle.

A typical meeting: a narrative account
If you stand in the street near 23 Hendene Road, Winbourne, at around 9.30 a.m. on a Sunday, you will see seven or eight cars turn into a steep, tree-lined driveway and

go down to a large, white, two-storey house. You will possibly see some children arrive on bikes or on foot, and enter the house as well. The children and the car occupants are all heading for the lounge room and kitchen of Naomi and John Whiting, and the regular Sunday morning house church meeting which is held there.

The early arrivals usually find Naomi and John and their boys tidying up the kitchen or lighting the fire in winter. There is kissing and greeting, conversation and lots of laughter, people putting their contributions to the mid-meeting morning tea on to the kitchen bench. Whoever has chosen the music for that week hands the list to John or Ivor (our music maestros) and they pull out the appropriate music.

At 9.30 sharp nothing very much happens. By about 9.45 most people have drifted into the lounge room and seated themselves, John or Ivor playing urgent introductions on the piano. Ian and Robyn get out their guitars to accompany. Colin seats himself at his drums. The week's meeting co-ordinator asks people to begin. (The meeting co-ordinator, as well as the study leader for the week, the childminders, the children's talk person, the communion leader, the morning tea organiser and the person who chooses the songs are all volunteer positions and are organised at the fortnightly members' meetings.) The children hand out hymn books, young Matthew goes round offering percussion-and-shake instruments from the instrument box, other children pull out any song sheets from under the lounge that are needed. Whoever is nearest holds up the song sheets required, usually assisted by a toddler standing on a stool, and after a piano introduction we begin to sing.

Mostly we sing between six and twelve songs. We chatter a little in between them and greet latecomers. If there are songs with actions, most of us do the actions. Sometimes some of us dance to songs like 'In the presence of your people'. The children rattle and bang their instruments, but in more thoughtful songs we ask them to put the instruments down. Whenever the co-ordinator decides, but usually about halfway through the songs, we stop for the children's talk.

The children's talk varies a great deal in format. Sometimes the person giving it just sits on a stool, surrounded by the children seated on the floor, and reads a story straight from the *Lion Children's Bible*, through which we are progressing more or less systematically. Sometimes the person giving the children's talk illustrates the story or a point in it with demonstrations (e.g. Soma cubes), gets the children to act the parts in it, or asks questions and gives out little prizes at the end. Sometimes there are drawings or maps. Sometimes we aim more at the older children, sometimes more at the younger ones. The older children often help the younger ones to answer questions or take their parts in activities. The children's talk can take from five minutes to about twenty, and the number of songs following depends to a degree on its length.

Anywhere between 10.15 and 10.30 a.m. we start our prayer time. Here, too, the format varies. When the group was smaller we usually stayed together, mentioned the things we wanted to pray about and then prayed together. Now the group has grown larger, we often talk together about prayer-points, but then split up into two or more groups to pray. Occasionally we split the group according to ages — children together, teenagers together and adults together — but more often it is split arbitrarily, with one section of the room going to the kitchen, another section adjourning to the sunny courtyard and another staying in the lounge room. (One of our bulkier members once suggested that he could be one group and everyone else the other!) When groups finish praying, they wander into the kitchen or lounge and some people begin to get the morning tea ready.

Naomi has usually put the urn on in the morning or filled the kettles if the fire is going, but the morning tea organiser now makes the tea and, with lots of assistance from other members, gets the table set, the children's drinks poured and the food people have brought taken to the table. There is a lot of chat and general enquiry while this is going on, the smaller children being encouraged to have a run around outside, if the weather permits, to discharge surplus energy.

When the morning tea is ready, we gather around the table

but, before the tea is poured, we usually have communion. I say 'usually' because at one stage we had it after or during prayer time, seated in the lounge room, and we still have it this way sometimes. At other times the person leading communion does something really innovative, like Adrian taking us outside to play with a parachute as an object lesson in how we must co-operate and work together as one. Once recently, too, Naomi organised a group 'encouragement session' as our communion. But mostly, the person taking communion will stand at the morning tea-table and read either from the Bible or some other book, perhaps talk about something significant, and pray briefly. After this, bread and drink may be passed around as a more formal communion, or we may just eat and drink our morning tea together as our symbol of communion.

When communion is finished, the tea is poured, the plates are passed and tongues go into high gear. Many of the children circulate with plates of food, offering them to others. If someone – old or young – has a birthday that week, we put candles on a cake (or a banana or the like if we don't have a cake) and sing them a rousing 'happy birthday'.

We don't hurry morning tea; it is as important as every other part of the meeting. But any time between 11.00 and 11.30 a.m., depending upon when morning tea began, the co-ordinator starts exhibiting signs of nervousness and asks who is taking the children. Then the one or two child-minders call the children and take them out. It is up to them to decide which activity they will pursue with the children. Some take them for bushwalks or to the park; others organise games or crafts; some follow up the children's talk of the morning. Often one adult will take the smaller children, another the older. The younger teenagers, who don't want to go to the study, usually play a game like Ungame or Monopoly or sometimes go on bushwalks with all the children. (We are currently trying to work out and organise appropriate activities for the teenagers.)

Meanwhile, back in the lounge room, the adults seat themselves while Noel sets up his tape recorder to tape the morning's study. Occasionally we might pray about some private or delicate matter which can't be mentioned in the general prayer time, and then the person leading the study begins.

In the past we have studied Gospels, epistles and books of the Old Testament, as well as various biblical themes or helpful Christian books. At the moment we are studying Richard Foster's book, *Celebration of Discipline*.[1] We listen to the study leader; we give opinions; we ask questions; we discuss. We go off at tangents and follow red herrings. We usually find the study time too short, because the children are almost always brought back very punctually at 12.00. Those who have time sometimes sit for another ten minutes or so, continuing the discussion.

After this, we whisk around tidying up and say goodbye. The cars go up the drive, escorted by Miffy, the Whiting's car-chasing dog, and the house church meeting is over for another week.

You will notice that the operative word in this description has been 'usually'. The order of procedure is not binding; members are free to suggest changes in order and content when they feel that this is appropriate. The aim, as one of our members says, is 'structured informality'. We quite consciously try to avoid rituals and ruts. But basically our meeting together is to honour, glorify and obey God, to upbuild one another, and to celebrate our unity and love as God's children and members of Christ's church.

Facets of home church life: personal journal entries
(a) A birthday celebration and its aftermath
We celebrated Bob's fortieth birthday last night. It wasn't meant to be a party, just the usual birthday cake at dessert time, but somehow the celebration atmosphere spilled over into the whole evening. Most of us had gathered when the Lesleys appeared. There were lots of wolf whistles and teasing when Bob came in wearing a suit. He looked very elegant and I saw an aspect of him that I'd never noticed. Wearing the suit seemed to temper his usual boisterous

---

1 R. Foster, *Celebration of Discipline*, Hodder and Stoughton: London, 1980

spirits and he was more at ease and charming than I've seen him before. He confirmed that he'd worn the suit to work as a way of marking the day as something special. Four-year-old Alex was almost beside himself with excitement as he shared 'Daddy's birthday' with us. Apparently the family gave Bob breakfast in bed and helped him open his presents – a new record and some books.

While we ate our meal the teenagers gave Bob quite a ribbing about being 'over the hill' and 'on the downward slope'. He takes such delight in teasing them that they were obviously pleased at this excuse to have the boot on the other foot. When Mary produced the cake ablaze with candles, the toddlers' eyes were like saucers. Martin and Sarah tried several times to count the candles and had to give up. When the moment came to blow the candles out, Bob invited the toddlers to help him. You should have seen the serious expressions on their faces as they puffed out their cheeks. After all the huffing and puffing, there was one candle still alight for Bob to extinguish to the sound of much laughter, clapping and cheering. It was a lovely cake – one of Mary's chocolate specials. Stephen produced a bottle of 'bubbly' and we all had a sip to celebrate.

The most moving part of the evening came during the prayer time when people one by one spontaneously gave thanks to God for Bob, Stephen suggesting that we all gather round and lay hands on him. There was such a feeling of being family, of being one. I couldn't help but reflect on how Bob has matured over the past ten years. Rare now are the days of self-doubt, of walking over others' feelings with hobnail boots and moodiness. In fact, he and Jane have been an example to us all! How effectively they have exercised hospitality: to us, their neighbours and those with whom they have contact at work, home and school. How regularly they keep contact with their non-Christian friends, giving them time and, in their low-profile way, seeking to witness to them.

(b) Some surprises in praying

We had a tremendous time of prayer tonight. It was one of those occasions when we were all on the same wavelength and were very conscious of the fact that God's Spirit was guiding us. I have learnt more about prayer since I've been part of this home church than I have ever done in my life before. Not that our prayer times are always like tonight – the very fact that I choose to comment about it should be testimony to that. In fact, sometimes they are so laboured that you feel you want to get out and crank them into life.

I've never been able to work out why there are these fluctuations. Sometimes it's obvious that at the end of the week people are tired and praying is hard work. Yet at other times when people have been just as tired, someone has begun with a prayer saying how weary they feel and, before you know it, we've been praying for an hour.

We've had some very funny prayer times. Like the time Edith prayed that God would help Stephen find a dentist who could relieve his toothache even though it was a long weekend – when all the time he was sitting beside Susan, a dentist! The group just roared with laughter. Then there was the occasion when the group was much smaller and we had what fourteen-year-old Andrew referred to as a 'prayer tennis match'. Apparently Edith and I were on the same wavelength over something and the prayers went back and forth between us. Andrew describes it thus: 'Edith smashed a prayer away down centre court. Anne scrambled forward, just got her racket to it and dropped a prayer over the net. Edith had foreseen this and was ready to send a prayer down to the back corner. Being younger, Anne raced across the court in time to lob a prayer high into the air which landed right at Edith's feet.'

He says the match went on for half-an-hour. I'm sure that's an exaggeration, but one thing's for sure, he's not going to let either of us forget it.

There was another occasion where a new baby was being welcomed and dedicated. A certain four-year-old prayed earnestly that if there were any other mummies and daddies who wanted to have another baby that God should let them know that he thought it was a good idea, too! The suppressed laughter of the adults had the foundations shaking.

(c) When things go wrong

Since most of the children now fall into the pre-school

category rather than toddlers, we decided three months ago to try meeting alternate weeks on Sunday afternoon rather than Friday night. It's gone reasonably well, with one exception – Adam.

One of the adults looks after the children while the others have a Bible study or discussion. All the other children have been very co-operative, but Adam has been coming in and out of the meeting like a yoyo. No one would mind that, if only he didn't insist on always drawing attention to himself, thereby interrupting the discussion or prayer. His parents don't seem to notice what a nuisance he is. Since they are fairly new members of the church, we're all a bit wary of stepping in. We're not too certain how they would react. Whoever has been minding the children has done their best to keep Adam outside, so far unsuccessfully.

One week it got too much for Bob. When Adam came in for the third time and his parents made no attempt to persuade him to stay with the other children, up jumped Bob, swung Adam over his shoulder and marched outside with him. We all held our breath, not daring to look at Mary and Brian. The meeting went on and there were no more interruptions. Bob spoke with Mary and Brian after the meeting, but he said they'd raised no objection. In fact, he got the impression that they were relieved someone had done something about it. Hopefully it's begun to teach them something about their own responsibility in the matter.

The following Sunday Monica minded the children and took them down to the park. That was a tactful way of dealing with the Adam problem. Others followed Monica's example and took the children to the park. Several meetings later it rained and David wasn't able to do so. To everyone's relief, although Adam came in towards the end of our prayer time, he was content to sit quietly at Mary's feet.

*   *   *

It was a rather frustrating meeting today. We were very small in number for various reasons and those who were there weren't, if you know what I mean. They may have been there in body, but appeared to be absent in spirit. I had the job of hosting the meeting and it was like trying to muster a recalcitrant herd of cattle. Half of those who did come arrived late, which meant that the rest of us found it difficult to sing with any gusto or enthusiasm.

Even when Thomas began to introduce the meal with a dramatic reading from one of the Gospels, one of Lydia's children had a tantrum. Although his mother removed him from the room, his screams were still a distraction.

After the meal we made a few plans for the coming week and I began to introduce our discussion. 'I have to go in ten minutes,' announced Larry, one of the bachelors in the group. 'I'm going on a picnic with some friends.'

'Yes,' said Lydia, 'I think we'd better go soon, too. The children are too obstreperous this morning.'

'But my study,' I thought. And while I was thinking Joanna began to speak as if she'd heard none of what had just been said.

'I've been watching the Olympic Games and I must say I'm really impressed with the dedication and discipline of the athletes. It reminded me of those passages in Paul's letters about running the race. I was challenged about the lack of discipline in my relationship with God.'

Someone made a half-hearted reply. But Joanna wouldn't let it lie there. She seemed totally unaware of the lack of interest and began to say something more about her admiration for the single-mindedness of the athletes. Bob, who had been sitting in the corner and appeared to be totally withdrawn, stirred into life to say he didn't think single-mindedness was necessarily a good thing. For the next five minutes we proceeded to talk at cross-purposes until our peacemaker pointed out that both sides in the debate were really saying similar things. Our discussion then took a more constructive turn and only came to a close twenty minutes later when Larry said he really had to go. We agreed that, as we had only begun to scratch the surface of a very important topic, we would return to it at a later date.

I felt exhausted when they'd all gone. There had been so many distractions and so much to keep an eye on that I hadn't got very much out of the meeting. I'm sure Lydia must have wondered whether it had been worth her while coming at all. As I sipped a cup of coffee afterwards and reflected on what a frustrating morning it had been, it suddenly occurred to me that I could never remember Joanna sharing anything of her inner concerns with us before. I thought about that for a while and concluded that, despite the distractions, in one respect it had been a red-letter day after all!

(d) A welcome and an argument

As David said to two guests after the meeting yesterday: 'Now you've seen the agony and the ecstasy of home churching.' The ecstasy was contained in the first half of the meeting. We'd gathered with the express purpose of welcoming the second child of Stephen and Rose James into our church. Emma was just ten days old – her first attendance at the group. Stephen had told us the previous week that when he and Rose brought her along to the group (most of us had seen her through the glass at the hospital, of course) they would like us all to dedicate her to God. So he and Rose encouraged us through the week to think of some contribution we would like to make to the occasion.

When the James' arrived tonight, they were the centre of attention. Some of the younger members had not seen Emma before, since the hospital forbids visitors under five years of age unless they are 'family'. Sarah, the James' other child, was obviously very pleased with her new sister and very protective of her. Stephen's chest was twice its normal size and Rose had a smile from ear to ear. Everyone made the usual noises about how small babies are, how much hair she had, what long eyelashes and so on. Emma seemed to accept all the attention as if it were her due.

We were later than usual getting under way with the singing and the meal. The children were just beginning to get restless when David suggested to them that he bring Emma (who was now asleep after a good feed) and put her bassinet on the floor in the centre of the room. David said a few words about why we'd gathered – to welcome Emma into our church family and to dedicate her to God. He then invited the little ones to sing a song for Emma, which they did: 'Bananas in pyjamas'! Monica and Reg spent twenty minutes or so reading out all the promises that they'd found in the Bible for parents with respect to their children. At the end of their reading they gave a typed copy to Stephen and Rose to keep so they could from time to time remind themselves of them. Mary and Brian sang a song of welcome which they had composed especially for the occasion. Jane read a poem out of A.A. Milne's *Winnie the Pooh* and presented Rose (who is a great A.A. Milne fan) with a copy to read to Emma as she grew up.

At the suggestion of eight-year-old Ruth, we sang 'Jesus loves me'. I read another Bible passage ('Suffer the little children...') and then we gathered in the centre of the room around Stephen, Rose, Sarah and Emma to pray. The prayers ranged from thanking God for Emma's safe arrival, prayers for Stephen, Rose and Sarah, prayers for Emma herself, and prayers for ourselves with respect to our responsibility to both Emma and her family. There was a quiet, encouraging and highly relevant prophecy from David for Stephen and Rose.

When we finished praying, Terry explained that Lyn wanted to do a dance of welcome – one she had choreographed herself to the tune of Brahms' *Lullaby*. However, at the last minute when they were leaving home to come to church, they hadn't been able to find the record. So we were requested to hum the tune while Lyn danced. It was a very moving occasion. In the truly unselfconscious manner that only a nine-year-old can manage, Lyn danced daintily around the bassinet. It's a pity Emma was asleep and missed seeing how Lyn, with arms outstretched in welcome and a perfectly executed bow, concluded her dance. Silence reigned for some time. Lyn with her final gesture had managed to capture the spirit of the whole occasion.

The 'littlies' went to bed while the dishes were done and we settled down with cups of coffee to make some practical decisions about our gatherings over the next few weeks. We planned a picnic to be held in the Botanical Gardens two weeks hence and then I suggested a change to one of our usual ways of doing things. Before we realised what was happening, we were in the midst of the most heated debate we'd ever had. Debate – it was more like a fight! How on earth could we have gone from the sublime to the ridiculous in so short a space of time? We were all very sobered by the affair and, as tempers cooled, we began to apologise to God and each other. Some of the tension still remains, however, and we're all likely to feel rather vulnerable for a while. None of us seems to find it easy to cope with conflict.

(e) Two divine interruptions

The funniest thing happened tonight during our prayer time. One of our thoughtful silences was interrupted by a voice from fourteen-year-old Andrew's bedroom, where the older children were playing. Instantly the adults as one person opened their eyes and looked quizzically around the room. No one spoke for fear of missing the reply to ten-year-old Katie's question: 'What do you think of abortion?'

'What's abortion?' asked nine-year-old Ruth.

'Oh, you know, getting rid of babies before they're born,' answered worldly-wise Andrew.

Twelve-year-old Robert then proceeded to instruct them all in the pros and cons of the abortion debate, ably assisted by Anna. It was a fascinating, quasi-theological discussion. Silence fell and then Robert asked, 'Did you see "The Thing" on TV last Saturday?'

'Wasn't it great!' enthused Ruth. We adults laughed softly.

Monica exclaimed, 'The things you learn about your children! I had no idea Robert knew all that about abortion.'

'I feel quite proud of Katie,' confessed her mother. 'I was nowhere near grappling with issues like abortion when I was her age.' There were a few grunts of agreement and we returned to our conversation with God.

*   *   *

I felt sorry for Stephen last week. It was the second time he'd come prepared to lead our next study on what the Bible has to say about Satan and the second time that it had been postponed. When I commiserated with him after the meeting, he replied: 'I'd be tempted to think that maybe Satan didn't want us to talk about him if I didn't believe that both discussions were God-sent.' I agreed. We've had to put off studies before, but usually only for one week as far as I could remember.

This interruption crept up on us unawares. We were sitting eating dessert when someone asked Mary how she was. (Mary's been sick for about six months and, despite repeated trips to the doctor and various tests, not to mention our prayers on her behalf, she continues to get slowly worse.) Mary confided that she was actually feeling very depressed about it all. After all, it's no fun trying to run a home and look after two active toddlers when you are lacking in energy. The group members then began to question and talk with her. As they did this over the next three-quarters of an hour, various experiences were recounted, Bible passages mentioned and thoughts shared. Certain people showed such discernment in the questions they asked and comments they made. Others like Steve conveyed how much they cared by their tone of voice and expressions on their faces. Only one person adopted a 'let me give you the answer to your problem' approach.

While this was going on Mary made several apologies for taking up our time, but we all hastened to assure her 'that's what we're here for'. Someone asked what we could do to be of greater assistance practically. Poor Mary and Brian were too embarrassed and said we already did enough by providing casseroles and cakes, and minding the children occasionally. Monica also offered to do the ironing – quite a generous offer on her part for we all know how she hates ironing! David suggested that Mary should sit on a chair in the middle of the room while those who watched could join him in putting their arms around her as we prayed. Then Stephen suggested that we should sing the song 'Farther along', the chorus of which runs:

Farther along, we'll know all about it,
Farther along, we'll understand why. . .

It was a moving event, with tears being shed by many. I have to confess to not being exactly dry-eyed myself. Afterwards Mary was given many hugs and kisses, while Brian didn't miss out on his share either.

(f) Some meals – and their introductions
It was the Mowbrays' turn to introduce the meal tonight. As

we gathered around the table, Peter read 1 Corinthians 15. Alice prayed a very simple and moving prayer, giving thanks to God for the gift of his Son and that through his death and resurrection we are made new, washed free of our sins. After that she passed around a loaf of bread which she'd freshly baked herself that afternoon. As we each broke off a piece, she reminded us that, just as the loaf was broken for us, so was Jesus' body. Peter produced a bottle of his best red and, as he opened it, he reminded us that just as the wine was poured out into our glasses so was Christ's blood for our redemption. It was done very simply but it had a real effect on everyone.

*   *   *

As we stood around the table tonight, David asked the children to name the food that was on the table. There was bread and butter, orange juice, wine, lasagne, a chicken concoction, some cold meat, a bowl of green salad and some coleslaw. We had to agree it was quite a mixture. But, as David reminded us, we knew from past experience that it would make a very tasty meal and that we wouldn't want to be standing around a table which contained only bread and butter, or only coleslaw. It was the *variety* that made the meal rather special.

Then he turned to four-year-old Alex and asked him if Stephen was like Reg. No! Was Rose like Mary? No! And so on, until it was determined that we were all different.

'Just like the food on the table,' concluded David, 'we are all different and we all have something special to contribute to our coming together as a family.' Then he invited each one of us to say a short prayer of thanks to God. As I waited for my turn to heap my plate with goodies, I looked around at the various members of our church and was struck anew by the diversity that exists. In many ways we couldn't be more different. Yet God in his wisdom has brought us together in order to make us one. Some of the differences are hard to take at times – and create some tensions between us – but how much would we lose if there were only a grey uniformity or superficial harmony among us?

*   *   *

We've decided to try some breakfast meetings. This came about as a sort of compromise. One small group of people within the church was finding regular Sunday afternoon meetings too much – first, because the children got too tired by the end of them and there was whingeing and fighting; second, because it meant they could no longer have Sunday afternoons for visiting relatives and friends. They were pushing for a return to Friday nights, but another group was just as opposed to that because they were too tired after the week at work. So a compromise was made – one Friday night a month (without the children), one Sunday breakfast (8.30 a.m.) and two 10.30 a.m. meetings on Sundays, one of which was to cater especially for the needs of the children.

*   *   *

It was so lovely this morning that we had breakfast out-of-doors. It worked very well. We had orange juice, cereals, muffins and coffee. David suggested we begin our meeting with 'Morning has broken' and a very appropriate choice it was! Not only were we able to sing about birds and dew on the grass, but we were actually able to see them around us. It was the James' turn to introduce the meal. Stephen read the passage where Jesus, after his resurrection, prepares breakfast for the disciples on the shore of Galilee. Rose prayed a very moving prayer, thanking God for the empty tomb and the resurrection of Jesus, for the fact that Jesus was present with us as we gathered in his name, and for the example of Jesus – that though he was Lord of Lords, yet he waited on his disciples. She asked that we might also seek to serve each other, rather than demanding that others attend to our needs.

During breakfast Rose read the children a story. I think the adults enjoyed it as much as the children. Then Don and I took the children off to the park. The adults, having decided that it was too hot to stay out-of-doors any longer, returned to the lounge room to begin their discussion of Jacques

Ellul's *The Politics of God and the Politics of Man*.[2] In view
of the impending elections and the fact that a number of
people in the group are involved in government administration, this should be most worthwhile.

A combined home church gathering: a letter

It was a wet Good Friday and members of three home
churches met to celebrate the source of all celebrations, the
death and resurrection of Jesus our Lord.

The meeting place was the converted double garage of one
of the member families (it had been changed some years
previously into a rumpus room attached to the house). With
carpets on the floor and comfortable seating, it made an
ideal venue for this kind of occasional get-together, as well
as for the leisure activities of the host family. People
streamed into the warmth out of the rain, shedding wet
weather gear at the door (excepting little Alex's new yellow
gum boots which he refused to take off, even for sleeping).
Contributions for our breakfast were taken to the kitchen.

By 9.00 a.m. all were assembled. There were fifty people,
all sizes and ages, including babies and toddlers. There was
no compulsion to attend, but not one member was absent.
We felt that God had drawn us together and this sense of
oneness continued through the meeting.

Members of one group had planned the outline of the
service and chosen some hymns, and had asked the other
groups to be responsible for various sections of the meeting.
No one really knew what the whole service would contain.

The first group started, when all were settled in chairs or
on the floor, with prayer and readings on the Last Supper.
Annette had baked some unleavened bread which was
passed around in a basket for all to share in silence. The
toddlers were free to move about, but at this early stage they
were all quiet. Peace settled on everyone as we thought
about Jesus and the disciples in the upper room, and the
events that were to follow.

Our thoughts moved to the crucifixion, members of

---

2 J. Ellul, *The Politics of God and the Politics of Man*, Eerdmans:
Grand Rapids, 1977

another group singing 'When I survey the wondrous cross' to a gentle guitar accompaniment. Alistair spoke on what Good Friday meant to him. God is not an absentee landlord, he said, but someone who chose to suffer as we do, to share our lot and be one of us. This had meant a great deal to him at a formative stage in his Christian life.

Another group took us on to the resurrection, and did this by means of a dramatic reading. The story was of a caterpillar who discovered the purpose of his life when he became a butterfly. He had spent all his life battling to beat his fellows in the 'climb to the top', had trodden on others in the process and had decided to withdraw from competition to live with a little yellow lady caterpillar. When that failed to satisfy him, he had gone back to the competition, finally to be led by the lady to his true future, which meant a kind of death before transformation. Parts of the story were shared out between children and adults in the group and no one needed an explanation afterwards to see the story as a picture of what Christ made possible for us through his own death and resurrection. We prayed and sang in gratitude and, before breakfast was shared, Arthur read to us what Jesus had said to his disciples when he shared food and drink with them on that last night.

Breakfast was hot cross buns and homemade breads of various kinds, with butter and honey and preserves. We drank fruit juices, tea and coffee and recalled other occasions in the past when we had shared bread and wine before the informal meal. On one memorable occasion, someone had brought champagne – an inspired choice, we felt, for such a significant celebration as Easter Sunday – and we had joined in a simple Jewish dance to express our joy and delight at Christ's living presence among us.

Breakfast continued with a shuttle service of hot tea and coffee, the sudden appearance (and disappearance) of hot sausage rolls, and good conversation. Members exchanged news, offered help, played with one another's children and finally carried away the breakfast things when there was no further need for them. Annette produced a basket of chocolate Easter eggs in brilliant wrappings; these were passed round, first to the children, then to adults who considered themselves children. The meeting broke up at the end of the morning. We had a strong sense that God had been with us, that something stronger than mere friendship was at work, making these larger meetings as significant to us as the smaller, more intimate ones.

Conclusion

As the narrative, journal entries and letter indicate, home churches contain a considerable variety both within and between their particular forms of meeting. There is no such thing as *the* home church approach, style of worship or way of gathering. As one of the extracts put it: 'Our order of procedure is not binding, and members are free to suggest changes in order and content when they feel it is appropriate. . . What we aim for is "structured informality".'

This means that the way an individual home church organises its gatherings will vary not only in incidentals from week to week, or in the general sequence its activities follow, but over a longer period of time may go through some major changes as well. Every new member who comes into the group, every step towards maturity that one of its members makes, every experience the group undergoes – positive or negative – can shape its life in a new way. In this lies the vitality and freedom of the home church when it is operating properly. It can alter its way of meeting from one week to the next if all the members discern that this will be more constructive.

Home churches also differ from one another. No two are alike. Sometimes the differences are relatively small, sometimes quite considerable. Of course, there are stable elements in all home church meetings, such as singing, prayers, learning, communion and sharing, but the form these take and the way they are mixed together can exhibit tremendous variety. Much depends on the class background or professional composition of the people in the group, their ecclesiastical upbringing or allegiance, the stage of maturity members or the group as a whole have reached, the age of the children within it and the intellectual level of the adults, the forms of Christianity which have influenced those who belong to it, and whether the group is city- or rural-based.

This variation is as it should be. It adds richness to the wider body of Christ, creating the possibility for diversity within a particular local congregation or denominational tradition, as well as between churches and Christian traditions. There is room for ethnic, cultural and educational variety between home churches, even within the one congregation, provided those who belong to them also express their unity by meeting together as a whole.

It is not only certain common elements which home church meetings share within their diversity, but a common spirit and ethos. The former includes such aspects as care, commitment, integrity and joy; the latter openness, informality, relevance and a concern to break down the artificial distinctions between worship and life. Not everyone possesses these to the same degree or displays them in the same way. Home churches seek this spirit and ethos partly because those who join them feel these qualities are important for their spiritual welfare. They also sense that they are crucial in any attempt to commend the church and the gospel today to the increasing number of people who are unimpressed with the impersonality and respectability – if not the aloofness and unreality – of many ecclesiastical institutions. Most of those who join or found home churches have experienced something of that impersonality and unreality themselves. They have partly felt 'outsiders' inside their own churches, as if only part of themselves was engaged in worship and service. For some, belonging to a home church is a way of staying 'in', rather than drifting 'out' into the no-man's-land of solo or purely para-church Christianity.

It is the hope and belief of those involved in home churches that their stories also connect up with the ongoing story of God's liberation of humankind from all that would imprison and diminish it. They seek to become a contemporary expression of the spirit, and Spirit, that they find in the pages of the Acts of the Apostles. There, too, we find singing, prayers, learning, communion and sharing – indeed Christian community in a genuine, provocative and, at times, disturbing form. But there, too, it is combined with care, commitment, integrity and joy – as also with openness, informality, relevance and a concern to break down the artificial distinction between sacred and secular.

Ultimately home church meetings, as with church services of any kind, stand or fall according to how faithfully they reproduce the life that the Spirit first released — and continues to release — into the world.

2

In the beginning:

Home churches in the New Testament

WE HAVE LOOKED AT SOME ACTIVITIES of home churches today. If the home church is more than a fad, what are the roots? How did this way of meeting affect the early Christians' life together and their mission to the world?

We will concentrate on Paul's writings in answering these questions, for they provide us with more information than any other. First, however, three matters require clarifying.

At the outset we are faced with a problem of definition. The word 'church' today refers to a wide variety of entities: the body of Christians in a particular locality, the building in which they meet, the denomination to which they belong, the totality of Christians in the world – even the full number of believers alive or dead. In the first century, word usage was much simpler. 'Church' generally signified the regular gatherings of Christians, whether meeting as a small home-based group or a larger, city-wide affair. Less frequently, it referred to the ongoing heavenly assembly around Christ in which all Christians now participate, by virtue of their inclusion in him, even as they go about their everyday activities.

These two ideas are closely related: the local churches are the expression in time and space of their heavenly counterpart. But it is in the *first* of these two senses that we will mostly be using the word. This means that we shall concentrate on the actual experience of community which small groups of Christians shared as they regularly met together to further their common ends. Strange as it may seem, this usage of the term does not result in a more restricted view. Instead, it has the advantage of preserving a vital first-century perspective.

Along with the problem of definition, we are faced with a second difficulty. How are we to visualise these small communities in operation? It is not only our use of the word 'church' which has undergone change, but our understanding of what it involves. It requires a considerable act of imagination to divorce our minds from what customarily takes place on a Sunday today and mentally re-create what happened in the house of Aquila and Priscilla in first-century Rome.[1] To begin, we have to remember that the 'church in the home' was the basic form of early Christian community life (cf. Romans 16:5; 1 Corinthians 16:19; Colossians 4:15; Philemon 2). Such groups were probably not very large: we can think in terms of a relatively intimate circle, centring on a host family. As well, the meetings possessed a high degree of informality. They were not purely religious, but also genuinely social occasions.

In the earliest writings, we find no suggestion that these meetings were conducted with the kind of solemnity and formality that surrounds most weekly Christian gatherings today. As the German theologian, Eduard Schweizer, says in his description of early Christian worship:

> The togetherness of the church and its services is not that of a theatre audience, where one or several paid actors act on the stage while everybody else is looking on. Each one takes part with his special gift... the body of Christ is not a body of soldiers in which one sees at best the neck of the preceding man... it is a body consisting of members living in their mutual addressing, asking, challenging, comforting, sharing of Christ and his gifts.[2]

---

1 For an attempt to do this, see my *Going to Church in the First Century*, Hexagon: Sydney, 1980.

2 E. Schweizer, 'The Service of Worship', *Neotestamentica*, Zwingli: Zurich, 1963, pp.335-336

Even the larger, congregational meetings of all the Christians in a city, as Romans 16:23 demonstrates, took place in a home. These were still relatively small and were characterised by a high degree of spontaneity and mutuality (cf. 1 Corinthians 11:17-34).

Third, in examining Paul, we must also attempt to discover how far his approach to church life is applicable to our twentieth century. This is far from easy and we have to guard against doing it in an inadequate way. For example, it is not simply a matter of isolating so-called 'enduring statements of principle' in Paul from his so-called 'culturally conditioned practice'. We have to take Paul's teaching about community whole and entire. Principle and practice, content and form, are too closely bound together in his writings to separate them out in this way. Indeed, it is only by examining his actual practice that some of his principles come to light. And clear statements of principle may be as culturally conditioned as certain of his practices. Besides, it is not just principles we are looking for. Alongside those, we should be concerned about the motives and dispositions Paul said people should have, the qualities of character they should possess, the models of behaviour he and his colleagues gave and the images of church life he put forward.

In any case, there is no way we can neatly distinguish what is relevant and irrelevant by considering Paul's writings on their own. We have to examine our present situation and allow it to ask questions of Paul. There is the need to develop middle principles or axioms, which can act as a bridge between his times and ours. There is also that extra prophetic touch of the Spirit which helps us to seek what is relevant to our varying local situations. Even then, it is only by testing what we have learned from our experience that we can discern how well we have done our work.

Distinctive features of early Christian church life

We can now identify certain aspects of Paul's idea of community which are fully relevant today. I want to single out three which are particularly significant for church life at present:

(a) Its family nature

There has been a considerable amount of talk recently about the church as a body. Although this has released new life, it has also obscured the pre-eminent place 'family' language had in Paul's thinking. Where family talk has gone on in congregations, it has tended to be superficial. So you will find members referring to their church as 'a family' or 'the family of God' when most have a very limited knowledge of one another. (Rather like those ads for building societies which project their clientele as members of one large, happy family!) In churches with a more informal atmosphere, you may find people calling each other 'brother' or 'sister' in a more personal way. Yet, for the most part, this is intended in a purely spiritual sense. The bridge between them carries only religious traffic.

Paul regarded his communities as genuine 'extended families'. They contained people who were to become fathers and mothers, sons and daughters and brothers and sisters of one another. It is clear that Paul did not intend this in a narrow spiritual sense. Sometimes these relationships replaced those with members' original families, which either the gospel message or social mobility had severed. In other instances, they supplemented these. In either case, a real involvement in each others' lives, based on a far-reaching commitment to one another, was Paul's intention. What a difference it would make to a congregation if its members, like the members of a family, determined to love and cherish one another 'for better for worse, for richer for poorer, in sickness and in health', so long as they all lived or until God called them apart! We may not live under the same roof with one another in the church. But, according to Paul, when I join with you in a church, I am to take care of you and you are to take care of me. You become my responsibility and I become yours. Both of us have, as Martin Luther put it, a responsibility 'to become to each other what Christ is to us'.[3] As the Danish Christian thinker, Søren Kierkegaard, so often stressed, the church is not a limited liability company

---

3 M. Luther, *The Liberty of a Christian*, Marshall, Morgan and Scott: London, no date, p.30

whose members are accountable to one another 'only to a certain degree'.[4]

Paul emphasised the diverse character of this Christian family. It is made up of people who are very different from one another; it is only as all combine that a unity and harmony emerges. Paul's most striking image for this was that of the body:

> For the body does not consist of one member but of many...
> God arranged the organs, each of them, as he chose...
> but... so adjusted the body, giving the greater honour to the inferior part, that there may be no discord, but that the members may have the same care for one another (1 Corinthians 12:14, 18 and 24-25).

This being the case, the group should have an inbuilt bias towards helping those who are, outwardly, the most disadvantaged. The way this takes place is through the co-operation of all members of the group according to the different capacities they have been given by God:

> Having gifts that differ according to the grace given us, let us use them... so that all attain to the unity of the faith... to mature manhood, to the measure of the stature of the fulness of Christ (Romans 12:4 and 6; Ephesians 4:13).

Paul saw this taking place in different ways, paralleling the different kinds of disharmony which might arise. For example, where there is severe disagreement between prominent members, they need the help of a respected third party who can persuade them to resolve the issue dividing them (Philippians 4:2-3). If a legal dispute has arisen between two members, they should put their case before someone who has considerable experience of God and can decide in the matter (1 Corinthians 6:1-6). When factions arise in the church, all are to be on the alert to distinguish

---

4 As throughout S. Kierkegaard, *Purity of Heart Is to Will One Thing*, Harper: New York, 1956 and his *Attack' Upon Christendom*, Princeton: Princeton, 1968.

those who are right from those who are self-seeking. Where differences concern matters on which more than one point of view is legitimate as distinct from matters of principle, there can be a variety of opinions. Those with a more mature outlook should bear with those who cannot rise to it (Romans 14:1-15). Should a person fall into some error, others should gently help them to their feet again, exercising care lest they repeat their mistake (Galatians 6:1). In notorious cases of misbehaviour, the whole community should take action to dissociate itself from the offending person or openly call him or her to account (1 Corinthians 5:1-5; 1 Timothy 5:19-20). For the rest, everyone should seek to admonish those who are not pulling their weight, encourage those who feel inadequate, assist those who need help and generally show patience towards all (1 Thessalonians 5:14; Ephesians 4:4ff).

(b) Its full-orbed character
We tend to think that Paul's view of the community's gathering was exaltedly spiritual. It was not, at least not in the way we generally use the word. Paul talked a lot about how practical everything has to be. What goes on should not be above people's heads and ought to help people in quite concrete ways. For we do not come to church to worship some far-off God in his mystical heaven. Through his Spirit he is here among us, becoming involved in all our personal lives. We are to imitate him by concerning ourselves in church with each other's actual needs. This does not mean that while church is on we are to move backwards and forwards from worshipping God to serving one another, from the heavenly and spiritual to the earthly and practical. We do *both* together. Whenever I pray, sing or share the Lord's Supper, I have you in mind as much as God. For I want you to enter into my prayer, take heart from my song, have fellowship with me as we eat the Lord's meal. And whenever I teach, prophesy or simply do you a good turn in church, God acknowledges it as much as if I was directing it to him personally. The two cannot be separated.

But there is a further implication. Paul believed that all parts of our personality should be involved in church. We are not there only as spirits engaging with spirits or as minds engaging with minds. We are also there as imaginative, emotional and physical beings, desiring to worship God with *all* our minds, hearts and strength, yet also concerned about the creative, psychological and bodily welfare of others. The capacities God gives us to worship him and edify others include all facets of our personality. As well, the various polarities in our make-up – for example, laughter and tears, introspection and intimacy, doubts and certainties – all have their place.

There is always room in church, even in the middle of prayer, to enjoy a good joke and, even in the midst of laughter, to convey a word from God. There are occasions when a meditative silence is the most appropriate response. There are times when a touch, an embrace or a kiss is the only satisfactory way we can convey what God wishes us to say. We should also be able to unburden our fears and leave them in others' safe-keeping, or allow our convictions to soar and carry everyone with them. There is room for the sublime and apparently trivial, for the occurrence of some profound experience of the reality of God and for the expression of the most everyday concerns. Unless we can draw in, talk about, pray into and work through our most insistent daily concerns and those of the world in general, then church is *less* than it should be. Paul's letters are full of allusions to such matters.

Paul also viewed people's financial and material needs as part and parcel of believers' ongoing responsibility. For those living within Christian households, these needs would have been met within the family context. In the ancient world, householders were under an obligation to provide for their immediate dependants, including slaves, as well as for relatives who had been deprived of their means of support, for example widows. Within a converted household, the head of the home should have a sharpened sense of responsibility in such matters. For 'if any one does not provide for his own relatives, and especially for his own family, he has disowned the faith and is worse than an unbeliever' (1 Timothy 5:8). We hear echoes of this household pattern of care in other passages as well: 'If a widow has children or grandchildren, let them first learn their religious duty to their own family and make some return to their parent; for this is acceptable in the sight of God' (1 Timothy 5:4). In these days of unemployment relief, student assistance and social welfare, it is easy to forget that Christians who belong to the same natural family have obligations to one another in these areas. But we have obligations to those who are part of the Christian family as well when they are in need.

Within his communities, Paul expected those who were better off to help those who did not have enough. One of the problems at Corinth stemmed from the failure of people from rich households to share the food they had brought for the common meal with those who came empty-handed, because they belonged to pagan households or to no household at all. To take another example, where there is 'a real widow. . . left all alone' with no one to provide for her, the church is to step in and look after her needs (1 Timothy 5:16). As James reminds us more generally elsewhere:

> If a brother or sister is ill-clad and in lack of daily food, and one of you says to them, 'Go in peace, be warmed and filled', without giving them the things needed for the body, what does it profit? (James 2:15-16).

Those who are single parents, those who are without work, those who are handicapped in some way should be of special concern to us when they are part of our immediate Christian community. God may call upon our abundance to remedy their lack. In this respect, too, church is a place where very down-to-earth concerns require attention and down-to-earth decisions have to be made.

(c) Its participatory style

All had something to contribute to the church as it was assembled, for all have one or more gifts from the Spirit to exercise for the others' benefit. This has the corollary that, whatever may have usually happened in these gatherings, they were always to remain open to the unexpected, e.g. a novel word from God (cf. Acts 13:2), a dramatic response to an entirely unforeseen event (cf. Acts 20:9-10), or a sudden awareness of Satan's designs on the community (cf. Ephesians 4:26-28). Although Paul insisted on an orderly meeting — *not* a fixed order — he urged the members to be 'open to the Lord's intervention whenever and wherever he is willing to interfere'.[5]

There was also to be an ever-present openness to those in the greatest need. This involved a willingness to drop everything else — however important it may have seemed — so that the fullest attention and help could be given. The test of any community is whether it can recognise that moment and devote its concentrated energies to it.

Paul also required a high degree of readiness on the part of each local church to look after its own affairs. That is why he constantly addressed his injunctions to everyone in the church, not to a special group or to a single leader. It is true that there were certain people in each community who possessed special abilities from God equipping them to further the development of individual and group maturity. Those who have the gifts of prophecy, teaching, wisdom and exhortation have a special part to play. But more important are those who exercise a pastoral or helping role.

It is not always clear what Paul regarded as the functions of this second group. Certainly they were less all-embracing than those exercised by ministers today. In all his churches there were several who contributed in this way. Such people were not employed in any full-time capacity. Moreover, to some degree Paul expected all church members to fulfil pastoral functions in relation to one another. What characterised this pastorally more qualified group was not any difference of status, such as that between clergy and laity. No such distinction existed in Paul's communities, any more than it did elsewhere in the first and second centuries.

While it is true that a few people in each church developed a greater pastoral ability, their task was to help others in the congregation develop an increasing control over their individual and corporate destiny. They did not decide for the members what was best for them, nor take some common activities out of their hands. No one person or group was in charge, led worship, preached, celebrated the Lord's Supper or directed the church's life. There were other

---

5 E. Schweizer, *op. cit.*, pp.338-339

significant people as well, for example the church's founding apostle and his colleagues. But these were involved in an itinerant ministry and only occasionally spent time with local communities. Even then, their function was to serve such communities and help them stand increasingly on their own feet, not insist that they remain forever dependent on outside ministry (cf. Ephesians 4:11ff).

We have people of both kinds today, in the form of ministers and denominational agencies. While these undoubtedly have their roots in Paul's approach, they also arose from other factors that are not so congenial to it. Though many clergy long for a less mono-ministerial situation, they are still the centre of too many expectations and the fulfillers of too many functions. Some of these right-fully belong to other members of the congregation or to the local church as a whole. And for all their desire to strengthen congregational life, denominational structures still fetter rather than free their member churches, keeping them in tutelage rather than helping them attain their majority. Only when ministers and denominations are able to hand over some of their responsibilities, and only when Christian people are willing to take them upon themselves, will the full resources of Christ in our local churches, his 'frozen assets',[6] become available.

Why do these three facets of Paul's idea of community possess continuing relevance? The answer is simple. Each of them flows directly out of the gospel he preached.

☐ We are to become a genuine Christian family because God has made us an integral part of his, sending 'the Spirit of his Son into our hearts, crying "Abba, Father!"' (Galatians 4:6). He calls us to enter into a real relationship with one another so that we love 'one another with brotherly affection' (Romans 12:10).

☐ Every part of us is to be involved in this because every cell of our body has become the 'temple' of his Spirit (1 Corinthians 6:19): every aspect of our lives is to be involved, for God has 'reconciled to himself all things, whether on the

---

6 The expression was used by R.T. Morton and M. Gibbs in their book *God's Frozen People*, Collins: London, 1964

earth or in heaven' (Colossians 1:20). The cross shows dramatically the lengths God went to in order to deliver the needy (cf. 1 Corinthians 2:9) and his resurrection released new abilities into people's lives through the pouring out of God's Spirit (cf. Romans 5:5).

☐ God took those who were of little account and turned them into something quite majestic (1 Corinthians 1:26-30). Since we will one day 'judge angels' and 'the world itself', we are not incompetent to deal with matters affecting our welfare in church (1 Corinthians 6:2-3).

All the things we have mentioned are simply the gospel itself expressed in corporate form. They are the shape it takes when translated into community terms. Paul viewed the church as a prism through which the light of the gospel is variously refracted. Yet it is not only the embodiment of something that has already happened. It also luminously reflects the shape of things to come. Nowhere is this more evident, and nowhere are the three characteristics of the church's life more strikingly fused, than in the community's meal. For this remembers not only the darkness of Christ's death but anticipates the delights of the Messiah's table. Here amidst sadness and laughter, reflection and conversation, deference and kindness, word and action, eating and sharing, we express the sacrificial love of Christ in our active concern for one another and experience the fellowship of the saints that will one day fill our lives.

Other aspects of the early Christian models
There are three related matters we must now consider.
(a) Witness by the early home churches
The attention of these early Christian home churches was not only directed to their internal functioning. In fact, we find among these Christians a powerful combination of inwardness *and* outwardness. The two go together.

It is only the person or group that develops an inner life that can develop the discernment and resources to carry out any vital outer ministry. A real inner life only develops if it is fed by the experiences, challenges and questions that an outer-directed life creates. One is not exclusive of the other. You cannot have one if you do not have the other. The way we often set the two against one another springs from a mistaken understanding of how authentic inner growth and outreach take place.

In his discussion of *Evangelism in the Early Church*, Michael Green summarises the place of the home – the same homes in which church meetings were held – in the witness of the early Christians to the world around them:

> One of the most important methods of spreading the gospel in antiquity was by the use of homes. It had positive advantages: the comparatively small numbers involved made real interchange of views and informed discussion among the participants possible; there was no artificial isolation of a preacher from his hearers; there was no temptation for either the speaker or the heckler to 'play to the gallery' as there was in a public place or open-air meeting. The sheer informality and relaxed atmosphere of the home, not to mention the hospitality which must often have gone with it, all helped to make this form of evangelism successful.
>
> Jason's house at Thessalonica was used for this purpose; so was that of Titius Justus, situated provocatively opposite the synagogue (with which Paul had broken) at Corinth. Philip's house at Caesarea seems to have been a most hospitable place, where not only visiting seafarers like Paul and his company but wandering charismatics like Agabus were made welcome. Both Lydia's house and the jailer's at Philippi were used as evangelistic centres, and Stephanas apparently used his home at Corinth in the same way. His household was baptised by St Paul in person, no doubt after some instruction in basic Christianity and a profession of faith, and we subsequently learn that he used his home 'for the service of the saints'. The very earliest Christian community met in the upper room of a particular house, owned by the mother of John Mark in Jerusalem. It is hardly surprising that the 'church in the house' became a crucial factor in the spread of the Christian faith.[7]

The early Christian home churches also developed an interest in what was happening to churches elsewhere and

7 M. Green, *Evangelism in the Early Church*, Hodder & Stoughton: London, 1970, pp.207-208

were willing to give aid to other Christians when the need arose. For example, they shared their possessions with those who were geographically far distant. Paul's gathering of funds from the Gentile churches for the poverty-stricken Jewish-Christians in Jerusalem is an example of this (Acts 24:17; Romans 15:24-29; 1 Corinthians 16:1-4). Although it was their surplus wealth that the Gentile churches were asked to contribute, some congregations 'in... their extreme poverty... overflowed in a wealth of liberality', giving 'beyond their means, of their own free will' (2 Corinthians 8:2-3).

(b) Difficulties in the early home churches

We should not forget that the communities Paul addressed often failed to embody the vision he had for them. Too often we have romantic notions about church life in the first century. Not only do these distort our understanding of the earliest communities; they also encourage us to have false expectations about what we can experience today. To guard against this, we need to look at some of the problems which arose in Paul's churches, especially in connection with the three aspects of life together already mentioned.

Paul wanted the members of his churches to see themselves as part of a Christian family. But relationships in a family are not always warm and supportive. Families have their ups and downs, periodic problems and occasional crises. Because the members of a family have so much to do with each other, there is both the promise of deeper intimacy and the potential for greater disharmony.

A number of the early communities experienced these tensions. At Corinth, for example, some members had fallen out with one another and were resorting to a court to settle their dispute (1 Corinthians 6:5-7). Various groups in the wider church were quarrelling with one another as to who was the best (1 Corinthians 1:11-13) or who was in the right (1 Corinthians 11:18-19) and were also inclined to act in a cliquish way (1 Corinthians 11:20-22). Some individuals were behaving without any regard for the way their actions might affect the more sensitive members of the family (1 Corinthians 8:7-9). Others were tending to show off and make others feel inferior (1 Corinthians 14:16-19). There was a general lack of discipline in the church (1 Corinthians 14:23 and 26-27) and too little attention was given to those who were older and more mature (1 Corinthians 16:15-18).

Paul also encouraged people in his communities to be themselves in their gatherings. While this meant opening up their whole selves to others and the possibility of real change, it also exposed them to the temptation of accommodating themselves to strong inner drives and powerful social pressures. Thus some of the Corinthians adapted themselves too much to the prevailing ideas of their time (1 Corinthians 15:32-34). Others were attracted to the sub-Christian moral standards of the day (1 Corinthians 6:15-16). One particular group gave too free a rein to their emotions, allowing these to get the better of them, even to the extent of swearing in a blasphemous way (1 Corinthians 12:3). Many of them looked at their fellow citizens and talked about them in a judgmental way (1 Corinthians 3:1-3). One person had even outstripped his pagan neighbours by the physical and moral crudity of his action (1 Corinthians 5:1). Strangely enough, much of this behaviour went hand-in-hand with a rarefied spirituality.

We have also noted that Paul's view of church placed a high emphasis upon participation, far more so than any other religion during the first century. Since everyone had a particular contribution to make, this magnified the resources at the disposal of each community and conferred real worth on even the least gifted of the members. But it could also lead to excesses, especially at the hands of those who had not experienced such freedom before. As a result, gatherings at times became unruly. Too many people attempted to speak at once (1 Corinthians 14:27), some going on longer than they should (1 Corinthians 14:29-32). One group kept interrupting with questions (1 Corinthians 14:35), while another was so caught up with their private worship that they ignored others' inability to enter into it (1 Corinthians 14:23). In these and other ways the meetings were disorderly, lacking in decorum. Paul was therefore forced to explain that freedom has its forms, spontaneity its rhythms, and participation its responsibilities.

In spite of the fact that such abuses crept in, however, Paul never retracted his understanding of how the church should operate. He never moved away from his view that the church is a genuine extended family in favour of a less personal, more institutional entity. He never suggested that the local church should occupy itself with only one aspect of activity – the allegedly 'religious' – and only one aspect of the personality – the so-called 'spiritual'. He never lessened his belief in mutual ministry and shared authority for one based more on liturgical order and hierarchical leadership.

Even in the case of Corinth where the most extreme distortions of his understanding arose, Paul unceasingly continued to stress his fundamental principles. He also looked through and beyond the Corinthians' failings to the potential they had to be the church in the fullest way. For all his realism about the actual situation, he envisioned them in Christ, confident that in him they had the resources to overcome their present problems.

(c) Relevance of the early home churches

Not all aspects of early church life are applicable to us today. Here we need to look briefly at three respects in which changes in social and cultural conditions have resulted in certain facets of Paul's approach to community no longer being relevant in the same way.

First, there is a difference in the *form of relationships* within the church. In establishing churches around the Mediterranean, Paul utilised the prevailing social structure of his day. Though some first-century families were not very different from nuclear families today, others included slaves and their dependants, friends and freedmen, older kin and single relatives. The first Christian churches were generally based on converted, extended households, as many passages in Paul's writings and Acts testify. This resulted in a greater continuity between the social network people belonged to before and after their conversion. Frequently, the two may not have been very different, Jesus' words about the gospel dividing families notwithstanding. It is different today: churches are mostly made up of nuclear families and single people, few of whom knew each other beforehand.

The particular social divisions that existed in the first century (for example between masters and slaves, patrons and clients) would have given a flavour to the dealings of Christians with one another that has no exact parallel today. Social conventions governing relationships between husbands and wives, parents and children were also much more formal (cf. 1 Peter 3:6). No matter how strenuously a church group seeks to restore the New Testament pattern of church life today, it cannot reproduce the same social atmosphere in its gatherings. Nevertheless certain distinctions between people remain, even in our egalitarian society, and should receive appropriate acknowledgement in Christian relationships.

Second, there is a difference in the *lines of authority* within the church. The authority within a first-century household generally centred on the husband/father/master. One household could also have authority over less socially advantaged families or individuals. The household in this position became the fulcrum around which pastoral oversight in a new church revolved. This did not happen automatically. It was only those households which turned their positions of privilege into a basis of service that received Paul's commendation. This approach to authority, despite the dominant role of men in ancient societies, was flexible enough to allow women to share in the oversight of the churches in their homes (Colossians 4:15, Romans 16:3-16, Philemon 1-2).

The abolition of slavery and the movement for women's liberation, both in part prompted by Christian impulses, have since altered the balance of authority within society. The availability of education and employment to all – and the opportunity for all to take on responsible positions in unions, voluntary organisations and the like – has also diminished the social gap between men and women, employers and employees. As well, the separation of work from home life and the separation of the aged from their offspring has tended to alter the kind of authority which parents previously possessed. These changes create the conditions for a more varied approach to authority within the local church than was possible in Paul's day. Even so, the continuing existence of minor social, sexual and familial distinctions in our society has to be taken into account. For all our distance from Paul in this area, a small degree of overlap remains. This means that alongside his insistence on the mutual subjection of Christians to one another, Paul's view that some people in the church play a different role from others has a modified application today.

Third, there is a difference in various *details of the church's meeting*. In the first century, bread and wine were people's basic food and drink. The breaking of the one and the drinking of the other marked a meal's commencement and conclusion. So the Lord's Supper was really an ordinary meal given an extraordinary significance, not a separate ritual! Insofar as bread is still the basic element of our diet, this presents no problem, but meals no longer normally begin with the breaking of bread. And while wine is becoming increasingly present at evening meals, tea or coffee are still drunk much more frequently and almost always bring the meal to a close. If we wish to restore to the Lord's Supper its character as a meal, we need a modern counterpart to the breaking and distribution of bread and the prayers over the wine.

This meal, like Christian meetings as a whole, took place uniformly in an apartment or home. Other religious groups in the first century met mainly in temples or special buildings for the purpose. The early Christians could not bring themselves to associate with the first and did not possess the second. So private dwellings or flats provided the venue for both smaller, weekly meetings and city-wide, less frequent gatherings. Although these meetings were based in the household, we should not think that a home was the only place in which church could be held – a rented room was also appropriate.

Similarly with the question of time. While it is true that meetings mostly took place on a Sunday, the early Christians felt free to worship on other days of the week (Acts 2:46). What underlay the choice of a venue and day was the conduciveness of the surroundings and the convenience of the time – factors which remain just as applicable today.

Conclusion

Although in this chapter we have drawn on Paul's writings as a whole, much of the material has come from his first letter to the Corinthians. This is understandable. It is there that Paul went into the greatest detail about what happens when Christians meet together. But this material is not untypical of practice in Pauline churches generally as the well-known New Testament scholar, James D.G. Dunn, shows:

> In Paul's picture of the church in Corinth met for worship (1 Corinthians 14:26-40), we are probably confronted with a gathering which was distinctive for its time. It did not meet on consecrated or special premises; its context was the home of one of its members. It did not centre round a sacred text or particular ritual acts; its *raison d'être* was rather the sharing of the shared grace (*charis*) of God in its particular expressions (*charismata*). It was not characterised by an established pattern or liturgy nor did it depend on an official leadership to give it direction; rather it was to be expected that the Spirit would exercise sufficient control through the interplay of gifts and ministries ordered by him. Its aim was to bring about the mutual edification of all through a being together and through a doing for one another in word and action as the body of Christ in mutual interdependence on the Spirit. . .
>
> We should perhaps simply add that this picture of the church should not be confined to Corinth as though that were a special case. Of course, we can hardly assume that the Corinthian church with its various disorders was typical of the churches established by Paul elsewhere in Greece, Macedonia and Asia Minor. On the other hand, the brevity of an exhortation like that in 1 Corinthians 14:29 implies that Paul was alluding to teaching already known and 1 Thessalonians 5:9-22 confirms that this was part of his regular notes of guidance for the ordering of his churches' assemblies even before the Corinthian problems arose. So, too, the parallels between 1 Corinthians 12 and Romans 12 imply that in 1 Corinthians 14 Paul was making specific applications of more general principles, rather than responding in an *ad hoc* way to the particular challenge of

the church in Corinth. In short 1 Corinthians 14:26-40 can be taken as Paul's picture of how any local church should function when it meets for worship. As such, it remains a challenge and inspiration to any group who meet today as the body of Christ.[8]

And so it does. This is true not only of the 'whole church' meeting described in the latter part of 1 Corinthians, but of the 'home church' structure the letter presupposes. This structure, as we have seen, surfaces clearly in other Pauline letters, as well as in other parts of the New Testament. The two-tiered approach to church life that the New Testament brings before us is not something we can regard as of purely historical interest. It remains just as important today. Rather than attempting to restore the New Testament church, however, what we need to do is give appropriate twentieth-century form to this approach to church life and to the way of meeting associated with it.

---

8 James D.G. Dunn, 'The Responsible Congregation (1 Corinthians 14:26-40)', *Charisma und Agape* (1 Corinthians 12-14), 1983, pp.235-236

3

A great cloud of witnesses:

Home churches since the first century

THE IDEA OF REGROUPING CHURCH LIFE around the home has had advocates down through the centuries. Today, in many different parts of the world, it is already becoming a reality. Arguments in its favour are now coming from an interesting range of Christian leaders.

It is not possible to cite all these various witnesses here. We want to draw attention to the more significant ones, quoting some key – and at points lengthy – extracts from their writings. These will convey not only the content of their thought, but also something of the spirit in which they wrote.

The witness of church history

(a) The earliest Christians

We have looked at Paul in some detail, but not closely at later passages in the New Testament which demonstrate the importance of the home as a context for church. From the birth of the Christian movement, as recorded by Luke, the first believers met 'day by day', not only 'in the Temple', the gathering of the whole congregation, but 'in their homes, eating with glad and humble hearts, praising God and enjoying the good will of the people' (Acts 2:46-47). In this passage we have underlined the centrality of the meal and the joyful nature of the fellowship which accompanied it, the thankful recognition of God's role in the lives of the group, and the influence of the lives of the people gathered upon those around them. With respect to the latter, it is surely not accidental that Luke adds 'and every day the Lord added to the group those who were being saved' (Acts 2:47).

Luke also provides the only detailed description of a meeting of all the Christians in a city. This took place in a home, possessed considerable informality and flexibility, and was a decidedly social as well as religious occasion:

> On the Saturday night, in our gathering for the breaking of bread, Paul, who was to leave next day, addressed them and went on discussing with them until midnight. Now there were many lamps in the upper room where we were assembled; and a youth named Eutychus, who was sitting on the window ledge, grew more and more sleepy as Paul went on talking. At last he was completely overcome by sleep, fell from the third storey to the ground, and was picked up for dead. Paul went down, threw himself upon him, seizing him in his arms and said to them: 'Stop this commotion; there is still life in him'. He went upstairs, broke bread and ate, and after much conversation, which lasted until dawn, he departed (Acts 20:6-11).

The author of Hebrews also throws light on the style and content of early Christian gatherings in homes. He confirms the highly participatory nature of those meetings and their emphasis upon what we would call 'fellowship' as well as what we term 'worship':

> Let us be firm and unswerving in the confession of our hope, for the Giver of the promise may be trusted. We ought to see how each of us may best arouse others to love and active goodness, not staying away from our meetings, as some do, but rather encouraging one another, and all the more as you see the Day drawing near (Hebrews 10:23-25).

During the following centuries, a change began to take place in the way Christians met, particularly with the move from the original home setting. William Barclay discusses what happened to the celebration of the Lord's Supper:

> When we turn to the Lord's Supper itself we find in it what we might call a series of movements.

1. There is the movement from the house to the church. It is not in doubt that the Lord's Supper began as a family meal or a meal of friends in a private house. This was inevitable for the simple but sufficient reason that more than a century was to pass before there was such a thing as a church building... worship was therefore a thing of the house church and the small group and the home. It was there that the Lord's Supper was born in the church. It was like the Jewish Passover which is a family festival at which the father and the head of the household is the celebrant. There can be no two things more different than the celebration of the Lord's Supper in a Christian home in the first century and in a cathedral in the twentieth century. The things are so different that it is almost possible to say that they bear no relationship to each other whatsoever. The liturgical splendour of the twentieth century was in the first century not only unthought of; it was totally impossible. The Lord's Supper began in the house and moved to the church.

2. The Lord's Supper began from being a real meal into being a symbolic meal. The very way in which in the early accounts excesses of eating and drinking are condemned shows that it is a real meal that is in question... the Lord's Supper originated in a meal of hungry men, for the Jews who sat down to the Passover late in the evening had not eaten since at least midday. For many, for the slaves and the poor, the Lord's Supper must have been the one real meal of the week. The idea of a tiny piece of bread and sip of wine bears no relation at all to the Lord's Supper as it originally was. It was not until the Synod of Hippo in AD 393 that the idea of fasting before communion emerged. The Lord's Supper was originally a family meal in a household of friends.

3. The Lord's Supper moved from bare simplicity to elaborate splendour. This elaboration of worship and liturgy had certain moving causes... That which had been a family occasion became a service at which the bishop dispensed the sacrament, surrounded by the presbyters detached from the congregation. It inevitably became something to be watched from a distance...

With the increasing idea of the conversion of the elements into the actual body and blood of the Lord, the sacrament became less and less the grateful memory of the death of

Christ and more and more the awestricken encounter with the glorified King of heaven and earth. It was coming into the presence of the King, and all the trappings of the court began to be used.

4. The Lord's Supper moved from being an act of the heart's devotion to being a centre of theological debate. It moved from being a dramatic and concrete picture into being an exercise in abstract and metaphysical thought. It began by simply confronting a man in dramatic and pictorial terms with the sacrifice of Jesus Christ. It began by saying quite simply, yet very vividly: 'Look what he did for you!'. It ended with complicated questions of the real presence of Christ in the elements and whether or not it was a propitiatory sacrifice, questions which in the early days it would never have occurred to anyone even to ask.

5. The celebration of the Lord's Supper moved from being a lay function to a priestly function. In the New Testament itself there is no indication that it was the special privilege or duty of anyone to lead the worshipping fellowship in the Lord's Supper. In the *Didache* again there is no mention of any special celebrant. In fact, the prophets are to be allowed to hold the eucharist as they will. In Irenaeus the celebration is not confined to any special person.[1]

These five movements – from the home to the church building, from real to symbolic meal, from simplicity to elaboration, from experience to dogma, from the concrete to the abstract, from the layperson to the priest – have continued to impoverish the Lord's Supper ever since. Though we cannot go into detail here, this is also true of other aspects of early Christian meetings as well.

(b) The Reformation

The significance of the home as a focus for church life arose again during the Reformation. As he did with so many other neglected aspects of the scriptures, Martin Luther gave the most powerful expression to this.

His intentions are set out in a little-known passage in the Preface to his *German Mass*. Until recently this writing was more or less completely ignored by theologians and church

1 W. Barclay, *The Lord's Supper*, SCM: London, 1967, pp.101-104

leaders. In it Luther identifies three kinds of worship. The first, he says, is the Latin Mass; the second is the German liturgy:

> These two kinds, then, we must let alone and allow it to happen that they are held publicly in the churches before all the people, among whom there are many who do not yet believe or are Christians... For here there is not yet any ordered and certain assembly in which one could govern the Christians according to the gospel... But the third kind which should have [the] true nature of evangelical order would not have to happen so publicly in the open among all kinds of people, but those who seriously want to be Christians and to confess the gospel in deed and word would have to register their names and gather themselves somewhere in a house alone... Here one could also conduct baptism and communion in a brief and fine manner, and direct everything to the word, prayer and mutual love... In brief, if one had the people who earnestly desired to be Christians, the order and manner could quickly be brought about. However, I cannot and do not wish yet to set up or to organise such a congregation, for I do not yet have the people for it. I do not see many who ask for such a thing. But if it comes that I must do it and am compelled, so that I cannot with good conscience leave it undone, then I shall gladly do my part in it and give the best help I can.[2]

As D.M. Lloyd-Jones points out, it was Luther's profound depression at the general ecclesiastical situation which led him to this radical view of the 'church':

> From 1513 on to 1520 and even 1521 he was on the crest of a wave as it were. There was great excitement and everything seemed to be going well. But then a reaction set in, the reformed impetus seemed to be pausing, nothing much seemed to be happening. A spirit of caution arose, people were hesitant, political considerations came in and Luther

---

2 This passage is quoted, inter alia, in E. Brunner, *The Christian Doctrine of the Church, Faith and the Consummation*, Lutterworth: London, 1962, pp.175-176

became profoundly depressed. But still more important, and still more serious, he was disturbed at the condition of the church to which he himself belonged, the churches which had responded to his teaching. He felt that they were lacking in true spiritual life and vigour. . .

Another thing that greatly aggravated this feeling which developed in him was the phenomenon of Anabaptists. . . He had to admit that there was a quality of life in their churches which was absent in the churches to which he belonged. So he reacts in two ways to them; he has got to discipline his people against them, and yet he wishes to have in his church the kind of thing that was working so well in their churches. The result of all this was that he felt that the only thing to do was. . . to gather together the people who are truly Christian into a kind of inner church.[3]

Unfortunately, Luther was initially hindered from acting on his insights by the lack of understanding and unpreparedness of the people in his churches. When later the situation was changing and Luther was planning to counteract the appeal of the Anabaptists by setting up home churches, he was distracted by the possibility of a large-scale political takeover of whole regions for the Protestant cause.

Luther, however, was not the only one who saw the value of a smaller Christian community within the parish church. Martin Bucer advocated something very similar in Strasbourg.[4]

(c) The Great Awakening

In the period of the Great Awakening in the eighteenth century, the significance of the home as a locus for church life once again came to the fore. The catalyst was John Wesley, who realised that the new wine produced by his

---

3 D.M. Lloyd-Jones, 'Ecclesiola in Ecclesia', *Approaches to the Reformation of the Church* (Papers from the Puritan and Reformed Studies Conference), 1965, pp.60-61

4 R. Peter, 'Informal Groups in the Reformation: Rhenish Types', *Informal Groups in the Church*, eds. R. Metz and J. Schlick, Pickwick: Pittsburgh, 1975, p.231

innovative preaching had to be poured into new wineskins if it was to survive and mature. As a result, Wesley sought to create new structures as well as adapt older ones. Howard Snyder has provided a fascinating account of Wesley's approach, demonstrating how radical Wesley was in his understanding and organising of the church. Snyder argues that the original Methodist class structure constituted the heart of the movement. It also contains, he feels, a forceful alternative to the present church scene, especially in view of Methodism's later departure from Wesley's basic ecclesiastical emphases:

> The Methodist societies were soon divided into classes and bands. Perhaps it would be more accurate to say the societies were the sum total of class and band members, since the primary point of belonging was that this more intimate level of community and membership in a class was required before one could join the society. . .
>
> The class meeting was the cornerstone of the whole edifice. The classes were in effect house churches (not classes for instruction, as the term *class* might suggest), meeting in the various neighbourhoods where people lived. . .
>
> They normally met one evening each week for an hour or so. Each person reported on his or her spiritual progress, or on particular needs or problems, and received the support and prayers of the others. 'Advice or reproof was given as need required, quarrels were made up, misunderstandings removed. And after an hour or two spent in this labour of love, they concluded with prayer and thanksgiving.'[5]

Snyder goes on to quote one of the early leaders of the Methodist movement, Henry Fish, who wrote one of the first manuals for class leaders:

> It is clear as daylight that that kind of communion [experienced in class meetings] has the express warrant of holy scripture; and that something more than church communion in the sacrament of the Lord's Supper was

5 H. Snyder, *The Radical Wesley and Patterns of Church Renewal*, IVP: Downers Grove, 1980, pp.53-54

enjoyed by the primitive Christians. They had 'fellowship' as well as 'breaking of bread'. How, for instance, could they exhort one another daily? How could they comfort and edify one another? How could they provoke one another to love and good works? How could they confess their faults to one another and pray for one another? How teach and admonish one another in psalms and hymns and spiritual songs? How bear one another's burdens? How weep with those who weep and rejoice with those who rejoice, if they never met together for the purpose of conversing on experimental religion and the state of each other's souls? Whatever persons may say to the contrary, those churches, the members of which do not observe or in which they have not the opportunity of observing the foregoing precepts which are enjoined in the New Testament scriptures, are not based on the model of the apostolic churches.

The three witnesses I have cited – Paul, Luther and Wesley – are major figures in Christian, and indeed world history. Down through the years there were also many others who, from a less prominent position and in a more low-key way, accorded a central position to the home in church life. As William Barclay notes, long after the New Testament early Christians continued to meet in homes. This was the norm until well into the third and in places even fourth century AD. It is often forgotten that the Christianity which conquered the Roman Empire was essentially a home-centred movement. This is one of the most paradoxical and extraordinary aspects of early Christian development. It stands as a continuing challenge to those who claim that only large, highly-organised institutions with powerful, publicly-recognised representatives can make a real impact upon the mores and structures of the surrounding society.

In the century following the Reformation, other circles, conventicles and so-called 'ecclesiola in ecclesia', i.e. 'little churches within the church', sprang up and flourished. While these took a variety of forms, all stressed the importance of an informal setting for prayer and edification. A number of them encouraged the sharing of experiences and the creation of genuine bonds of fellowship. They were lay-oriented, often encouraging women to participate along with the men. Most of these groups were cells for devotional exercises within a congregation. Others were more conscious of their functioning in some sense as 'church', initially within but later alongside an institutional framework. For example, the Quakers originally met as cells in homes while they continued to attend official places of worship. However, although George Fox began by calling the church to renewal, he gradually came to see the movement as an independent entity and ceased participating in formal services.

During the early days of the Industrial Revolution, pietists in the Lutheran Church in Europe, evangelicals in the Church of England and members of newer religious movements in North America rediscovered the value of informal meetings for instruction and prayer. Few of these thought of themselves as church, though some did. Our own family history contains a Church of England clergyman who encouraged and attended a home meeting in his parish in Kent in the 1820s. This was a meeting for church and supplemented the weekly morning service. He and others were prosecuted and fined for doing so, for all such meetings had been proscribed by law since the mid-seventeenth century. This prohibition partly explains why there was less of this kind of activity than otherwise might have been. Outside the established and dissenting churches, other groups in England, Ireland and the United States also met informally to sing, pray, teach one another, help the needy and break bread together, holding a strong belief in the ministry of all believers. These groups predated the emergence of such movements as the Brethren and continued alongside them.

The witness of non-Western countries
In our own century, particularly during the last two decades, the church has begun to 'come home'. While this has happened in the West only to a limited degree, since the 1960s Bible-study, prayer and fellowship groups have tended to become more relational in character, more home-oriented in location and more open to including elements of 'worship'.

The impact of the charismatic movement upon the churches and the influence of various secular groups has contributed to this movement, not always constructively. Nowadays other groupings – cell groups, family clusters, pastoral circles, cross-generational classes, home dialogue meetings and other types of informal gathering – have emerged. Few of these, however, have developed into home churches after the biblical pattern.

It is outside the West that Christians have made more substantial moves towards home churches: especially in Communist and Latin American societies.

(a) Communist China

It is in China that the greatest developments in a home church direction have taken place within communist countries. These date back to the Communist Revolution in 1949. Shortly after this event, an official policy caused the closure of buildings used for religious purposes. Christians were forced to meet in other settings, indeed wherever they could do so without coming under scrutiny. In order to escape attention, they also had to meet in fewer numbers. Sometimes open fields became places for worship, especially when volunteers were called upon to work and believers could put themselves forward as a group. Forests occasionally provided another venue. But mostly Christians met secretly or semi-secretly in homes. The Cultural Revolution in the 1960s intensified the need for and danger of meeting.

Despite the freer atmosphere of the post-Mao period, few of these groups have been able to come out into the open. Hong Kong's Chinese Church Research Centre estimates that there were some five million Protestants in 'home churches' around the country during the Cultural Revolution, with Catholics sometimes participating, and that these still make up the mainstream of Chinese Christianity. Throughout the whole period from 1949 the number of such groups has continued to increase, particularly in rural areas, and now tens of millions are involved.

The key characteristics of these house churches have been summarised as follows:

1. Indigenous in nature, they are no longer associated with Western imperialism.

2. Stripped of all the outward organisations and denominations associated with the church in the past, with no church buildings, fixed times of service or paid ministry, Christians continue their witness.

3. Rooted in the home, the church depends upon the loyalty of family members.

4. With a hunger for the word of God, they have spread the message of the gospel by circulating handwritten copies of the scriptures.

5. Without pastors, they have experienced the fellowship and teaching of the Holy Spirit, and lay leadership has been raised up.

6. During times of suffering, they have experienced the reality of prayer and the power of God in the healing of diseases.

7. Witnessing through humble loving service, they have impressed non-believers through the quality of their lives and their ability to help in time of trouble.[6]

Some personal accounts of these communities – their origins, history and character – have been gathered by Raymond Fung, the World Council of Churches' Secretary for Missions and Evangelism. Here is an excerpt from one of them:

Yes, we regard our meetings at home as a local church in spiritual fellowship with the worldwide Christian community. We began as a prayer group for Christian students at the University about 1952 when it had become untenable to have our meetings on campus ground... So we met in my quarters in the professors' compound at four every Wednesday afternoon. We did the things we had always done in varsity fellowship – singing, Bible studies, intercession, fellowship, but with, I believed, more depth and more openness...

Between 1952 and 1964, the prayer group had its ups and downs. We never had more than thirty or so students. In 1962, there was only my wife and me. But the important

---

6 Courtesy the 'Pray for China Fellowship'

thing was that God had left a Christian witness on campus. . .

Unknowingly, our group turned itself into a church. By 1964 our church had about thirty people worshipping on Wednesdays. Only seven were students or members of the faculty. Others came from the neighbourhood. We had a weekly communion service. . .

The years of the Cultural Revolution were a blank so far as our home meeting was concerned. We had no meeting. I was assigned to work in a fruit-preserving factory. My wife went to live with her parents. There was not much to do. . .

Now I am back teaching physics and I have also got back my quarters. We have resumed our house worship, but of the twenty we had before the time of the Red Guards, only eight are still around. Five younger people will probably eventually come back from the north-west. However more new people have joined us. . .

I am in two minds about our future. On the one hand I would love a pastor to come to us, have a small church near the University and do good evangelism work. On the other hand, I can't help feeling that, given our peculiar situations, it might be best for us to continue to meet in homes, away from the limelight, quietly refracting the light of the Lord.[7]

Contacts with Jonathan Chao of the Chinese Church Research Centre in Hong Kong and with a member of a Chinese home church visiting the West confirm the representative nature of this report.

(b) Latin America

It is in Latin America that the most significant reorientation of church life is taking place. This has been happening since the late 'fifties, chiefly within the Roman Catholic Church. Other denominations have their small groups and Pentecostal churches are still multiplying rapidly, but a new kind of populist movement has spread in Catholic circles in a quite extraordinary way. From Honduras to Chile, from the Atlantic to the Pacific, people have formed 'communidades de base', basic Christian communities. The

---

7 R. Fung, *Households of God on China's Soil*, WCC: Geneva, 1982, pp.24-28

term 'base' was chosen to underline the low economic status of their members – they come from the base of society. It is mainly in countries that suffer under a military dictatorship – generally of the right – and contain a large disadvantaged population that such groups have been formed. In 1982, it was estimated that there were more than 150,000 such groups in various parts of Latin America.

These communities differ in size and in the regularity of their meetings. Some are more tolerated by the institutional church than others. Yet they strive towards a common goal and express a number of common characteristics. James O'Halloran, a Silesian missionary and developer of small ecclesial communities, identifies these, though acknowledging that only fully developed groups share them all:

> The small Christian community is an integral part of the church. It ought therefore, at least when fully developed, to reflect all the essential characteristics of the universal church... The members of the church throughout the world *share the same faith*. So also do the members of the small Christian community, which is not just any agglomeration of persons, but a gathering of those who believe...
>
> *Christian love* is the most fundamental quality of the church in all its manifestations. 'By this all shall know you are my disciples, if you have love for one another' (John 13:35)... Worship is an essential element of the worldwide church. It must also be found in the smallest unit. Indeed, a group that is not centred on prayer, the word of God and the Eucharist has absolutely no chance of survival...
>
> The church is *missionary* (reaches out to people, especially the needy) and *prophetic* (stands up for justice). We are a church of servants...
>
> Finally if the church is not to stagnate, it must constantly renew itself. Frequent *renewal* is also vital for the small Christian community.
>
> In the end it is not just the place or the persons that make small Christian community; it is the *commitment* or the total giving of themselves to Christ which the members undertake...[8]

8 J. O'Halloran, *Living Cells: Developing Christian Community*, Orbit: Maryknoll, 1984, pp.29-33

All these basic Christian communities seek to revolve the church around the actual needs, questions and aspirations of their members. They seek to integrate faith and life, indeed discover the reality of God, the Bible and each other as they grapple with the oppressive situations in which they find themselves. That situation is very different from home churches in the West. Base communities can appeal to a popular religious piety and sense of community that has long dissolved in advanced industrial societies. They also arise in a relatively monochrome ecclesiastical culture far removed from the fragmented post-denominational world of contemporary Western society. Both these features of the base community context help to explain its extraordinary growth in societies influenced by Spanish or Portuguese Catholicism. But this does not negate their challenge to the West, and at the heart of this challenge lives an insistence on the 'church-like' character of base communities. As the Brazilian theologian, J.B. Libanio, points out:

> They are *not a movement*, an association or a religious congregation... They are *not a method* (or the only method) of building up the church: they are the church itself. They are *not a miraculous recipe* for all the ills of society and the church. They are the church renewing itself... They are *not a utopia*: they are a sign of the kingdom, though they are not the kingdom... They are *not messianic*, but they can be prophetic and produce prophets like the church should. They are *not a natural... community...* identified with a race, language, people, family... They are the church... They are *not a protest group*, although their life is a protest against the mediocrity, sloth and inauthenticity of many... They are *not special groups for special people*. They are the church committed to the ordinary man, to the poor, to those who suffer injustice... They are *not closed*: they are open to dialogue with all. They are *not a reform of anything* in pastoral work: they are a decisive pastoral option, made in order to construct a new image of the church.[9]

9 Quoted in D. Prior, *The Church in the Home*, Marshall, Morgan and Scott: London, 1983, pp.16-17

Different kinds of small ecclesial groups have been developed elsewhere, particularly in the Philippines – another ex-Spanish right-wing dictatorship. In the Philippines, they possess the same character as the Latin American base communities. The internationally reported trial of Frs Brian Gore and Niall O'Brien, and several members of a base community, highlighted their predicament in that society.[10]

We could cite other examples of this rediscovery of the home as a fundamental context for church life in non-Western countries – for example, the emergence of clandestine groups, particularly among young people, in Russia within the Orthodox Christian tradition. There is the gradual growth of base Christian communities in Africa. On the Indian sub-continent, some Christian leaders are beginning to realise the potential that the home church approach has for remote, poverty-stricken villages. Home churches in states such as Kerala demonstrate that vital Christian worship, fellowship, outreach and social action can flourish without the aid of church buildings, ordained pastors or denominational agencies. Indeed, in many places this is the only hope of anything at all happening corporately among Christians or evangelistically among their neighbours.

The witness of Christian leaders

While it is mainly in non-Western countries that the most thoroughgoing experiments in regrouping the church around the home are taking place, a number of voices in countries with a longer Christian tradition have called for the same kind of change. These have not been confined to any one denomination, form of Christianity or position within the church. So far these voices have gone relatively unheeded but, if anything, their arguments for the home church approach have become more applicable in the intervening years. During the last decade their number has increased significantly. Endorsements of 'home churches', 'base communities' and the like have also begun to appear in the

---

10 A.W. McCoy, *Priests on Trial*, Harmondsworth: Penguin, 1984

reports of various ecclesiastical, inter-denominational and ecumenical bodies.

(a) From a traditional denomination

In his book *On Being the Church in the World*, Bishop John A.T. Robinson presents the extension of this two-tiered approach to include a third level of organisation. He begins by insisting that 'the house church' should not be regarded as merely a temporary expedient in a new area, nor as simply an evangelistic weapon for reaching outsiders:

> Both these conceptions are inadequate in the light of the New Testament. For it, the church in the house... is a theologically necessary part of the body. The implication is, rather, that these were churches within the 'parish' church, in much the same way as today the parish church is a church within the diocese... This conception... has been grievously lost to the modern church. We should never think of a diocese being an agglomeration of individuals or a federation of local organisations... but always as an organic union of parishes. But on the smaller scale that is precisely how we *are* content to think. Our parishes are for the most part collections of individuals; or, if these are brought together, it is in organisations. These latter are not units of the whole church in miniature but sectional groupings founded on some specifically limited basis of sex, age or interest... I believe that the theological recovery of this idea of 'the church in the house' is one of the most important tasks of our generation. Whereas the organisation is an optional extra... the cellular structure of the church will be rediscovered as a necessity of its life.[11]

In a later passage, J.A.T. Robinson isolates three elements of permanent significance for the church as a whole emerging out of his own experience of the church in the home:

> 1. The first is a living experience of a *form* of the church different from that which most people in this country have ever actually known. And it is a form which compels those

---

11 J.A.T. Robinson, 'The House Church and the Parish Church', *On Being the Church in the World*, SCM: London, 1960, pp.84-85

who find themselves within it to face questions which other levels of Christian living still allow them to evade. When there *is* no church to *go to*, one *can* only *be* the church. At this level, there is a new constraint both towards mission and towards deeper involvement with one's neighbour in Christ. One cannot ignore either the house next door (there is no real 'next door' to the parish church) or the Christian next to one (the parlour is very different from the pew)... At the same time there is being built up in the house church something much less vulnerable to disintegration from *without*. In the event of persecution, the church does not have to go underground; it *is* underground, even if the superstructure has to go.

2. The second thing that is being discovered is the meaning of holiness. By uniting the words 'holy' and 'common', hitherto defined as opposites, Christianity created something entirely new... By taking the Holy Communion from the sanctuary... nothing of reverence is lost, but rather that henceforth the most common is sensed as holy.

3. The third question that is being thrown up is the nature and future of the ministry... The significance of the house church is that it raises this question precisely in the right form and with immediate urgency. It shows a new type of ministry to be a necessary requirement of the normal (parochial) form of the church's mission and not merely of evangelistic adventures that might (very wrongly) be dismissed as side-lines or stunts. It shows the real need to be not mere assistants at the parish church (lay readers, permanent deacons, etc.), but the breakers of bread, priests of indigenous churches.

Robinson concludes his essay with the admission:

The experiment is full of dangers and shortcomings, of which those are most conscious who are most deeply quickened. But I should like to put on record for what it is worth — and I measure my words carefully — that I believe this development of the church in the house to be the single most important new thing that is happening in the Church of England today.[12]

---

12 *Op. cit.*, pp.93-95

(b) From a newer denomination
In his excellent book, *A New Face for the Church*, Lawrence
O. Richards argues that the 'small group' meeting as church
is 'the basic building block of the life of the gathered
church.' This is so partly because we 'need to know others
intimately in order to become the church. . . Another reason
lies in the nature of spiritual growth.' This 'cannot be understood merely as a change in ideas or in belief systems', but
'in terms of character change − transformation of attitudes,
of values, of personality. . . These are learned in our association with others', particularly in 'a community in which the
word of God is made flesh. . .'

The church today, as the church of the New Testament,
needs the 'church in the house'. 'Nevertheless,' he says,
'making the small group the basic unit of congregational life
will not be easy. Such decentralisation goes contrary to the
centralising structure that has grown up. And because the
two trends are not compatible, to the extent that small
groups become basic in church life, the total church organisation will necessarily change.'

Lawrence Richards sees the following pattern emerging:

> 1. The smallest churches. . . are neighbourhood gatherings,
> no larger than can comfortably fit in a home. In these
> meetings all the functions of church take place, and this is
> the prime location for mutual ministry. . . As gifts emerge
> and are recognised, church leaders are selected.
> 2. The church at times will assemble as a larger group for
> a variety of purposes, for the Sunday meeting, or to consider
> some problem facing it as a whole.
> 3. The leaders of the church meet together. . . one or more
> may be supported to free them for full-time ministry. . .
> There is no one prominent man in the local fellowship: no
> single pastor to whom we all look.[13]

Lawrence Richards' chief interest is in Christian
education, particularly in developing a thoroughly biblical

---

13 L.O. Richards, *A New Face for the Church*, Zondervan: Grand Rapids,
1970

or 'nurture' model of ministry to children. This model differs from the prevailing 'schooling' pattern that informs most education in local churches, Christian organisations or even theological seminaries.

> There is no hint in the organic world of the New Testament of the formal classroom or of culturally defined 'teacher' roles. Instead there is simply the warmth of closeness. There is the impact of life upon life, as faith and the great truths of the faith are shared from person to person.
> Both New and Old Testament nurture systems rely on involving children in the life of the faith community. Even today, some local fellowships follow this model of life together.
> One significant impact of adopting the schooling/instructional approach in our churches has been a resultant segregation of children into narrow, graded groups... But the segregated approach is not the only one available. In a variety of ways we can, and some *do*, restore children to significant participation with adults in nurturant groups.
> One of the most promising ways to touch the life of children is to let them become part of the support group of which their parents are members.[14]

Although Richards lists two other ways alongside the 'house church model' in which this kind of nurture can be cultivated, the author has indicated elsewhere that it is only the home church approach which permits the fullest implementation of the biblical model.[15]

(c) A post-denominational view

Finally, here is someone who speaks for those who, even where they belong to small groups within denominations, have found themselves frustrated, isolated and ignored. He is J.C. Hoekendijk. In *The Church Inside Out*, he argues that:

---

14 L.O. Richards, *A Theology of Children's Ministry*, Zondervan: Grand Rapids, 1983, pp. 201 and 281

15 In personal conversation with the authors

...only one road remains open: the crossing of the boundaries. For many of us this is probably the only way left. And
it is precisely here that the house church comes into view
again, but in a different context, namely, at that place in the
world where members of various denominations live and
work with those who come from elsewhere and also wish to
express their faith in communion with one another. There is,
of course, nothing new or original in this. The great majority
of mission congregations are constituted in the same way...

The traditional pattern of community life of the parish
church will have to be tested as to its missionary usefulness
as well... It emerged during the early Middle Ages and
served the expansion of the church from the city into the
surrounding area... We have canonized the parish church;
from an incidental pattern it became a normative model;
from a historically conditioned phenomenon it became an
unchangeable divine institution...

On this point a consensus is growing that can be
summarised concisely as follows: *the parish church
functions only in a stable society* for which it was originally
intended... In the modern world, in which the people are
becoming 'mobilities', a church that wants to enter into the
missionary situation in an adequate fashion will have to
structure itself as a mission church.[16]

Hoekendijk's strictures about the 'parish church' have more
relevance in a Western European situation where a more
stable society still exists. In newer industrial countries some
local congregations have adopted a missionary posture and
have broken out of their geographical boundaries. But they
continue to have difficulty in reaching the more mobile
members of our community.

Hoekendijk is particularly concerned about the need for
the development of home churches to be essentially a lay
enterprise rather than dominated by those who hold office
in the church. This, he feels, is critical if they are to become
effective agents of mission and complete expressions of the
church. Consequently:

---

16 J.C. Hoekendijk, *The Church Inside Out*, SCM: London, 1967,
pp.93-97

never can the establishment of a house church – or any other form of church life – be made dependent on the functioning or non-functioning of the (regulative) offices. In other words, we do not need to wait for anything. (If that had happened in history, very little would have come – in my opinion – of missions.) The laity have the privilege of the initiative. They ought to use it.

There is no reason, he says, why lay people should not celebrate the Lord's Supper in house churches. But it will only have its full power if it is a common rather than cultic meal. Hoekendijk concludes by saying that we are so unused to the notion that 'what happens on Sunday in the sanctuary can take place every day in the house church,' that:

> A house church that really functions is so improbable and mysterious for those who come into contact with it that one scratches one's head, and at the same time it is so common and so sensible that one finally feels that one gets his feet on the ground.[17]

Summary
The main aim in this historical overview has been to show that the idea of the 'home church' is not as novel as it appears. The 'home church' was central to the first Christians and continued for some time afterwards. At key points in the renewal of Christianity, the 'home church' has surfaced again in the thinking or practice of significant reformers.

Today, in Two-thirds World countries where the Christian gospel is making the greatest headway, the 'home church' – or something like it – is increasingly the fulcrum for spiritual and numerical growth. From different denominational backgrounds, Christian leaders in the West have begun to advocate that the 'home church' become the ecclesial basis or missionary spearhead of the congregation. Restructuring the church for community and mission

---

17 *Op. cit.*, pp.102-107

around the home, then, is not so strange a suggestion as it sometimes sounds. Despite this, few still launch out into the deep. John V. Taylor comments:

> Much has been said in the last twenty years about Christian cells and house-churches, yet their establishment as the normal unit of Christian community is still so patchy and experimental that it is easy to despair. The marvel is that the 'little congregations' are already coming to be regarded as normative in so many places. The process is bound to go on as the mobility and fragmentation of human societies increases.
>
> These small units of Christian presence are emphatically not a halfway house through which the uncommitted will eventually be drawn back into the parish churches. Nor are they an interim structure which ought to grow into new parish churches in due course... Too many people in the church insist upon regarding any other form than the conventional parish congregation as sub-normal and peripheral. They will not believe that such groups may have the fulness of Christ and should be allowed to possess all the resources and all the responsibilities of a local church.
>
> I believe that the parish structure will continue to minister to certain of the various areas of life... but it is the 'little congregations' which must become normative if the church is to respond to the Spirit's movements in the life of the world.[18]

If Taylor is right, there is a clear challenge to the church at large to discern the work of the Spirit in the formation of home churches today and to co-operate with him in this way.

---

18 John V. Taylor, *The Go-Between God*, SCM: London, 1972, pp.148-149

See further on the theme of this chapter the more recently published books by G. Cook, *The Expectation of the Poor: Latin American Basic Ecclesial Communities in Protestant Perspective*, Orbis: New York, 1985; R. Paul Stevens, *Equipping All the Saints for Ministry*, IVP: Downer's Grove, 1985; Lois Barrett, *Building the House Church*, Herald, Scottsdale, 1986; and B.J. Lee and M.A. Cowan, *Dangerous Memories: House Churches and Our American Story*, Sheed & Ward: Kansas City, 1986 — the last three from Brethren, Mennonite and Catholic backgrounds respectively.

4

Small is beautiful:

Testimonies to the home church experience

GIVEN THE BIBLICAL WARRANT and historical precedent for home churches, why has so little been attempted within the main denominations to make the church in the home the basic unit of congregational life?

Hindrances to the development of home churches
We can think of five main reasons:
(a) Lack of awareness
Up to a point, church members have been encouraged to head in this direction. One only has to think of the many small groups that exist in churches today or the proliferation of cell groups on campuses. But mostly Christians have been encouraged to think that by attending a service on Sunday and a group midweek, they have fulfilled their biblical duty to 'gather together'.

An added problem is that in large services the emphasis is on formal worship of God, with fellowship as only a secondary element. Meanwhile, small groups tend to focus on a particular interest, for example Bible study, prayer, the exercise of gifts or ministry, with members not necessarily in a substantial relationship with one another.

What is generally missing in both large and small meetings is the commitment to a *specific group* of people with whom we are in close relationship and for whom we take practical responsibility. Yet, only as we do this, can we actually fulfil such injunctions as: 'love one another earnestly from the heart' (1 Peter 1:22), 'care for one another' (1 Corinthians

12:25) and 'bear one another's burdens' (Galatians 6:2).
These words must become flesh; they cannot remain
abstract. God asks us to incarnate them and live them out
among a specific group of people. Otherwise these
injunctions remain comfortably general in scope or become
merely pious sentiments which have only occasional
application.

In a home church, we can get to know and take an interest
in a manageable group of people who will also get to know
and take an interest in us. In such a group we can in time
take off the masks we wear and begin to share our
weaknesses, doubts and fears as well as our strengths,
certainties and abilities. By doing so we start to overcome
the ironic situation that it is in the *church* that we are often
less open and honest with each other than elsewhere, least
able to share and deal with the concerns that most deeply
touch us. In a home church we learn to give and receive, to
teach and understand, to help others and have our own
burdens carried, to love and be loved. In brief, in such a
group we can become more like Christ and assist others to
become more like him as well.

(b) Cost of commitment

At a meeting to arrange a day conference on the subject of
community a couple of years ago, one of the organisers was
overheard to say: 'The more I hear about the contents of this
conference, the less sure I am that I can afford to come
along.' She had already begun to feel the challenge of a
greater commitment to others and started to ask herself
whether she was really prepared for it.

This small incident shows up what contradictory creatures
we are. We are capable of both wanting and not wanting to
commit ourselves at the same time. There is nothing
surprising about this. When some of us first heard the
gospel clearly, we were drawn to it but also hesitant about
it, knowing that it was demanding something of us as well
as granting something to us. Similarly, some Christians feel
both tantalised and threatened by the prospect of joining a
home church.

In a way we do well to hesitate before we move in this
direction, just as we do well to count the cost before we

accept the gospel. For in doing so we are recognising that community does not come cheap, at a bargain price or on a discount. Yet we do not really need to hold back in fear that we will become too exposed or lose our individuality. As Art Gish reminds us, genuine community does not involve 'a loss of individuality and personal freedom', but 'a living relationship which gives us the freedom and power to be who God wants us to be... It does not mean we are destroyed, but transformed into something new and better... It is not so much the end of the old as the beginning of a new life.'[1]

We do not really need to be told this. Many of us have had experiences at a houseparty, parish conference or church camp where we began to open up more of ourselves to others and God, only to discover that we found more of ourselves and God in the process. It is a sad comment on the quality of our church life that we have to arrange such events in order to deepen the bonds between members. Church ought to be a sort of houseparty each week and that is exactly what a home church becomes when it is operating properly – and what a meeting of the whole church can become if loosened from some of its traditional moorings.

(c) Shortage of time

Probably the main reason why so much is said and so little done about community is lack of time. We live in a busy world. Few people have much time at their disposal. Those who are most interested in developing a greater experience of community – young marrieds, couples with growing families and single people – tend to be overly committed already. The demands of small children, establishing a home and increasing responsibilities at work, as well as involvement in church and other Christian organisations, are often heaviest upon such people.[2]

Who has the time to participate in a home church?

1 A. Gish, *Living in Christian Community: A Personal Manifesto*, Albatross: Sydney, 1980, p.52

2 For a fuller discussion of this theme, see Robert Banks, *The Tyranny of Time*, Sydney: Lancer, 1983 (Exeter: Paternoster; IVP: Downer's Grove, 1984)

Frequently, the time does not seem to be there. Even where people make a determined effort to participate in a home church alongside their other commitments, they do not have the time nor energy to make it a priority. As a result it receives only their second-best attention.

If a home church does not receive more than that, it will only ever be second-best in character. Second-best attention means second-best results, and the members of such a home church will fail to love both God and the other home church members. This is one of the reasons why many home churches never really get off the ground. They are not anyone's top priority and therefore never develop their real potential. Even where people do make room for them, they often prefer to gather fortnightly rather than weekly and are prepared to come together only for a couple of hours rather than for a longer and more fruitful period. Because of people's initial uncertainties, a two-hour meeting once a fortnight may be the only way to begin. But unless there is the possibility of meeting weekly for a longer period of time, little will come out of the home church.

The cult of busyness and activism that infects Christians so much today is one of the greatest barriers to the church becoming what it should be. If only Christians were willing to *be* more with each other and corporately with God, they would find that although they *do* less, they actually achieve more. We can all do this. It is simply a matter of working out what is important and giving it the priority it deserves.

(d) Loss of capability

In an article entitled 'Christian Community: A Painful Union for Australians in Particular', Spencer Colliver notes: 'An Australian, because of his socialisation, the particular patterns of his culture and the structure of his society, faces much greater difficulty in achieving deep and lasting inter-personal relationships than people from other cultures'.[3] He identifies as contributing factors the lack of emotional intimacy in the family (especially between father and sons),

---

3 S. Colliver, 'Christian Community: A Painful Vision for Australians in Particular', *Comfort or Crisis: Living Christianly in the Eighties,* Hexagon: Sydney, 1980, p.50

the dependence upon bureaucratic institutions rather than other people, and the authoritarian, repressive streak in the Australian character (for all its alleged egalitarianism). Thus many small groups in the church find it difficult to establish a genuinely communal lifestyle. This is a pervasive Anglo-Saxon, not just an Australian problem.

We could add a related difficulty. Most Westerners, female as well as male, have suffered imaginative as well as emotional deprivation. This means that when we meet together in small groups or home churches, our minds are active but our imaginations and feelings are less so. (One of the indicators of this is that when our imaginations or feelings are given a free rein, they are often uncontrolled.) Yet we cannot understand or help one another properly unless we are emotionally sensitive, able to get behind surface conversation. We also need to be capable of placing ourselves in others' shoes, to appreciate why they come at things a particular way. In many groups people are only listening and responding to others superficially, missing the important things underneath. Moreover, the Bible reveals to us a passionate and creative God and is itself, from beginning to end, full of emotional appeals and warnings, of imaginative symbols, parables, metaphors, similes, dreams and visions. We can only understand God himself and his revelation to us in the Bible if we are willing to open up our emotions and imaginations and let the Spirit stir them into life.

Yet many churches and groups have so allowed secular models of teaching to affect them, that it is only the cognitive activities that receive much attention. That is why doctrinal teaching and Bible studies dominate so many small group and home church meetings. This excludes those who are intellectually less advantaged, those who think through images and associations rather than deduction and inference and those who have valid experiences (e.g. parables and stories, intuitions and experiences, dreams and visions) to share. Where emotion and imagination are given little place in a group, there will be only a minimum of communication – and therefore of community with one another and with God.

(e) Weight of structures

There are two main ways in which congregational structures can hinder home church development. Since the structures of most congregations revolve around the minister, if he is resistant to the idea of home churches, it is very difficult for them to emerge. As David Prior, himself a clergyman who has initiated home groups, says:

> For many pastors and ministers, including bishops and archbishops, such home church life is very threatening. The reasons for this fear are profound and manifold. Clergy have not been trained to operate in this way. Orthodoxy in doctrine is usually seen to be of prime importance, and such home churches look like potential seedbeds of heresy. The human need to control situations for which we are held responsible becomes very urgent. There is, moreover, a crisis of identity and role amongst most clergy today. For many, uncomfortable experience of small groups in the past obstructs openness to the Spirit now. Even when scope is given for this pattern of church life, it is very tempting to keep tight control even while decentralising and delegating. To many clergy, delegation looks and feels like abdication, especially when the actual teething troubles begin.[4]

Yet actually ministers have an enormous amount to gain from the contribution of home churches, especially where they are prepared to belong to such a group themselves. Quite apart from what they may gain in terms of personal support and spiritual vitality, closer contact with some of their people puts them more in touch with the actual needs of their parishioners and with the main pressures in society. It also enables pastors to become more relaxed in their relationship with other people and less the players of an ecclesiastical role. A home church will help them discover their actual gifts as opposed to those others expect them to have.

Where a number of home churches exist in a congregation, the mutual care that goes on within them – as well as to

---

4 D. Prior, *The Church in the Home*, Marshall, Morgan & Scott: London, 1983, p.25

outsiders in need – reduces the pastoral work of ministers enormously. As such groups take hold, they can also render the existence of a number of typical congregational organisations unnecessary, thus reducing the amount of time ministers and the overworked few in their congregations must spend on planning and in committees. Even the provision of formal training to help people identify their gifts becomes superfluous in properly functioning home churches which help people discover and mature these organically. Home churches are also able to take responsibility, as a whole, for specific aspects of the congregation's life, such as organising and leading public worship, interviewing those seeking marriage or baptism, visiting the sick and bereaved, praying for and writing to a missionary.

There is a second way in which the structures of the church can create difficulty for home churches. Some denominations as yet do not permit the decentralisation of certain aspects of public worship into a home setting. The most frequent casualties are the sacraments. Unless the minister is present – and, perhaps, a particular liturgy used – the Lord's Supper cannot be celebrated. The same situation applies to baptism. Given the importance of these two sacraments for the life of a Christian community, restrictions upon them limit the extent to which home churches can become fully operational. Some creative ways of dealing with this situation are discussed in chapter 8.

But even with these restrictions, people can begin to meet together, include a meal regularly in their meeting and welcome children into their church. This enables them to go a long way towards gathering as a church in the fullest sense of the term and in time limitations upon their fellowship with God and one another will hopefully disappear.

Testimonies to the value of home churches
If these are some of the factors hindering people from developing home churches, what are some of the benefits? These have been implicit, even explicit, in what has been said already.

The best way to portray the value of gathering in a home church is to let those who have done so for some time speak for themselves. What follows is a number of testimonies from people involved in different kinds of groups. A minister, and some of his people, talk about participating in a home church within the context of a local congregation. A whole group shares what they have gained from belonging to an interdenominational home church. A number of people in another group explain why they joined independent home churches instead of remaining in their local congregation.

□ *A minister speaks. . .*

After more than twenty years as a minister, I came to the conclusion that I was not well and all manner of things were not well with the church. Looked at as an institution, there was much in St Paul about the church and much concerning the kingdom of God that was as a dream from another age – something gone and unrepeatable. Bible studies were largely repetitious, with a certain lack of mutual affection between the members.

After a major change in the structure of our church, I found myself one of three in a team ministry. This promised something new, but actually was one of the loneliest, saddest times I could remember. The three of us did what seemed good in our own eyes. Each being fiercely individualist, we largely passed each other by. We planned together occasionally and prayed together not at all. There were five congregations to be ministered to: each one also by itself and for itself, each one further fragmented into a number of 'fellowships'. Apart from Sundays, there was no meeting of men or women sharing life and faith. There were very few who had nerve enough to share themselves with others, apart from the usual pleasantries.

After a year or so in low spirits, even physically ill, I came across *A Staircase for Silence* by Alan Ecclestone.[5] In the chapter entitled 'Do you pray the Parish?' I read this:

> The parish means a body of people drawn and held together in a spirit that prompts the members to care for, respect and

5 A. Ecclestone, *A Staircase for Silence*, Darton, Longman & Todd: London, 1977

love each other... small enough to permit a true understanding to grow up between its members. Such a body must
extend their lives by confronting them with diversities of
character and achievement, encouraging each person to be
himself... Scattered among the people in our fragmented
churches today there are those who hunger for something
other than they see, who are in pain because the church they
belong to seems hopelessly stuck fast in a way of life that by
no stretch of the imagination can be described in terms of
leaven or salt or light, who realise daily that the words which
are used to speak of the church are far from being embodied
in it.

This and much more addressed itself to my condition, and
illumined the path ahead. I found by asking that there were
others who did 'hunger for something other than they see'.
Two young mothers and I met one afternoon and, after some
cheery conversation and prayer, decided to ask permission
of the parish to meet in one of its halls. Most of my sickness,
I found, had left me before I reached home. We established
a pattern of shared meal, an informal eucharist, singing,
praying and Bible studies which has remained constant. We
meet on Wednesdays from 6.30 to 9.30 p.m.

We have been a house church for five years, meeting in
homes during winter and using a large room attached to a
church building at other times. When thirty-five people
came the first night, it seemed then like the end of a siege.
In fact, it was the beginning of a way that was as difficult
as it was joyful. We found that other parishioners viewed
our activities with unease so that, with the customary
departures and change of location, some winter evenings
our numbers dwindled to five or six. It was my hope to have
a house church at each of the five meeting-places of the
parish, but that unfortunately did not eventuate.

When we began, some members who had been meeting for
twenty-five years in conventional church settings discovered
that they did not know each others' names. That initial
shock gave the core members added incentive for staying
together through thin times. What we valued most, apart
from our fellowship and study, was that we had a group to
which we could invite others. As a consequence of the

fellowship, most members of the house church (we average twenty) have developed a form of ministry, some of exceptional quality, simply by picking up the leads that became evident in their relationships. In consequence, people hostile or indifferent to the appeal of 'Sunday church' have come, blossomed and brought into the fellowship people from other denominations who have subsequently participated fully. And though they have not left their own churches, they relate to us as essential friends. The faith as it comes to us in the body has been eminently exportable.

☐ ...*and two of his parishioners*
We started as a small group of Christians, feeling that something was missing from our lives, something that the structured church services and regime couldn't fulfil. We met with really no firm ideas of what format our meetings would take, and we have now 'put together' a meeting which is worshipful, joyful and vital. We are always seeking new ways of getting to know Jesus Christ better and, through him, each other.

On a personal note, I have grown as a Christian since I have learned to know and accept the almost unbelievable fact that God loves me just as I am. Our prayer has been an enriching and rewarding experience: prayers for healing, spiritual strengthening and guidance have been answered.

The group has also grown together. We not only sustain each other in our worship, but give – and receive – positive help in many areas. It's a real joy to share thought-provoking, sad, and even mundane experiences with friends. The meeting has become for me a weekly happening that I don't want ever to miss.

*   *   *

For me, coming to the group was, at first, a tentative gesture of someone reaching out in a state of depression, for companionship and the need to belong. Although unable to join in, I came away from the group with a sense of warmth and well-being. It gave me the strength and incentive to carry on living. Now that I am a new person – having found Christ, swiftly and unexpectedly – coming to the group gives me a new meaning of growth, learning and love. Christ is ever-present in the quiet caring prayers, the sharing of weekly experiences, in a smile or a ready joke. To forgo the meeting for even one week would be a far greater starvation than forgoing daily food.

☐ *Two ex-fulltime Christian workers...*

When people ask us 'Why did you start a house church?' it is interesting that the discussion that follows highlights several definite reasons rather than one simple answer to the question.

My wife and I were on the staff of an interdenominational tertiary student ministry. We were fully involved in encouraging and assisting people to become Christians, to grow in their faith and in turn to help others do the same. However, by the time we had four young children, we realised that it was requiring an increasing amount of personal energy to build and maintain relationships with students – people that we would not naturally be spending time with as a young family. What we needed was a form of ministry which worked through everyday relationships and which had a natural focus on the family, bringing the family together rather than fragmenting it.

During this same period we were clarifying our perspective on the fundamental purpose of the church. Basically we see it as providing an environment which helps Christians become more like Christ, in-depth personal relationships with other Christians being essential for this. This environment should encourage and sustain Christians in their ministry to other people, whether to Christians or non-Christians. We believe that, measured by the actual results in people's lives, the priorities, activities and quality of relationship in many churches are called into question.

A third strand of thought crystallised for us at the same time. We had noticed the increasing financial strain experienced by the church in our society. For many churches there is a tension between the maintenance and mortgage payments for church buildings and payment of a minister or church staff. Missionary societies are also acutely aware of the shortage of funds for their staff. Alongside this, we observed a stereotyped perspective of ministry. Very often a Christian young person who wanted his life to count for God came to the conclusion that he must go 'full-time' and be a paid Christian worker to achieve this. All Christians should earnestly seek to fully invest their lives for God, but if this requires that all Christians be paid Christian workers then this is clearly not possible. This caused us to explore a model of church which was simple and efficient, and a model of ministry which could provide effective pastoral oversight without the accompanying financial support.

When we concluded that we needed a change from student ministry, we had a number of options open to us. However, none of the options in the conventional church or in parachurch organisations could give adequate scope for the vision we had. After reflection, we decided that the most suitable model to encompass this was the first-century concept of house churches as basic units of a wider Christian community. So we decided that I would take a job in the regular workforce and that we would start a house church, but retain our involvement with our local church.

□ *...and others in their group*
I have gained from our house church a new vision for church growth, a new sense of direction and the development of a personal ministry. . .

I have a group of friends that I call and relate to as a family — my own family live in another city. Now that I've resigned from work, the studies have become extra valuable as a means of mental stimulation as well as learning practical ways of Christian living. (A toddler doesn't stretch your mind very much — bend it, yes, but not stretch!)

With our house church I have an unusual sense of wholeness, of belonging to a vital Christian organism which has a network of interdependent relationships. The beauty and meaning of 'the body of Christ' is unfolding for me. . .

Membership of a house church has provided me with a vital resource and learning atmosphere that I can use in my personal living as well as for input in my mainline church. The fellowship facilitates caring and love for each other where we are accepted and welcomed, a family atmosphere in which I can be myself and not have to assume roles I don't

want to. The Christian fellowship also helps me from sliding
away.

□ *Two married couples. . .*

Our feelings after our first night at a house church were
mixed. We enjoyed the people in the church and a number
of things which were done. We were made to feel quite at
home, different people introducing themselves and showing
interest in us: where we were living, what we did profes-
sionally, what our church background was and generally
getting to know us. But we felt the meeting moved too slowly
(it had lasted about four hours). Being used to liturgical
services which were briefer and brisker, we had wanted
things to get moving.

As time went on, however, we settled to this style of
churching. We found that, while not 'clear cut', when the
church met there was quite clearly 'form without structure'.
Indeed, it didn't take very long to see that a great deal of
thought, prayer and effort by members went into the preparation for the meetings. Yet there was plenty of room for flexibility and adaptation, depending upon the circumstances of
the evening or specific issues which may have arisen for
individual members during the week. Interestingly, when
we had cause to return to our former church and attend a
morning service, we found it all very rushed and
regimented, with no time for reflection or opportunity for
questions, discussion or sharing.

Much has happened since our attendance at that first
meeting. Our church has gone through various changes in
terms of membership, numbers and composition. The
advent of a number of babies has led to some rescheduling
and re-arranging of meetings. It has been good to see the
adaptability of the home church in these circumstances and
the 'seasons' or 'passages' that a church, as well as an
individual or family, goes through, though we wouldn't
pretend that the changes have always been smooth or easy.

Notwithstanding these changes, a number of core
elements of our meetings have been maintained throughout:
the provision of a meal (central to the meeting and providing
its fundamental orientation and context); opportunity to
relax and catch up with one another, as well as address

particular issues if necessary; freedom to sing and express ourselves creatively; time to pray and reflect, study, talk or meditate.

Of course, the meeting is only part of our church life. More informal contacts through the week allow relationships to grow and develop. But the time spent at our regular meetings allows the opportunity for God's Spirit to help us in particular ways.

*   *   *

We have been members of a house church for thirteen years. From our previous experience of small groups, we came to realise how much Christian growth can take place in such a setting. However, these groups were often frustrated in their purpose – through inexperience and the lack of priority given to them in the formal life of the church. In such groups we also often felt obliged to put people right and solve their problems for them. The house church to which we now belong is a top priority for its members and this makes a considerable difference to the quality of our fellowship in it. We have also come to realise that it is more important to accept one another as we are than to try to set one another right.

Jean Vanier, whose work in community with the handi-capped has given him valuable insights in this area, argues that 'to accept our weaknesses and those of others is the very opposite of sloppy complacency... It is essentially a concern for truth so that we do not live in illusion and can grow from where we are and not where we want to be, or where others want us to be.'[6]

We have come to experience, in a way we had not known before, three important aspects of church life. First, we have discovered the importance of just *being with others and valuing them for themselves*, the worthwhileness of being committed to them as they are. This commitment to one another is seen in prayerful concern as well as practical help in time of need.

---

6 J. Vanier, *Community and Growth*, St Paul: Sydney, 1979, p.18

Second, we have investigated *the truth of God's character, his values and his perspective*. As we have studied together God's nature, we have found that the Holy Spirit does act in people's lives to change their long-established attitudes, opinions or behaviour patterns. A well-developed atmosphere of love and acceptance allows people the dignity of responding to God's Spirit in their own time, whether in the area of personal lifestyle, the call to social action, or special witness to the truth of the Christian gospel.

Third, we have learnt afresh that *each member is able to make a unique contribution to the whole*. The setting in which this happens generally takes the form of a meeting lasting about four or five hours. This is made up of the fellowship meal, personal sharing, prayer, singing, study and discussion. Spending this amount of time together encourages participation by all members, including children, and the full expression of the gifts of the Spirit.

We have personally gained great benefit from being able to 'recognise the meaning of the Lord's body', i.e. the church (1 Corinthians 11:29), through sharing in the fellowship of the Lord's Supper as an actual meal. In preparing and sharing the fellowship meal, we have come to appreciate and care about other aspects of one another's lives that would not otherwise be revealed.

We appreciate the contribution that the various traditional forms and structures of church life have made to the edification of Christians. These differing expressions emphasise facets of God's truth. However, we have over the years become satisfied that small-group church life as expressed in home churches is most conducive to the New Testament goals of mutual ministry, sound teaching, caring fellowship, and personal and corporate edification.

□ *...and some single people*

Why do we belong to a home church rather than attend a local church?

There are a number of characteristics prevalent in local churches which have moved us to seek an alternative. Many local churches have become so big that people can remain anonymous, becoming spectators rather than real participants. We have consciously sought to avoid the masks which people put on in that environment – the masks of security, niceness and personal piety. Because of their large numbers and lack of participation, there is a greater risk of activities, worship services especially, never rising above a superficial level. People can attend church for years without taking part or becoming known. The minister alone is often responsible for the church's organisation and delegation.

This lack of personal involvement is related to other difficulties we have experienced. Local churches are generally hierarchical. This means that decision-making is mostly in the hands of a few. There is a large emphasis on formal teaching, especially from the minister in sermons, at the expense of discussion and sharing of insights within the congregation. We have serious doubts about the effectiveness of this kind of meeting.

There is a further problem. The local church, as part of the institutional church, also presents itself to some members of our group as part of the establishment in society. It is often found supporting the status quo, even pursuing self-interested ends. Also the local church does not see the small groups within it as the key focus of the church's life and energy. This is despite the fact that these small groups may be providing effective opportunities for discussion, participation and friendship, while the large services, which are the main focus of church life, provide none of these.

Our home church is small and less structured. This promotes free, honest and meaningful discussion, a closer understanding between members and, as a result, genuine caring for each other. There is greater involvement, partici-pation, activity and responsibility within the group. Over time, a small group offers greater intimacy and deepening fellowship where trust is engendered. Worship, we find, has greater reality and more meaning when we are sharing our lives in this way. Worship is also more readily related to the rest of our lives. In a home church we have the opportunity to experience love in action, to focus our energies and to enjoy each other's company.

Our home church is non-hierarchical. People all take responsibility for the structure and process of the group.

People have a commitment to each other in a way which is not possible generally in a large, anonymous group. There is also greater flexibility, spontaneity and variety, with more sharing of resources and gifts where everyone, to some extent, is responsible.

*   *   *

What does being part of a home church mean? Home church is participation in an environment of faith in which I am being opened, nurtured, challenged and supported and where I in turn can be open even about my doubts, nurturing, challenging and supporting. It is an occasion from which I go out to be more effective during the week as a result of the focus which the group offers. Home church is a place where I belong, where people are concerned for each other and I can be who I am without any facade. Home church is a forum where we can receive and consider new ideas and challenges, where we can worship in the context of shared lives. So home church offers an experience of, and the chance for experimentation with, old and new ways of worship that reflect the interests and personalities of the individuals involved, be it praise, prayer, meditation or learning.

However, the commitment and responsibility of home church is not always easy. Home church is also the place where my busyness and tiredness prevent me from participating as I should, where my narrow-mindedness prevents me from being open, makes me judgmental and resentful and where my contribution is yet another burden at the end of a week of demands. But in this conflict between the opportunity for and the burden of giving, as well as the opportunity for and the burden of receiving, we find real growth. At the moment we struggle with the difficulty of being open to a diversity among group members, while maintaining some cohesion. We are fearful of a sterility which springs from our middle-class outlook, and we have not been able to meet the needs of a few people who did not share our interest in the intellectual pursuit of our faith.

Some further observations
(a) A personal confession
Why do we belong to a home church ourselves? Despite the risk of repeating some of the things said already, we feel that this is a question we should answer as co-authors. For here we come to our most basic reasons for writing this book.

We belong to a house church because we find that God is there in a fuller, more real and intimate way. This has something to do with the fact that we meet in an ordinary home – or occasionally out-of-doors. In the familiarity of a home or the beauty of God's creation we come to experience him in a closer and more vivid way. It also has something to do with the fact that when we come together we see him, feel him and overhear him in the others who are there. As everyone relates to God and to each other – as they talk and sing, laugh and cry, give and receive – he relates to us, shares with us and gives life to us through them.

Our time together keeps us in touch with the different personal struggles, family responsibilities, work situations, social concerns, cultural pursuits and specific types of ministry that we're involved in outside the group. It's these that are taken up in conversation and prayer and scrutinised in the light of biblical teaching, prophetic insight and Christian experience. In this way many of our strengths and weaknesses, dreams and doubts, encouragements and hurts, hopes and fears are acknowledged, shared and sifted.

As a result of our meetings, we have gained a clearer insight into what is happening to people and society around us, and a stronger desire and power to do something about this. Others directly benefit as a result, as we see God working through us outside the group, sometimes in quite natural, sometimes quite unexpected ways. We find there is a definite flow-over from our sharing in the group to our sharing with those in need whom we meet from day-to-day. We don't feel embarrassed to ask some of these to come and join our group, so that they too can enter into what we ourselves experience.

We find church by turns provoking and stimulating, disturbing and comforting, demanding and heartening. It's full of variety, as people come with differing backgrounds and beliefs. There's no fixed order for what we do or how we do it. It's full of change: every time a new person joins our little community or some new problem and opportunity is worked through, its character alters. It is full of surprises, too, as we discover our own unconscious needs and desires and hear God's unpredictable response to us, either directly through an individual or gradually through the group.

It's the genuine family character of our church that means so much to us. We've gained some additional sisters and brothers whom neither of us had in our natural families. We also have some young nephews and nieces, several of whom look upon us as more their uncles and aunts than those who really are such. As an extended family we try to do things for one another, not only inside but also outside our meetings. This isn't always easy, as distance separates us and some are heavily burdened by their jobs. But we do make an effort.

We have our high points and low points, agreements and conflicts, ups and downs. Doesn't any family? Sometimes we also disappoint and fail one another and feel down or let down as a result. But we often do that to ourselves in our own Christian lives anyway. The key feature is that we're committed to working through our difficulties with one another, not running away from them. This is just as well, for tensions emerge more in the open in our kind of group than in a normal church, and you're forced to come to terms with your own and others' limitations. But we find that these are often the growing points of our own and the church's life. Although there is always some pain involved, what comes out in the end is really worthwhile.

There are some real benefits apart from a sense of belonging and the growth that comes through conflict. For example, as we grow closer we're discovering that we're able to open up to one another emotionally as well as intellectually, more capable of giving our affection or concern for one another some physical expression. We have also discovered that in the supportive environment our church provides, we and others have been able to take some risks for God which otherwise might have daunted us. Or we've been able to cope better with crises in life that otherwise we might have found too overwhelming. We have also come to see that the quality and character of our common life, and the way we relate to and handle each other, is going to affect and change us more than anything else except our individual family situations.

Last, but by no means least, church is generally the social and humorous highlight of the week, especially as we eat and drink together in the Lord's name, delighting in the simple but superb meal before us, good company around us and presence of God among us. There we catch a glimpse of what it will be like when we sit down and celebrate together with Christ in his kingdom. If what we experience week to week is a little foretaste of it, then we can hardly wait to get there!

(b) A general recommendation

For ourselves, then, and for the others who have spoken in this chapter, belonging to a home church is an indispensable part of the Christian life. In fact, we cannot conceive of living and growing as Christians without it. To lose it would be to lose the most vital means of the Spirit's working in our lives. That is why we plead so strongly for the development of home churches within existing congregational and denominational frameworks and that they become the basic unit of church life.

We say 'home churches' deliberately, not 'small groups'. The latter do not encompass all aspects of church gathering and are rarely the fundamental aspect in a congregation's life. Establishing home churches is the most effective way of creating a far-reaching family bond between the members, of earthing their gatherings in the realities of everyday life, and of enabling them to exercise their gifts and fulfil their responsibilities.

When the home church gets beyond a certain size it becomes impossible to establish genuine relationships with and take real responsibility for everyone in the church. Beyond a certain size meetings are too formal for us to show certain sides of our personality and to share many of our everyday concerns. Beyond a certain size everything becomes too regulated to permit everyone to play a part in determining the community's affairs. For these reasons, in church as well as in society, 'small is beautiful'! Just as we need an intermediate technology to balance the big structures that surround us, so we need intermediate institutions to complement the churches' larger organisations and gatherings.

How realistic is this? Does it make sense in the light of contemporary social conditions? This is an important question and not one alien to the outlook of the early Christians. Their idea of community touched the raw nerve of certain changes taking place in first-century society. At that time many people were searching for a more intimate form of family or communal life. Some were joining various religious societies and social clubs in order to find their own identity and a little human warmth. Others were dreaming of a new view of society, worldwide in scope, which would enable them to have a say in the running of their own civic and political affairs. In a quite remarkable way the early Christian communities met all three needs at once. No wonder they proved such a strong attraction to the spiritually jaded, socially isolated citizens of the Mediterranean world!

Some of these same tendencies have now come to the surface in advanced Western societies like our own. The break-up of family ties resulting from increased social mobility, and the nuclear family's inadequacy to carry the burdens imposed upon it, have given rise to a longing for more extended family networks or semi-communal arrangements. Many people want to get more in touch with their emotions and imaginations, and to bridge the gap between their private selves and their social responsibilities – witness the growing number of personal development courses, community discussion groups, continuing education programmes and mature age enrolments at universities. There is interest in new forms of religious experience and a desire for more participatory approaches to decision-making.

Some of the people affected by these trends are among those most open to the gospel today. They tend not to look in the direction of the institutional church. Its stress on the private at the expense of the social sphere, its preoccupation with dogmas at the expense of life, and its authoritarian rather than participatory structures do not appeal to them. Only a form of church life that runs counter to these trends is likely to provide what they are looking for.

There are other groups outside the churches which are also uneasy with institutional forms of church life. Many people who come from a working-class background still place a greater emphasis upon the family and communal networks. They are less inhibited, more down-to-earth, preferring a more informal way of relating. Other people are disadvantaged by the overly individual, cerebral and institutional character of our society, some of whom are instinctively looking for an alternative as their only hope for justice. Home churches provide a form of church life far more compatible with the values and longings of these people.

These trends in society at large are as observable inside the church as outside it. The move towards cross-generational educational programmes as well as home, cell, cluster or pastoral groups precisely parallels the broader interest in more extended family and communal arrangements. The new concern with Christians' moral and social responsibilities, and desire on the part of many Christians to give greater expression to their emotional and creative capacities, demonstrate the search for a more relevant and balanced way of life. The new interest in spirituality illustrates how much longing there is for a more personal expression of faith and many people wish to play a greater part in deciding the church's affairs.

Even many of the most conservative of church members are feeling the impact of the broader cultural changes that are taking place in our society. A study of a congregation in the United States some years ago came to the conclusion that establishment adults were in transition, reassessing their values, their identity, their relationship to authority, reassessing how the past relates to the present, institutions and structures, how decisions are made, and the importance of intellectual-verbalisation and acting-feeling.[7]

---

7 Quoted in C.M. Olsen, *The Base Church: Creating Community through Multiple Forms*, Forum House: Atlanta, 1973, p.48

Conclusion

There is also a growing number of people for whom none of these changes is enough. Some manage to hold on at the edges of congregational life. Some find a temporary resting place in parachurch activities of one kind or another. Some withdraw into a private Christianity too disenchanted with institutional church life to find a home there again. What binds these people together is a deep sense of desperation. They literally ache to belong to an informal, compassionate community. For them this is no general desire or optional extra. It is a life-and-death matter, a case of spiritual integrity and survival. They will not settle for anything less for they cannot get by on anything less. Nor can they venture out into experiments of an evangelistic, social or cultural kind unless they have the support of a genuinely caring community.

For the sake of the vitality of the church as a whole, on behalf of those who are feeling marginal in it and those most open to the gospel, we need to rediscover that 'small is beautiful' and restructure congregational life accordingly. The conditions are ripe for doing something about this. It's time we rose to the opportunity.

5

First steps:

How home churches can come into being

WE ARE NOW IN A POSITION to ask: how should a home church come into being? We have deliberately put the question this way rather than asking: how can you start a home church?

This second way of putting the question places the emphasis on us and what we can do, not on the role of God and his Spirit. Yet any church first and foremost emanates from God. Unless he wills it, it should not be commenced. The fundamental question anyone must ask when considering forming a home church is: does God want this to happen or not? It is not enough that people are in need of it. It is not enough that some are asking for it. It is not enough that some have the gifts to sustain it. God himself must be consulted to find out whether he wishes a group to commence and whether he wishes it to commence now.

Some fundamental factors
Being divine rather than human institutions, churches, like marriages, are made in heaven, not upon earth. To think otherwise is a serious mistake.
(a) A sound foundation
Over the last fifteen years too many home churches have started and later stopped because God's approval to start was assumed, not discerned. It is true that some that began on a false foundation were later re-formed on a proper one. Not so others, which eventually came to grief. So it is very important to know what is in God's mind when there is the possibility of a home church coming into existence.

This is not something individuals can find out for themselves. Anyone who goes ahead on the basis of some personal revelation from God has taken a dangerous step. God makes his intentions in these kinds of matters known to a group, however small. While he may give a lead to an individual, encouraging him or her to initiate discussion and prayer with others, it is not until others have corroborated the initial lead that anything definite should get under way.

Some years ago before we left Sydney to return to Canberra, we considered whether God wished us to join an existing home church in Canberra or to begin a new one. After talking over the matter for some time, we were fairly confident that he was asking us to commence a new group. Although we had come to this conclusion jointly, we knew that we had to test it out on several others also interested in a home church.

After our arrival in Canberra, we did this. It was an unhurried process, taking several weeks, before we all decided that it seemed good not only to us but to the Holy Spirit to form a church. We have since helped another group, some of whom were friends but some strangers, to discover whether God was calling them to begin a home church. This took longer – about four months in all. Three of the original number decided that they were not ready to commit themselves to the enterprise. If the group had regarded itself as a church from the beginning, their departure could have seriously disrupted and weakened the venture.

If a group of people cannot be certain that they should form a church, there are still other ways of meeting that are open to them. In other words, just because they are not yet sure they can start a home church, or even if they are convinced they should not, they may well gain from coming together for other purposes. For example, in one case where there were insufficient people and gifts to commence a home church, two couples agreed to meet regularly to give support to one another. They decided to do this until God added to their number and provided a wider range of gifts – which, incidentally, he did not – or until a group formed in their vicinity which they could join – which is what ultimately happened.

(b) A basic commitment

We certainly need to know whether it is belonging to a home church that people have in mind. Sometimes people are only wanting to join a more helpful Bible study, prayer meeting, discussion group or charismatic circle. Sometimes they are merely seeking closer fellowship or some avenue of social action. These are valid concerns which have their place in a home church. But in themselves they only justify the formation of some other kind of group.

Even the desire for fellowship is not sufficient reason for beginning a home church. Those who wish to found a home church must be sure that they are not coming together primarily to engage in a certain activity or to fulfil a particular need, but to share in a common *life*: as a Christian family, based on commitment to one another and to God.

It is true that some home churches do begin their life as a particular interest group. Those who came together may have done so originally to study the Bible, pray together or support one another. Over a period of time, however, their fellowship deepens and they realise that they wish to go beyond this and 'church together'. There is nothing wrong with this, so long as they realise that churching together does not merely involve a broader range of common activities, for example celebrating the Lord's Supper, but also a deliberate choice to pursue a common life.

Not everyone in the group nor everyone who subsequently joins it, needs to have this depth of commitment. This means that the home church is able to include, even invite, others who may come to it initially or temporarily to fulfil a certain interest or meet a particular need – provided such people understand that it is not fundamentally an interest or therapeutic group. On the same basis, the home church is able to include someone who is not a Christian or has lapsed from the Christian faith.

These remarks imply the need for a core group. This may consist of only three or four people who make some kind of expressed or unexpressed commitment to one another under God. This provides the foundation of a home church. Unless this is present at the beginning or develops over a period of time, a group generally deteriorates into an interest or therapeutic group, or becomes superficial in character and irregular in meeting.

The type and content of this commitment can vary greatly as can the point at which it emerges. A few groups draw up a written statement. Others use such a statement to indicate the general spirit of their relationship. Some simply say a sentence or pray a short prayer which expresses their commitment to one another. There are some groups which do not do any of these and a core within them simply grows into a commitment to one another. Each home church needs to work out what is most appropriate for itself. But, in our view, it is helpful if the core members of a group do eventually give some tangible indication of their commitment to one another.

We are not talking here about something which the whole group should consent to, nor about something imposed as a precondition even upon members of the core group. It is a few people at the heart of a group that we have in mind, not everyone. Others can, and will, come into a group with all sorts of reservations about how much they wish to be involved in it. Such should be accepted as they are and allowed to grow into whatever level of commitment they are capable, under God, of having. Even in the core group we are thinking of a quality of involvement that springs naturally out of people's relationship with God and one another, not a demand to be met or a standard to which they must aspire. This quality of involvement may be present at the beginning or may develop gradually over a period of time: it may be articulated or may be present in an unspoken way.

Though it may not appeal to everyone and it has its limitations, an analogy may be helpful here. The commitment that develops within a core group is *in some respects* similar to that which exists in a marriage. It is the quality of involvement between a husband and wife that provides the stable basis on which a family can be built. As children become part of the family or outsiders are welcomed into it, they are not required to make the same kind of commitment to one another or even to their parents.

But they do have the benefit of seeing a depth of commitment modelled before them which they in turn can voluntarily emulate as they grow up in the family and when in turn they start their own families. Just as a commitment between a man and woman develops from a friendship, through engagement to marriage and then deepens within marriage itself, so it works among the members of the core group. While in some cases this commitment will be an unspoken or low-key affair at the beginning – in others it will be there from the start – hopefully it will develop and deepen into something rich and life-giving. There are certain dangers in pressing the analogy between core group commitment and marriage too far, and other analogies could be utilised instead, such as friendship, but it does highlight an important aspect of home church formation.

Some agreement as to the general belief framework of a home church *may* also be necessary. We say 'may' because a group which begins under the auspices of a local congregation will already have a denominational tradition of some kind. Some groups also start with people who have a common allegiance to a certain form of Christianity, such as evangelicalism. This does not mean that people coming into a home church should not feel free to re-examine such a tradition or allegiance. This can be a very healthy exercise and often such people want to find out what is authentically Christian as opposed to humanly superimposed. But there does need to be an expressed or unexpressed agreement that, to quote C.S. Lewis, there is a 'mere Christianity',[1] that is, a basic core of convictions distinctive to Christianity which has been held by believers down through the centuries. These convictions include the reality and person-ality of God, the centrality and liberating work of Christ, and the presence and guidance of the Spirit, and it is in the Bible that they are to be found.

If a group is radically uncertain about these convictions, it may be better for it to begin as a discussion group rather than as a church. But there would be no need to do this if one or two of its members were re-evaluating basic beliefs

---

1 C.S. Lewis, *Mere Christianity*, Collins: London, 1952, p.6

or even searching for God. And on other matters, agreement is not necessary at the outset, nor may it come in the long term even within the core group. But that is another matter which we will discuss more fully later.

(c) A pastoral centre

We have seen that a core group of members is a basic element in the formation of a home church. There is one other factor: the eventual presence among the core members of a 'pastoral centre'.

Every church needs at least a couple of people who can provide the essential pastoral contribution that any group requires for effective functioning. Such people have a general concern for the welfare of the whole group, not just for particular individuals within it. They often have an intuitive sense of where the group is at in particular situations – and how it can best move from there to where it needs to go. They also have confidence that God will direct and sustain the group.

They are welcoming and hospitable and, since their relationship with God and each other is relatively stable, are free to give themselves generously to others. They have the capacity to understand the differing attitudes and values of people in the group, and are able to act as intermediaries when misunderstandings or disputes arise.

Though they can discern weaknesses in the group and confront problems when they arise – and are also aware of their own weaknesses and problems – they are primarily 'encouragers'. By constantly seeing the potential of others, they give confidence to the church that it can mature and grow. They also have some vision of what the church can become.

Above all, such people 'model' God to those in the group, insofar as they have come to know and imitate him. In doing this, they embody the qualities of 'faith, love and hope' which Paul regards as basic. They also have a definite conviction from God that their home church is the top priority in their personal ministry.

Such people, however, are not necessarily the most gifted teachers in a group. Often they are self-effacing and are not generally charismatic leaders. They may only partially possess these pastoral attributes. Nor should they be regarded as different from other members. They do not have to be formally appointed and designated 'elders'. They do not have to be men. Indeed, in our society women often possess greater pastoral insight and skill.

Normally the pastoral centre of a home church will contain both men and women, mature people who have been raising children for some time and who have the confidence of other Christians. However we have known groups that commenced with women alone at the centre, with a number of younger, still maturing Christians, or with people who had each other's endorsement. But unless such churches develop a more balanced pastoral centre, they tend in time to succumb to real difficulties.

Unfortunately where a home church is formed within a congregation, what often happens is this: the minister looks around for someone who has teaching or organisational skills to lead the group. He then appoints this person, usually a man, as the group's leader – overlooking the fact that an ability to teach or organise does not necessarily include a capacity for pastoring others. As a result, those with pastoral sensitivity are not given time to gain the recognition of the group in which they are placed. It is far better for a minister to ensure that a new home church has some people in it with pastoral concerns, but then wait and see what emerges from the actual dynamics of the group. He can then informally underline the importance of such people or publicly endorse them in some appropriate way.

So far we have mentioned three factors that should be an integral part of a new home church: a sound foundation, a basic commitment or core group and a pastoral centre. Where these are altogether lacking, people should not deceive themselves into thinking they are a 'church'. Where these ingredients are only embryonically present, a group can work towards becoming a church in the fullest sense of the word. This will only happen gradually; the group should not rush ahead of its actual capacities.

If over a period of time the above fundamental factors do not emerge, the group will need to settle for something less, or disband itself and pray for something else to emerge. What is needed is a realistic attitude to home church formation – one that recognises the creative work of the Spirit in a group, but does not abstract this from the actual capacities and development of the people involved.

Some guiding principles

There are three principles which apply to commencing home churches, whether in a congregational or independent setting. These principles do not only stem from practical experience. They are rooted in the very nature of God. They identify the way in which the providential activity of the Father, the saving work of Christ and the transforming operation of the Spirit bear upon our corporate Christian lives.

Founding home churches is not a matter of human organisation, wisdom and techniques, but is a divine process in the fullest trinitarian sense. It is one which springs from and is patterned upon the character of the Father, Son and Spirit. Failure to recognise this ultimately leads to the weakening of any attempt to commence home churches themselves.

(a) The providential principle
The first principle is this:

In forming home churches we must take into account those networks of personal relationships that God has already established in a congregation or between people outside one.

These are part of God's providential arrangement of people's lives. It does not matter whether the networks of relationships are based on geographical proximity, mutual interests or spiritual affinity. What matters is that we build on them. Building churches on pre-existing relationships strengthens the possibility of their success.

Such groups should not be introduced in a managerial manner. When this happens maps are consulted, lists of names are drawn up and people are flung together who hardly know one another. They may live in the same area, but one's neighbourhood and neighbours these days are more defined by the telephone, car and work situation than by locality. While ultimately it may be beneficial for the communities we live in to bring groups and locality closer together, this should be a goal reached through growing contacts between people in home churches, not the initial point of departure.

There is a corollary to this. As well as bringing people together, God also works providentially in individuals' lives, preparing them for certain types of ministry. This is complementary to the way the Spirit develops gifts in certain people. For example, the list of qualifications in 1 Timothy 3 for 'bishops' (the first century equivalent to those who are the 'pastoral centre' of a home church) indicates that the experience of raising a family and administering employees, if successfully negotiated, is part of the training for ministry to others. While not all who undergo these experiences succeed from a Christian point of view and while other qualifications are also necessary, it is from this group of people that potential 'servant-leaders' in a home church will most frequently come.

Too often, however, this kind of providential training is overlooked in favour of those who have undertaken some theological education, displayed some leadership skills, or possess some charismatic credentials – irrespective of their ability to handle relationships. While the former may become good teachers, organisers or prophets, there is no guarantee whatever that they will function effectively pastorally.

(b) The organic principle
The second principle is this:

It is only as small churches grow from seeds the Holy Spirit has sown and with the guidance he provides that they will prosper within themselves and fulfil their proper role in corporate or personal life.

All too often the introduction of such groups is organised from the top down on a church-wide basis. It is essentially an administrative rather than a spiritual matter. Human planning rather than divine initiative is at the controls.

Something may come out of all this activity, but certainly not what we have been talking about. What generally happens is this: several groups run for a while then wither; some barely manage to survive; one group makes good — and the majority of people are well and truly insulated against ever attempting anything similar again. No, the real thing begins quite differently: in discerning prayer to see whether the Spirit is really preparing the way.

You may only begin with a small number of people. The task is to find these, encouraging them to make a start and be available to help them where appropriate. It means being content with small beginnings and being prepared to wait for others to catch the same vision before proceeding further. Throughout, a home church is to be organic rather than contrived. The possibility should always exist that tiny initiatives may eventually lead to a partial or total reshaping of the life and structures of the congregation. Where someone desires a whole congregation to meet in home churches, some patient groundwork is necessary. Even then, it is only likely to work in certain circumstances. Those circumstances include living in an area which is itself a natural community (such as a semi-rural or geographically distinct area) or where there is the opportunity of creating community from the outset (for example a relatively new congregation or a congregation that has virtually dissolved.)

It is generally in inner-city areas, in new housing estates or on the fringe of large cities that these circumstances are present. Even then, a lot of patient teaching, consultation and corporate prayer is needed before a congregation will be ready to move on the matter. It is crucial in such cases for the final decision to be a congregational one, not just a committee decision, and that every member of the congregation — women and older children as well as men — be able to express their feelings.

Once one or more home churches have begun this way, it is important to give them room to grow: at their own pace, in their own way and primarily out of their own resources. The temptation exists for those in authority in a congregation — or people with some theological training, leadership expertise or charismatic ability in a home church

— to seek to control its activities or channel its growth in predetermined directions.

Appointing a leader at the outset is only one way this might take place. Others include prescribing the shape of the meetings and the content of the studies conducted in it, setting sacramental limits beyond which a group cannot go, and limiting the range of activities. It is one thing to provide wise counsel, pastoral support and helpful resources for a group — mostly it is those with some authority in the congregation or expertise in the group who are best positioned to act. But this is very different from seeking to exercise power over or in a group, with all the crippling effects this has upon its growth to maturity.

(c) The resurrection principle
The third principle is this:

It is only through death that new life comes: 'resurrection' only takes place if a person or group is willing to endure the 'cross'.

For this reason it is illusory to think that a new form of church life can spring up without any alteration to present attitudes. These have to be opened up to reconsideration, challenge and, in some cases, change. Unless those who come together in a group are prepared to do this, their home church will ultimately fail. If there is no willingness to allow their views and lifestyle to come under the scrutiny of the communal study of scripture, mutual exercise of spiritual gifts and combined wisdom of the group (especially of those with greater maturity), the home church will soon begin to suffocate for lack of air to breathe. After a while, the home church will become a sharing of personal ignorance and prejudices, rather than a searching for the mind of God.

Fortunately, members of most groups soon come to realise how limited and secondhand most of their knowledge is. Thus begins a fresh search of the Bible so that they can fully understand and live by it. Gradually they begin to ask how much they, their culture and even their denominations have overlaid authentic Christianity with other beliefs, values and traditions.

There is another aspect to consider. It is unrealistic to

think that this kind of home church involvement can simply be added on to existing church responsibilities that most Christians already have. If home churches are to work effectively, they must have top — or at least equal — priority with the weekly gatherings of the whole church. In other words, those who begin them must be encouraged to see them as more important than any other small group, committee or ministry. Many Christians need permission to be released from certain of their existing church commitments.

Although this may appear to result in an initial loss of involvement in the local church, ultimately this process will bring great gain. It may well become obvious that some groups or committees in the local church are unnecessary anyway, or that their aims are fulfilled in home church meetings. So long as members of a home church regard their involvement as an extra, an addition to their other obligations, they cannot give the time, prayer, thought and energy required to fulfil the group's potential. Such groups function at a relatively superficial and, finally, unsatisfactory level. Numbers begin to wane and sooner or later the home church will come to an end. In one sense it does not even really die; it never really lived. Such is the fate of groups which are an appendage to existing congregational structures rather than the basic unit of local church life.

Those forming a home church may find it helpful to invite people from an already existing home church to share with them. It is far better to ask in a group rather than just one person. Quite apart from the fact that there is something strange about *one* person speaking about community, a group of people can express something of the diversity that a community possesses and, above all, through their relationships and behaviour actually 'model' community. Those invited on this basis ought not come to prescribe how home churches should be developed. They should come to listen as well as speak, to identify key concerns rather than lay down ready-made formulae, to portray a vision rather than present a programme.

Each congregation and each group is unique. God is very versatile in his operations. We need only add that follow-up visits have a valuable part to play.

Some general guidelines

Once a group of people have come together on the basis of these principles and the factors mentioned earlier, what are the most important things they should do to enable their home church to get off the ground?

At this point group dynamics, discussion methods and interpersonal techniques tend to rear their head. While these are of potential interest, they are not the place to begin. They tend to introduce a selfconscious, even artificial note into gatherings. If someone feels informed in these areas, it is better for that person to embody them, only bringing them into the open where it is strictly necessary.

In any case a home church is different from other types of groups. The model for the church is more that of the family. To some extent this affects the goals of a home church as well as its permanence, its size and the nature of its leadership. Also, while the dynamics, methods and techniques of small-group life echo some of the ways the Spirit works in the church, they do not exhaust them. The role of forgiveness, the influence of the fruit of the Spirit and the presence of spiritual gifts add a dimension to church life that is not generally captured by psychological or sociological analysis.

The following are more crucial factors in the development of a home church:

(a) An interpersonal focus

The less people know one another, the more necessary it is for them to lower the barriers between them. Even where they have rubbed shoulders in a congregation over a number of years, in reality people may have had only limited contact with each other. Only as they get to know each other will they be able to share, pray, learn and celebrate together in a wholehearted and meaningful way.

Most people come into a group with their guards up to some extent. As Jean Vanier says: 'when people join a community, they always present a certain image of themselves. . .'[2] It takes time for people to feel at ease and allow their masks to drop.

---

2 J. Vanier, *Community and Growth*, St Paul: Sydney, 1979, p.30

This process of breaking-down-the-barriers can be assisted in two ways:

* *Keep the group small for a time*

There is much to be said for beginning a home church with only a handful of people. While initially this limits the range of gifts within the group and restricts the effectiveness of certain group activities, like singing perhaps, it has other more basic advantages. Smallness of size enables us to open up more to one another and to forge proper relationships with one another. This is especially important in the inter-personal climate of Anglo-Saxon societies, where so many people feel unsure of themselves and inhibited in their encounters with others. In other societies it would be different – the original unit could be larger – but once a group gets beyond a certain size most of us feel ill at ease.

This means that, if twelve people are interested in beginning a home church, in most cases it would be better for two smaller groups to commence rather than one large one. At one stage we formed part of a group that began with only five adults, a teenager, a primary school child and a baby. We felt it was important to establish our relationship with each other and with God firmly *before* the group increased in size. Since we knew we would find it impossible to say 'no' to anyone who wanted to join us, we asked God to hold people off until we were ready to receive them. This was rather like a young couple deciding not to have children immediately after their marriage, so that they had time to lay a proper foundation for it. Six months later, when we decided our preparation was complete and that we would like to widen the group, a few people began to ask if they could come along.

* *Don't rush into 'religious' activities*

In the situation just described, the people who came together had known each other previously. However, what about a group which forms around people who do not know each other very well? Here, members need to allot time to learning something about each other before plunging into prayer, Bible study and charismatic sharing.

Another group did this by encouraging one family (or single person) each week to tell something about their 'life story' up to their joining of the home church. Initially this sharing something of people's personal history was the key activity. Commencing the group this way proved very beneficial. It helped everyone understand where others were coming from, threw light on why they held certain beliefs or used a particular kind of religious language, and enabled all to begin to see what others' particular needs and contributions might be. The whole process gave some clues as to the most appropriate content of the first studies, and helped people to begin to pray for one another more specifically. If the group had majored on more traditional 'religious' activities, it would have disguised some of people's real concerns and situations and, given the spiritual games Christians often play, masked the real nature of their relationship with God. Consequently, it would have taken longer to develop genuine openness in the meetings. As so often is the case, the most direct route is not always the most effective.

(b) A healthy openness

As mentioned our largely Anglo-Saxon heritage inhibits many of us from revealing our inner selves and deepest needs. Those who come from a Celtic or southern-European background are less disadvantaged. Women are undoubtedly far more open than men in this respect. Younger adults are less reserved than the generations before them.

A complicating factor is the legacy of some denominational traditions. Some Christians feel that their hopes and problems are too personal or trivial to be of interest to others – sometimes even to God himself! Class backgrounds also play a part. Middle-class people tend to find it easier to talk about personal details; working-class people are far more down-to-earth in what they discuss. Again, there are at least two lines of action a group can adopt to begin overcoming this problem:

* *Make a meal an integral component of every church meeting*

We have already noted that, for the early Christians, the common meal was as much a social as a religious event. Indeed, the separation of the social from the religious, fellowship from worship, love from truth, shows how far we have strayed from a biblical perspective. The 'Lord's meal' (in England the word 'supper' refers to the normal evening meal) is not only an occasion when we can thank God in a heartfelt way for Christ's giving himself for and to us. It is also an opportunity for us in like spirit – indeed, in the Spirit – to give ourselves to another.

In twos or threes around the edges of a room, or as a whole group, sharing a meal helps us naturally open up to one another. We can talk about the things that have been happening to us and what we make of them, how we are feeling at present and have been coping, whether anything particular is coming up and the way we are preparing ourselves for it – and so on. If a group has a time formally set aside for 'sharing', many people tend to remain silent or find it difficult to say exactly what they want. There is something about a meal, however, which enables them to speak more easily and openly with others. It is God's natural setting for such interchange and nothing else is better designed to encourage it. That is why prayer for one another is always easier after than before a meal.

* *Recognise the importance of asking questions*
  and volunteering difficulties

One of the main reasons why people keep so much to themselves is that they do not have the skills or confidence to open up to others. Yet quite often they find they can do this if someone asks them the right questions. Certain people have this gift: it is actually one of the many gifts of the Spirit. Others could acquire it, for it develops with practice. All you need to begin is a genuine interest in others. (It is not only adults who need to have questions asked of them, but children as well. In between songs, during the meal and at times especially for children, members of a group can ask the younger ones what news they have to share, what interests they have and what concerns them at present.)

Probably the best way of helping people to open up is to do so oneself. This is undoubtedly the most precious gift anyone can give to a church. It takes courage. It is risky. You can never be sure how others will respond – even if they will respond at all. This kind of open confession takes place not only through conversation with the group, but through prayer with God. More than anything else, it encourages, permits and frees others to say what is on their minds and in their hearts.

(c) A sense of liberty
Many grown-ups have an inability to let themselves enter wholeheartedly into play. That is why we have to be exhorted: 'Life. Be in it!' Yet there is a definite link between human enjoyment and celebrating God. What could be less joyous, less enthusiastic, less passionate than a typical worship service? This is where we should be able to love God with all our 'heart and strength' as well as with our 'mind and soul'. But something holds us back.

In beginning to break down some inhibitions, charismatic Christians have tended to introduce some standardised, culturally-imported responses. We need to discover ways of celebrating that are more natural, flowing out of who we are as individuals and as a church. Only then will we be able to introduce a more spontaneous, festive note into our gatherings. We can best go about this as follows:

* *Ensure that play has a regular part in group life*
Children are particularly important. Since they still possess what adults generally lack, they are the ones who can most help recapture some of the unselfconscious and unreserved zest for life that God delights to see. Quite apart from the fact that by this means children learn more how to worship together, our playing with them helps meet our needs as well. Indoor games and outdoor games, quiet games and noisy games, silly games and clever games, games for young children and games for older ones – all have their place at some time or other in a group's life.

A good idea is to incorporate a game every time the church meets. Now and then a group can also have a 'games day' when both adult and children's games, uncompetitive play and sporting activities can be enjoyed. In our own group we have also engaged in biblical 'play' – miming a favourite story from the Old or New Testament or devising our own versions of well-known biblical events to help recapture their freshness and vitality.

* *Encourage non-verbal communication in the group*
There are a number of possibilities here. Having a stock of
simple percussive or other instruments helps: children and
adults are able to play these as they sing. Others, once they
know it is all right, will enjoy clapping or moving to the
music in ways with which they are comfortable. A few may
find they can take the children's hands and join them in a
simple dance – or even dance a little themselves!

Music and praise are not only intended for our lips; they
are for our whole bodies. The Old Testament makes no
secret of this, nor of God's pleasure in it. But most of us
need to begin with activities we would find less embar-
rassing. These will lead us in time, step-by-step (sometimes
quite literally) from shaking hands at the door to greeting
and farewelling one another with a kiss, from prayer for one
another at a safe distance across the room to a hand laid on
a shoulder or an embrace as we speak, from reserved
expressions of pleasure or sadness to spontaneous gestures
of delight or sorrow when God or others touch us in an
unexpectedly personal way.

There is one very practical way in which a new home
church can begin to implement the three guidelines we have
mentioned. That is to go away for a weekend together,
preferably a long weekend. The earlier the group can do this
the better. However the group should not structure such a
weekend as it would a houseparty or conference. While it
will want to build in opportunity for informal worship and
set aside time for discussion and praise, the main purpose
of the weekend would be to get to know one another better,
hear each other's hopes for and reservations about becoming
part of a home church, join in games with the children and
appreciate God's world round about.

In one sense, the more primitive the conditions are on such
a weekend the better. People tend to be thrown together
more and reveal some of their underlying attitudes and
feelings. It helps us begin to see others as they are, rather
than as they pretend, or even as we would like them, to be.

These guidelines may seem too 'down to earth' – too
horizontal or 'relational' in character, lacking the more

vertical or 'spiritual' dimension. Our experience is that the majority of people who seek a home church already have a reasonable knowledge of the Bible, some experience in prayer and, less strongly, an awareness of spiritual gifts. Indeed, all these are often *overdeveloped* in comparison with their ability to share their real selves, enter sensitively into others' concerns, carry their burdens, and delight in the gifts of God in a guileless, childlike way.

It takes time to develop such skills. Study of the scriptures, prayer and exercise of God's gifts only have practical effect when they are brought into contact with our innermost selves, are undertaken within an open, discerning and loving community, and involve our imagination, feelings and bodies as well as our minds and wills. As Paul reminds us, we are to offer our whole selves as a living sacrifice to God, dedicated to his service and pleasing to him. This is the true worship we should offer if we wish to become fully conformed to him (Romans 12:1-2).

Conclusion

It will be clear from the foregoing that home church meetings should not be programmed or rushed. If they are too planned, there is little room for deep things to come out from people or for the Spirit to lead the group in the most fruitful direction. If they are too brief, there is insufficient time for all that needs to take place to develop the fullest communal life. The activities of a home church should take place in an orderly way, but this does not necessitate a fixed order. The meetings of a home church should take account of people's other commitments, but this does not mean that attending merely fits in after everything else. Freedom and form are equally important while church is in progress. Meeting at a time that is most convenient to people yet also is most open-ended should govern the choice of a day and hour.

While certain patterns of meeting may be followed more often than others, there should always be room for the unexpected to happen and to be given its head. Some groups have different patterns of meeting from one week to the next, for example a breakfast meeting, a children's day, an evening meal and a 'child-free' gathering. Most groups find that the pattern of their meeting changes as the group develops.

This is also true of the time at which meetings are held. Much will depend on the ages of the children in the group. The number of people coming may also be a factor. The pattern of working hours some members must follow, or church services which members may attend, has to be taken into account. All this is negotiable. Indeed, it needs to be renegotiated after any significant enlarging of the group or alteration of its constituency.

Venues for its meeting should also be those which are most appropriate for the number coming, most conducive to fellowship with God and one another taking place, most marked by the spirit and gift of hospitality, and most suitable for the use of the children present. Most groups find that some regularity in the places where groups meet is a decided advantage. This means that a group should mostly meet at one home and only occasionally at others, or is best meeting at one home for a number of meetings before moving on to the next or, if gathering in homes by turns, ought to do so in such a way that the meetings fall in the same home at the same time each month.

In all these matters – format, time and place – there are two basic principles which should govern the decisions that are made. Let everything be decided so that everyone can gain the maximum benefit from the meetings. This is the principle of edification. Also, let everything be decided by everyone in the group. This is the principle of consensus. Both principles come to clearest expression in Paul's writings and are as relevant today as they were when he advanced them. So long as they are adhered to, whatever diversity of application they may have, everything that is decided will serve the best interests of the home church.

6

Experiments in progress:

Current models of home churches

SO FAR WE HAVE OUTLINED the basic factors, principles and guidelines that should be taken into account in commencing a home church. We now look at various experiments in starting home churches with which we have had contact. Before we look at these, however, let us attempt to make clear the difference between home churches and other types of small groups.

The differences between home churches and small groups

The clearest way to present this difference is diagrammatically. Small groups are of two main kinds. We may describe these as 'interest groups' and 'action groups'.

The first kind of group draws people together around a common interest that they wish to engage in for their own benefit. It can be represented in the following way:

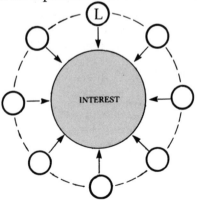

Here the various members of a group (represented by the small circles) gather primarily to concentrate on whatever personal interest they have in mind. They may come together to study the Bible, to pray, to discuss a book, to exercise charismatic gifts, to learn to meditate, even to experience fellowship. While these interests involve encountering each other (represented by the dotted lines), they do not meet primarily to develop a common life under God. Such a group has a defined leader (L).

The second type of group brings people together around a common activity that they wish to pursue for the benefit of others. It can be represented in the following way:

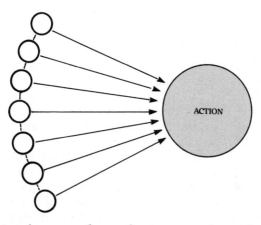

Here the various members of a group gather primarily to concentrate on some external activity that they feel requires attention. They may come together to visit the old and unwell, engage in evangelism, stage a political protest or campaign for some disadvantaged minority. While participating in this activity enables them to experience some fellowship with one another, they do not meet primarily to develop a common life under God.

A home church has similarities with both kinds of groups, but also crucial differences. Members of a home church come together to deepen their common life with God and one another as a group. This may be represented in the following way:

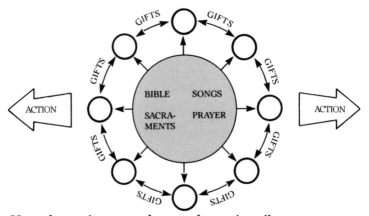

Here the various members gather primarily to concentrate on God and each other, not only so that they might grow personally more fully into God or act externally more effectively for God, but so that they will become a more closely-knit community. To achieve this they will also study the Bible, pray, discuss books, exercise charismatic gifts and meditate together, but they do not meet primarily to do any one or all of these. Such are a means to an end, not ends in themselves. The members of a home church will also wish to engage in various activities outside their group so that they introduce the life of God more broadly into the world. But they will chiefly do this as individuals or families, rather than engaging in some united action. They do not primarily meet to plan and engage in such activities. Unlike either of the other groups, they also share the sacraments together and view these as a vital way of building up their common life in God.

While the many house groups that congregations have established over the last ten years occasionally move beyond being interest groups, they rarely become home churches in the full sense. Some of the limitations of these groups spring from this. Since children are generally absent, both adults and children miss out on an important dimension of fellowship and growth. 'Worship' activities have only a secondary place and such groups do not tend to celebrate the Lord's Supper. Fortnightly meetings, which are often the norm, do not sufficiently challenge the tyranny of busyness to which so many Christians succumb. The continuing existence of too many other organisations in a church results in competition between these and the house groups, tending to dissipate people's energies.

1. The decentralised home church/congregational model[1]

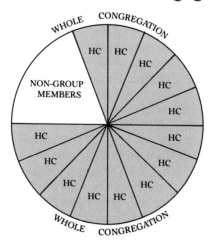

On the fringes of a major Australian city is a Baptist congregation with about 120 members. It has established house churches as a basic unit of its life, while still maintaining central congregational leaders, worship and administration.

The move to home churches developed out of two concerns on the part of the pastors and congregational leaders. First, a desire to come to terms with what it means to give practical expression to being the people of God in the local community. Second, an awareness that traditional congregational life was not providing adequate opportunities for fellowship, pastoral care and participation in worship. After working through a booklet entitled *Going to Church*

1 On what follows, see C.M. Olsen, *The Base Church: Creating Community through Multiple Forms*, Forum House: Atlanta, 1973, pp.73-87

in the First Century[2] together with some other materials, pastors and leaders concluded that home churches were a fundamental concept of church life as seen in the New Testament. With the approval of the congregation, a working party of five men and three women began to explore the implications of home churches and eventually drew up a submission for congregational discussion. This submission included both theological foundations and practical proposals.

Here in essence are the practical proposals which were accepted and then implemented with only minor changes.

Operation of house churches

(a) Everyone will be invited to become part of the fellowship of a house church. It is hoped that all will be able to participate but, if some cannot, they will still be under the care of a house church pastor. House churches will consist of fifteen to twenty adults, together with the children of the families involved.

(b) To begin with, the house churches would meet fortnightly. A limited choice of nights of the week will be given, with Wednesday or Friday being the most appropriate. These nights will be chosen to fit in with other church activities. It may be necessary to form a house church which meets during the day for those who find it impossible to meet in the evening.

(c) Homes of a suitable size, location and facilities will be chosen from amongst those offered by members of the congregation. Preferably the homes chosen will not be those of the house church pastors. The host and hostess will be asked to have meetings in their home for at least six months to provide continuity and the situation will be reviewed at the end of that time.

(d) The meetings will generally occupy a two-hour timeslot, with some flexibility to cover different needs. The time suggested is either 7.00-9.00 p.m. or 7.30-9.30 p.m. If desired, there could be an earlier start at 6.30 p.m.,

---

2 See Robert Banks, *Going to Church in the First Century*, Hexagon Press: Sydney, 1980

allowing time to share a meal. Communion could be part of the meal.

(e) Activities in the house church meeting would include many elements of worship with which we are already familiar. Singing, prayer, sharing, Bible reading and teaching, a children's programme, a meal and supper with an informal time of fellowship are some of the elements which could be included. We hope that each house church will arrange common social activities and interaction with other house churches.

(f) The teaching will be generally related to the Sunday services, using notes prepared by the congregational pastors. To prepare for house church teaching, the house church pastoral team will meet fortnightly. Initially, all the house churches will be studying the same topics at the same time. If particular issues or topics arise in a particular house church, the pastoral care team will consider how they could be incorporated into the teaching ministry. Various members will be encouraged to lead the house church in devotional teaching.

(g) Leadership in the meetings will be primarily the responsibility of the house church pastor. When people have come to know each other, say after three months, it will be possible to choose from the house church a deacon and deaconess to look after the practical needs. A person who is able to lead in worship through music will be allocated to each house church (guitar, piano etc.) and also a person responsible for the children's programme. It has been agreed that an overall co-ordinator of children's activities will be needed.

(h) It is hoped that children will share in the meetings as part of the church family. The degree of participation by the children will depend on factors such as age, homework and the need for sleep. Activities for children could be singing, specially produced story or Bible-study materials, tapes, videos, more active games, outdoor games in summer, picnics or barbecues.

(i) Teenagers will participate on the same basis as adults, while recognising that they may have extra pressures from school and homework. A continuing youth group is held apart from the house church programme.

(j) Ministry will be an integral part of the house church. It is hoped that the Spirit's gifts will be exercised more freely in the context of the house church. At the same time, there will be an opportunity for evangelism to occur through the natural reaching out of members into the wider community. Community needs, missionary support or worthwhile humanitarian projects should also become part of each house church's ministry. A regular offering would be encouraged to help meet these needs.

(k) Our aim is for the members of the house church to be committed to each other in a caring and open way. There is a real need to learn to be a community of people who do more than just meet together. We must learn to encourage each other, pray with each other and meet each other's practical needs day by day. This will involve a true sharing of our lives with each other as a family of God's people within the house churches as well as in the wider fellowship.

House church pastors

(a) The title of 'pastor' has been chosen because of the shepherding nature of the position. The general qualities of house church pastors are those of elders and deacons as listed in scripture.

(b) Some important attributes of a house church pastor would be initiative, commitment and concern for people, and a personal maturity. However, the most important quality is that they be filled with the Holy Spirit and living demonstrations of what they teach.

(c) The house church pastors will be responsible to work together with the congregational pastors and elders in a spirit of mutual submission and accountability. It is out of this context that their authority will be exercised within the house churches.

(d) Initially a twelve-month commitment is expected of each house church pastor and he should be prepared to give at least two nights per week to house church ministry.

(e) In general terms a house church pastor is committed to regular training as arranged by the congregational pastors and is responsible for:
   * Leadership and arrangements for each house church meeting and activity.

* Visitation of each person and family in the house church as a ministry of encouragement.
* Being able to identify and arrange follow up of practical needs within the house church.
* Being available to be involved with members of the house church in any weddings, funerals, child dedications or baptisms in liaison with the congregational pastors.

The whole process took a period of eighteen months, the working party being aware that successful change depends on the understanding and co-operation of the members involved. This new congregational structure has now been functioning for over two years, with more than ninety per cent of the congregation being involved regularly. Each group is different, some having more children than adults, two containing almost all the teenagers and several having meals together only irregularly. There is common agreement that the new arrangement has deepened the life of the congregation and made pastoral care more effective. It has also led to a re-evaluation of the constitutional structure of the congregation, together with its leadership style. Leadership is based less on a managerial approach and more on a servant model. At the same time there is evidence of more people using their gifts and abilities for ministry both within the congregation and the house churches.

There is still some reassessing of what should happen on Sunday mornings at the congregational gathering. The present arrangement includes a teaching hour for most adults (with children in Sunday school), a coffee break and a family service (the sermon being studied in the home churches in the following week).

The house churches have recently conducted a comprehensive evaluation of their development after two years in operation. This has revealed both strengths and weaknesses – as is to be expected. Some of the more general comments from the evaluation reflect this. 'I feel we are growing and being matured slowly.' 'House churches have enabled a more intimate situation and hence a meeting of some particular needs that would otherwise have been overlooked, or more than likely would not have surfaced.' 'In varying degrees our folk are living out the aims, but it is understandable in a group of such wide age-differences and years as Christians that we are not all at the same level and have to make allowances for this.'

It is possible that the fortnightly meeting pattern and the relatively short meeting length are a factor here. These could limit the rate at which people can develop relationships with one another and pursue questions in depth.

2. The pilot home church/congregational model

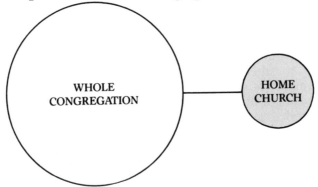

The following example was not founded intentionally as a home church, but gradually developed in this direction. Although a clergyman initiated the group, it was laypeople who were largely responsible for its development. The congregation concerned is a long-established Anglican church in an upper-class suburb in a medium-sized Australian city. Not all members of the church, however, come from high income families.

Here is a report by one of the members of the group:

Back in 1974 the curate saw the need for biblical teaching within our youth fellowship. He formed *Koinonia*, a group to bring together those interested in serious Bible study. At the end of his two-year curacy he moved on, but *Koinonia* stayed, albeit with changes to venue, meeting day, meeting time and emphasis.

These changes were largely due to the different needs of people who came into the group. In general, the new people were older. Most of the original youth group had married and moved out to other suburbs. After about three years, only five people were involved: two couples and one girl. This group of five thought many times about giving up, but each felt the need for fellowship and had the conviction to go on meeting. Every Wednesday at 6.30 p.m. we would gather in someone's home, each bringing a contribution to the meal. After the meal, we would study the Bible, particularly Paul's letters. Then we would share and pray together. Later, as the group grew in number, we added singing to our activities.

Koinonia provided a level of Christian community which did not seem to be evident or available in the regular life of the congregation. It was not as if members of *Koinonia* were not committed to the local church – they were all involved in activities of various kinds. Three members were successive leaders of the Sunday school and another was the longest serving Sunday-school teacher in the parish. At various times six members were parish councillors. One gave strong leadership to the Girls' Friendly Society. One member was at various times an organist, Sunday-school leader, parish councillor and youth leader in the parish. But this involvement in itself did not meet the needs of the individual members. They were principally giving out to others without replenishing their own inner resources. *Koinonia* provided a sense of identity, an opportunity for learning and an experience of community not available in the Sunday worship service.

So strong was the sense of community that for a number of years members were asked to commit themselves to each other in a covenant. The intent of the covenant was to bring people into a close relationship with Christ through mutual support – expressed in daily prayer and practical help. The practical help was probably the harder part, since in our prosperous society physical needs are sometimes hard to find. When they do exist, it can be even harder to accept help from others.

Confessing a need to another also seemed to play an important part in experiencing the body of Christ in a tangible way. Having members of the group pray in a spontaneous way for that person and their need became a crucial part of our life together and strengthened our commitment to each other. As our commitment to each other increased, so did our faith, our endeavour to live the Christian life and our desire to reach out to others.

Not everyone is gifted in evangelism, but everyone is called upon to witness. In *Koinonia* we found that we could support one another in the exercise of our particular gift. Through those with the gift of evangelism, the whole group was able to reach out to others. Through those with the gift of hospitality the whole group was able to care for those whose faith was young and weak. Through those with the gift of teaching the whole group was able to learn more about the Christian life.

At a more mundane level *Koinonia* has not been without its difficulties. Initially there was a great deal of uncertainty about leadership. Then there was the difficulty of accommodating teenagers. Finding sufficient time to spend together has been a perennial dilemma. More recently the high ratio of females to males presented a problem. Not all these difficulties were overcome simply, though one was. Appointing a co-ordinator who then chose two others solved the leadership problem. Several members have left, some because of transfers to other places and others for reasons known only to themselves. Many of these difficulties have been a reminder that it is God who has brought together *Koinonia* and it is his body to do with it whatever he will. God does not give guarantees to any group, but he has developed in us a deep sense of commitment and community. Perhaps that is all he wants to do.

The pilot home church, whether commenced by lay people on the fringes of a local church or by the minister from the centre as a matter of policy, has much to contribute. It provides a model which others in the congregation eventually may want to emulate. The pilot home church releases ideas, ministry and life into the congregation, especially where it serves aspects of congregational life or pioneers a new area of ministry.

The pilot home church is open to misunderstanding, particularly by more traditional churchgoers. They will often view it as elitist, self-centred or judgmental, even when it is none of these. Despite some criticism, this particular group was fortunately viewed by the minister as the 'lynchpin' of the church. Another problem is that such a group will frequently not feel free to celebrate communion, lest they upset people within the congregation or because certain members of the group have scruples about it.

Even greater difficulties arise, however, when the home church begins to question some of the basic goals, activities and structure of the local church. Such a reappraisal led the members of the home church in one parish to relinquish their positions on the church council, in the Sunday school and on other organisations in favour of more novel forms of witness in the suburb around them. This was seen as a betrayal by many people in the congregation, though not by the minister. Although he had initiated the home churches and belonged to one of them, however, he did find himself pulled increasingly in two opposing directions. Because of the life produced by the home churches, he was prepared to live with this tension.

The clergy vis-à-vis the home church
Before considering more independent approaches to home church life, we should take up a question which so far has not been addressed directly. Should the minister in a congregation be a member of a home church or not?

The answer to this is very simple: yes. The minister, above all, needs the ministry of such a group and a group benefits greatly from his candid, 'unprofessional' membership within it. Many ministers can testify to the way in which belonging to a home church has supported them through difficult times and helped them identify their real, as opposed to expected, gifts. The main obstacle to ministers belonging to such a group is not a fear of confidentiality being breached, but a fear of opening up to others about their inner weaknesses and doubts.

As for the relationship between the minister and home churches in the congregation, the best model is provided by the relationship between Paul and his communities. Paul felt he had a general responsibility for his communities, but encouraged all of them to develop a high degree of responsibility for their activities. Though he and his assistants visited them from time to time, advising them on various matters they raised, for the most part the communities looked after their own affairs.

Paul gave special attention to those in the communities who had developed a pastoral concern, but did not seek to supervise them closely. Apart from the authority he had by virtue of his founding these communities, it was Paul's personal example and practical experience which lent authority to his instructions. As far as possible he endeavoured to help his communities achieve spiritual adulthood, so that they became partners with him rather than subordinates under him. To this end he laboured in prayer on their behalf.

3. The inter-denominational home church

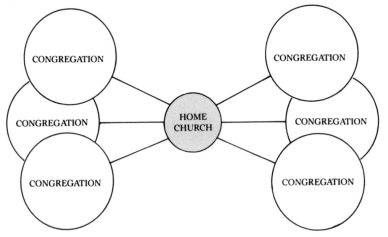

The group described below began in the early 1980s in one of the newer areas of a smaller Australian city. The couple who tell the story are in their early thirties and have four children. One of them was previously involved in a ministry to students. It was through this ministry that he and his wife developed relationships with a number of people who later became involved in their home church. Their reasons for commencing this group sprang from a vision of ministry which worked through everyday relationships, had a natural focus on the family, produced genuine Christian growth, encouraged and sustained Christians in their personal ministries, was simple and efficient and did not require paid Christian workers. Conversations with the authors helped clarify the way they could best proceed.

Here is the couple's account of what happened:

How did we start a house church? We had not been part of a house church before, but we understood one to be essentially an extended Christian family: a small fellowship of Christians who had a family type commitment to one another and who exercised all the functions of church. Relationships, then, were central to a house church: a common commitment to Christ and a mutual commitment to one another.

We began by sharing the vision of a house church model of ministry with Christians we already knew well. We spent about three months in conversations with couples and single people, discussing the concept and benefits of the house church model and comparing it with conventional church forms. We suspected that the most difficult aspect of the house church would be its initial functioning and stability. To avoid possible problems in the early stages, we invited people to join who could show care and respect for one another and who had previous study group experience. Although the initial members of the house church came from four different Christian traditions, we shared a similar commitment to the Lordship of Christ, the authority of scripture and the importance of personal ministry. One other point of interest was that everyone desired to retain an involvement in their local church.

The house church commenced with the interested people meeting to discuss their understanding of what the group would be like, to agree on how we would create the environment that would accomplish our aims and to commit ourselves to one another for a trial period of one year.

Our group began with seven adults and five children. Over two years it has grown to include fifteen adults and ten children. Although it is still functioning well, we sense that larger numbers will adversely affect its distinctive qualities of intimate relationships and maximum opportunity for involvement in discussion, leading and decision-making.

What interaction is there between the house church and the local churches to which we belong? We seem to have a significant ability to draw from what we gain in house church and contribute to our varied local churches, and similarly to draw from our local churches and contribute to the life of the house church.

In addition to this informal interaction, the house church has contributed in a variety of concrete ways to local churches. These have included:

* taking several series of expository sermons;
* providing a seminar series on marriage;
* speaking at evangelistic meetings for youth.

On another level, a number of house church members have become involved in the leadership of several local churches. They are helping shape the direction of their respective local churches, encouraging the formation of house churches within them.

While we actively seek to contribute to the local churches with which the house church has contact, we also appreciate the ways in which other churches have contributed to us. On a few occasions people have met with us to share specialist teaching or perspectives on areas which we had not researched ourselves. These times we count as most valuable.

The interaction we have seen between our house church and various local churches arises naturally from the conviction we share about church. We see the house church as our primary and most meaningful church involvement, but we also see ourselves as responsible members of a wider Christian community.

This particular model has considerable strengths. It supplements what happens in the local church and, in doing so, provides certain people with a supportive climate in which they can grow. The interdenominational home church may also enable some people to keep a connection with a congregation instead of dropping out or going underground. Its ability to contribute to the local church as well as draw from it has some advantages.

This two-way link can also create some tensions. One of these, disapproval by the minister or congregation of a person's outside home church involvement, is a potential problem. One minister gave his people an ultimatum: either you belong to the local church alone, or you have to leave. In a milder form, there is pressure on the time of those who have dual membership in a congregation and in a home church. They tend to find themselves overstretched or with little 'free' time to give to world-related concerns. Also, this particular group has not yet felt able to celebrate communion together.

There is one other kind of difficulty which some members of the above group are beginning to face, namely long-term lack of interest on the congregation's part in developing home churches within their own framework. This may result in members leaving their congregation so that they can concentrate their energies on creating new home churches for people they know who are not attached to any congregation.

4. The home church cluster or loose network

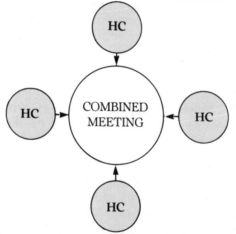

The following example, coming from the home churches to which we belong, is an independent variant of this and draws in people who feel religiously, relationally or physically disadvantaged in our society.

The membership of the various home churches involved is largely in keeping with the predominantly middle-class character of the Australian national capital, Canberra, though other class backgrounds are also represented. Many members once belonged to, but had frequently long left, mainline churches and are from a wide variety of Christian persuasions. Some have come out of a counter-culture context and several have worked their way out of quasi-Christian sectarian groups. Others have had no church background at all. Here is a summary of our development:

These home churches had their origins in a series of Bible studies among people who were dissatisfied with the low level of teaching that existed in their churches. These studies concentrated on the nature of Christian fellowship, worship and ministry. As a result of these, the group extended its activities to include more sharing and prayer – and a common meal. The group saw no reason why it should not meet as church rather than primarily for teaching. At this stage it was partially an interdenominational home church – most of its members were still heavily involved in other congregations – though for some, whose links with their congregations had been increasingly tenuous, it had become the *only* church they attended.

A number of those attending one local church were told they could not remain members of that congregation unless they severed all links with the home church. This was despite the fact that their home church involvement had given them a new vitality in fulfilling several responsible roles in the congregation. Such was the harshness of their treatment that they decided to leave the congregation in favour of the home church. This made the home church almost completely independent.

Today, although some members of our home churches (there are now several) maintain a connection with a congregation and others move regularly in denominational circles, the majority do not. However, we have continued to recognise the importance of maintaining links with one another. For us this takes the form of a loose network of home churches.

This informal association sprang from the fact that all the groups come from a common root. At the end of its first year, the original home church divided into two and later a third group was formed. While the present groups are the result of later developments – the number of home churches has contracted and expanded over the years – all stem from that common foundation. This gives them a shared history and common friendship which strengthen both the individual groups and the network as a whole. Although there is no formal organisation linking the home churches, they do meet together regularly for different purposes: combined worship/fellowship every six weeks, discussions of common concerns such as evangelism, Christian education and church growth, and evenings for pastoral reflection and prayer. Once or twice a year we also join in a combined service with other Christians in the city, either in connection with a common act of witness or an annual civic celebration.

While there is no formal leadership either within or over these home churches, most recognise that certain members within each group have an important pastoral role to play and that a few have a valuable wider ministry.

The main elements of this wider ministry are:
* support for those who are at the pastoral centre of a home church
* bringing home churches into contact with each other
* assisting new home churches to begin
* encouraging mainline churches to develop home churches themselves.

The strengths of the home church cluster are its strong links between the individual house groups, the sharing of personnel and other resources when appropriate, the possibility of one group helping out another when the situation arises, the existence of people who have a more general ministry among the various groups and the links the combined groups have been able to develop with other home churches in the city and elsewhere. Such a model demands strong lay involvement, with all members playing their proper part. The individual groups have no formal support system.

Although we are only aware of this model in its independent form in Australia, a congregation could be pioneered this way and be allowed to exist without buildings, programmes or hierarchical leadership.

Sometimes a home church is not able to form a cluster, but can find another home church with which it can have occasional contact. Some searching may be required on the part of such a home church to find another empathetic group. We still come across groups which have been in existence for several years, quite unaware that anyone else is meeting in a similar way. The more home churches develop, however, the less this will be a problem.

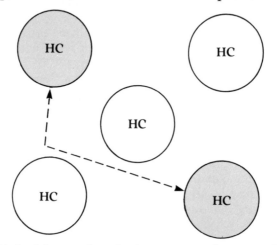

The linked home church shares some, but not all of the strengths of the cluster model. Its main difficulty lies in the more fragile connections with other home churches. Unless there is a continuing concern to develop links with other groups, such groups have the tendency to go solo.

The solo home church is a small group which is quite independent of any congregation or home church. Often the only way a home church can come into existence is as a solo group. This presents no problem so long as in time it develops some links with a congregation or other home churches, however informal and occasional. If not, it runs the risk of eventually withering through lack of cross-fertilisation with other groups.

Conclusion
We close with some comments on the possibilities and limits of the congregationally-related approach to home churches.

From our observations and the experience of others,

certain kinds of contexts appear to be more conducive to the development of home churches than others. On the whole, home churches are most easily established in decaying inner-city churches, new churches in recently-built housing estates and in churches located on the fringes of cities. In these settings there is a willingness to experiment, lack of tradition and quest for community respectively. An older suburban area which has retained a sense of community can also lend itself to the development of home churches. This does not mean that it is impossible to develop home churches in other settings: only that it is more difficult to do.

Much also depends on the length of time that a minister is prepared to stay. Someone has commented that it takes five years for a minister to really implement the changes he most deeply wishes to see introduced. Unless a minister is prepared to remain a few more years, the home churches may not consolidate in the way they require. If a change of ministers takes place before this has happened and the incoming minister is less committed to the home church approach, everything can revert to the original situation. It goes without saying that, where a minister is not open to the development of home churches, it is more difficult for lay-people to move in this direction. While this should not prevent them from trying, they should recognise the difficulties involved and tensions that might arise.

Given the nature of institutions, it is very difficult for a congregation to decentralise itself *completely* into home churches, changing its authority structure in the process and becoming a home church cluster. One overseas congregation which did this finally decided to return its building to the denomination, while its pastor voluntarily became a part-time elder. Although the whole congregation voted in favour of this, the denomination could not cope with the direction the member church had taken. Consequently, it struck both minister and congregation off its books.[3] This

3 The church in question is the subject of the books by R. Girard, viz. *Brethren, Hang Loose*, Zondervan: Grand Rapids, 1972 and *Brethren Hang Together*, Zondervan: Grand Rapids, 1979. See also Girard's more personal statement *My Weakness His Strength: The Personal Face of Renewal*, Zondervan: Grand Rapids, 1981

action indicates the limits upon congregational autonomy, *even when* the whole church is in agreement.

The problem is one of wineskins. The old wineskins just cannot contain the new wine that is poured into them. It is for these reasons that those seeking to establish home churches within a congregation need to appreciate the potential difficulties. Those who feel compelled to realise fully their aspirations in this matter may only be able to do this outside the institutional church. However, they should recognise that they also operate under certain limitations. These do not arise within the individual home churches to which they belong. They arise from the existence of the institutional church itself, that is its ongoing (if declining) prestige, attraction and influence. They also stem from the scattered, independent nature of home churches themselves, which sometimes makes it difficult to establish helpful contacts between them.

Where home churches begin on an interdenominational or independent basis, it becomes important to establish contact with others who are meeting in the same way, or at least with one or two people who have long-term pastoral experience in such groups, however informal or intermittent the link might be. As Jean Vanier points out:

> No community, whether large or small, can cope on its own. Very often its members are not able to resolve their tensions. They need help to grasp the way community is evolving and to find new structures for the different stages of its growth. Every community seems to need regular visits from a friendly outsider... above all someone who can counsel its leaders, so helping the community evolve and discover the message of God in its tensions.[4]

In the chapter after next we shall look at some of the main tensions that arise in a home church and consider how best to deal with them.

---

4 J. Vanier, *Community and Growth*, St Paul: Sydney, 1979, p.110.
  See also his remarks on p.93

7

Gathering together:

A discussion of home church principles

WE NOW LOOK AT DIFFERENT ASPECTS of home
church life that create dilemmas for the people within such
groups. Most of these situations only create difficulty if
handled wrongly. With God's help, these issues can
gradually be resolved through discussion, if informed by
study and prayer.

We have cast the contents of this chapter in conversational
form. Alan and Pat are husband and wife and part of a
congregationally-based home church. Carol and Tim are
single people attending an inter-denominational home
church which has only been in existence a short time. Ruth
and Graham, also married, have belonged to a home church
cluster for many years. We pick up their conversation
midway through the evening.

Decision-making

Pat: I've often wondered how you make decisions in your
home church. Do you have a leader who works out what to
do or does the majority have the say?

Graham: What sort of decisions are you thinking about?

Pat: Oh, how you organise your meetings, what you're going
to study, how to deal with problems which arise – those
sorts of things.

Alan: You see, in our group most of these matters are
decided by the leader appointed to our group. . .

Pat: . . .or, so far as studies are concerned, by the minister,
who preaches on them on Sunday mornings.

Graham: Personally, I'd have some problems with that. I can see that it has certain organisational advantages, enabling systematic teaching to go on. But the needs of groups vary so much that to programme their studies this way would prevent them exploring their specific concerns. I also wonder whether it fails to give a group sufficient responsibility for it to develop full maturity.

Pat: So you discuss things and then vote on them as a group, do you?

Graham: No, we came to the conclusion quite early on that we should decide all major issues by consensus.

Alan: You mean everybody has to agree before you can go ahead and do something?

Graham: Well, yes and no. When a question comes up we're all encouraged to think and pray about it and express our understanding as to what we should do. . .

Tim: Excuse me breaking in, Graham, but does that include new members as well?

Graham: Yes. It's rather like the parable of the labourers in the vineyard. Even those who begin work at the end of the day receive exactly the same treatment as those who were there the whole time. But even though all take part in making decisions, we don't always all have to reach the same conclusion before we can go ahead.

Pat: Well, isn't that the same as a majority vote?

Graham: No. To start with, working by consensus actually produces full agreement most of the time – far more than you'd normally expect. When it doesn't, we only go ahead if those who disagree are happy to trust the judgment of the rest. Even if only one person has a serious reservation, we hold fire until their misgiving disappears or the remainder come to see that it is divinely based.

Alan: I can see a real problem with what you're saying: surely it's very inefficient. If I ran my firm the same way, we'd take ages to make decisions. In fact, some things would never get done at all!

Graham: I agree that it can sometimes be rather frustrating. But then I don't think you can run a church like you run a business. Mind you, there's a lot more consultation in business these days than there used to be – more so than in many congregations! In any case, while striving for a consensus may mean it takes longer to come to a decision, it is far more efficient if you consider the way it helps people mature in their judgments and in their sensitivity to one another.

Ruth: And don't forget that because people know their views really count − that no one, even the majority, is going to ignore them − it is sometimes easier to reach a decision anyway.

Graham: That's true. The other thing I was going to say, Alan, is that when only one or two disagree, mostly they're happy to respect the combined wisdom of the others and give their consent despite their reservations. This is easier for people to do if they have *already* come to see that the judgment of certain people has proved itself right in the past. This builds trust within the group and strengthens its capacity to make better decisions.

Carol: You've spoken of the procedure in rather human terms, Graham. Where does the Holy Spirit come in?

Graham: I'm sorry if I gave that impression. For me, the Spirit is fundamental to the whole exercise. It's because I believe he gives different insights and knowledge to different people, and because he seeks to bring everyone to a common mind, that we must reach decisions by consensus rather than by decree or majority vote.

In fact, what I've described only works if people are discussing together with the intention of seeking the mind of the Spirit. If they're simply fighting for their own particular view, the group isn't going to get very far at all.

Tim: So prayer is also basic to what you're saying?

Graham: Yes, and not just in the sense that it should accompany discussion. For example, when a group reaches a stalemate, it's time to abandon discussion and start praying through the deadlock to see if God will throw fresh light on it as people pray. Remember that group we were in, Ruth, where we couldn't agree about which of two possible courses of action we should follow?

Ruth: Yes, we just seemed to be going round and round in circles at the time.

Graham: And as we were talking it over with God, roaming

in, around and through the dilemma, exploring and debating aspects of it with him, a third possibility unexpectedly emerged...

Ruth: ...which everyone then agreed was the path to follow.

Graham: In fact, I've come to feel that we ought to discuss much less at times and start praying much earlier. I suspect we'd get a lot further if we did.

Praying

Tim: I'm fascinated by what you say of the role of prayer in decision-making. I'd like to think we could make decisions that way, but honestly our group makes such heavy weather of prayer.

Graham: Why do you think that's so?

Tim: I'm not sure really. Perhaps it's because we don't know one another very well yet...

Carol: ...and that few of us are used to praying aloud in a group.

Tim: We had family prayers of a sort when we were young, but we never seemed to move into praying together as adults. I don't even know if my parents prayed together as a couple.

Ruth: That sounds very much like my own story. We didn't get much help at church, either. At youth fellowship we prayed, but it was as if God was only a giant question box into which we put our requests.

Tim: I doubt if our times of prayer are much different to that. What do you think, Carol?

Carol: It's not quite that bad. We really want it to be more than it is, but we don't know how to proceed.

Ruth: Now and again we also have some disastrous prayer-times, occasionally some really fantastic ones, but most of the time they are somewhere in between. It's certainly changed a lot since our early days. I expect we weren't very different from yourselves in the beginning.

Graham: Alan and Pat, you've been very quiet.

Alan: Well, I think you're being a bit tough on the institutional church. As I remember it, we had quite a lively fellowship. When it came to prayer-time, you could hardly get a word in edgewise.

Pat: Yes, but you've got to admit that your church was the exception rather than the rule in our suburb. I have to confess that it's only since belonging to the home group that I've really learnt to pray.

Tim: What made the difference?

Pat: I don't know that I've really thought about it enough. Certainly getting involved in the lives of people in the group has made a difference. Their concerns become your concerns. I think our group really took off in prayer when we discovered that the Browns' child was ill.

Graham: It's interesting how many times you hear something like that!

Carol: Yes, but if you don't have that kind of situation in your group, you can't manufacture it. What do you do in the meantime?

Graham: Well, you could do what one group does: keep a note of all the requests people make in prayer and then each week thank God for the answers received. It's been a great revelation to them of the way God works, even if he doesn't always answer their prayers the way they expect. It's helped them to praise God better, too.

Ruth: The biggest aid we had to prayer in our group was Arthur. He was an older chap with a very natural way of relating to God. Whenever he prayed, you felt as if God was there in the room, sitting in an armchair listening. And it wasn't 'chatty' in the wrong sense. It was just that Arthur truly walked with God and it came out in his prayers. He wasn't afraid to tell God that he didn't understand, or that he was angry with him over something. He was honest with God and that helped us over our hangups about using the right words, or only expressing certain things.

Alan: Like the fellow in *Fiddler on the Roof*?

Graham: Exactly!

Tim: I notice you're using the past tense of Arthur. Has he left your group?

Ruth: Yes, he had to go interstate for his family's sake.

Carol: What effect has that had on the group?

Ruth: It's left a big hole. In fact, it made us realise how much we'd come to depend on Arthur. Somehow when he prayed it made it easier for us to pray.

Graham : Not only that. God also frequently answered his prayers. He obviously had a gift for prayer.

Ruth: Many of us hoped that God would raise up someone else in the group to fit Arthur's shoes, but he didn't. We've had to struggle on and learn by listening to one another. One of the men in our group has taught me a great deal about relating to God. Another's prayers have a profound simplicity from which I've learned a great deal.

I guess the most significant thing I've learnt about prayer has been the value of just doing it together. I don't mean that our prayers become more effective when there are others saying 'Amen'. It's more what Graham referred to as praying 'through' things. The fact that the whole group can converse with God and that, through listening to the way someone prays about a matter and to God in the silences that arise, prayers of others are shaped. Slowly but surely we seem to come to a common mind on the matter we are praying about.

Tim: That sounds wonderful, but we're a long way from that. We need help to even take the first steps.

Carol: Well, Graham gave us that suggestion about taking note of our requests.

Tim: Yes, but isn't there something else we can do?

Pat: I think there is, but don't forget that your group is a fairly new one and that these things take time. Prayer doesn't come easily to people. They have to be willing to trust other members of the group with their stumbling sentences. People have to feel 'at home' with one another. So a good place to start is by working on your relationships.

Graham: That's right. And there are other things you can do. For example, you can encourage people to use prayers out of books and ones which they write out at home themselves. The best way of encouraging others to do this is to do it yourself from time to time.

Alan: We've used a sort of litany in our group from time to time. Whoever's leading the prayer-time says for example, 'Let us pray for the world'. People then simply state things they'd like to pray about, e.g. the current elections, nuclear disarmament, the famine in Africa and so on. Then the leader says, 'Lord, hear our prayers', and we all answer, 'And grant our requests'. This pattern can be followed under a variety of headings like 'our city', 'our neighbours', 'the church at large', 'other home churches' and 'ourselves'.

Pat: Some people who don't normally say a word join in those prayers.

Ruth: We do something similar. Every now and again we limit prayers to one or two sentences.

Alan: Well, there are a few suggestions.

Graham: And we also need to ask God to *teach* us how to pray. Sometimes we get so involved with techniques that we overlook the most obvious thing to do.

Teaching

Tim: Teaching! That's what we need – not just about prayer, but about the Bible.

Carol: There's no one in our group who's had any sort of theological training – not even at a Bible college. One or two of the members are a little concerned that we might end up in a 'blind leading the blind' situation – or drift off into some heresy.

Alan: I'd be concerned about that, too. It's vitally important to have a solid talk or Bible study at the heart of each meeting. How can you grow if you don't hear the word?

Pat: Alan and I often have disagreements over this. It's not that I feel talks and Bible studies are unimportant, but somehow I think there's more to it than that. I probably don't understand the dynamics of it enough to say clearly what I mean. For example, Alan, remember the time that Kevin gave that Bible study on prayer? He'd really put a lot of effort into it and people were participating well. I can remember thinking how much more I was getting out of it than from many sermons I'd heard. We sat back at the end of the study with a sort of satisfied glow. And then Peter said:

'That's all very well. I've known that in my head for years, but it still doesn't help me to pray as I want to, nor does it help me to understand why so many of my prayers go unanswered.'

I realised afterwards that it was only *then* that the study actually took off – or, should I say, touched earth, became relevant to our real situations. We must have spent an hour talking, sharing experiences, asking questions of one another – that's when the real learning took place.

Ruth: I think I know what you're getting at, Pat. In our group we've come to see that God is more concerned about the quality of the learning than the quality of the teaching. And learning is not confined to that part of our gathering officially labelled 'teaching'. The whole meeting is a learning experience.

Tim: How do you mean?

Graham: The sort of thing we were saying a minute ago with respect to prayer. We learn how to pray by listening to and being stimulated by others praying, not just by listening to studies on prayer. I came across a statement recently to the effect that 'Bible study of itself, vital as it is, doesn't ensure character development.'[1]

Ruth: And learning what it means to love is by being drawn into the concerns of others. I'm continually being challenged by the caring that I see others giving to someone in need. I often find myself saying, 'Why didn't *I* think of that?'

Graham: My understanding of the Lord's Supper and its significance has expanded so much in the past ten years – mainly by entering into the way in which others introduce the meal. They say that 'variety is the spice of life' and I find the variety of ways in which we approach the meal most rewarding.

Tim: I can see you've got a concept of 'teaching' that's different to mine. It's an attractive model in some respects, but I'm still not sure.

Carol: I'd be interested to hear what the rest of you have to say about something that happened in our group last week. As we sat eating our meal, we became involved in a discussion about the ethics of sport these days. One of our young people began talking about an incident that happened during a Davis Cup match and this developed into a general deploring of the lowering of standards in a variety of sports. Then someone else – a girl called Jenny – mentioned some problems she was having in this area in her hockey team.

---

1 The author was Ron Trudinger, *Cells for Life: Home Groups: God's Strategy for Church Growth*, Logos: Plainfield, NJ, 1979, p.38

At that point Tim reminded us that time was moving on and we'd better get started on our study for the night. Alice said she felt we ought to abandon the study in favour of addressing Jenny's problem. Jenny is a very self-effacing person and said she didn't want to take up our time. We got on with the study and prayed for Jenny briefly later in the evening. I've had this niggling doubt ever since that perhaps God really wanted us to take up Alice's suggestion.

Tim: And not the Bible study?

Alan: You couldn't do that. It's important to have a study every time you meet. Jenny's problem could be taken up by one or two after the meeting.

Pat: This is where Alan and I disagree. I think I'd want to do what Alice suggested. It's a matter of discerning what the Spirit is saying, isn't it?

Alan: You've got to have order.

Graham: I agree, but isn't it a question of whose order: man's or God's? And I'd want to argue with the inference that taking up Jenny's problem for discussion is somehow inferior to studying the Bible on such occasions. More than once we've begun talking over the meal about some issue affecting one of our members and chosen to pursue that rather than taking up the study planned for the night. These are always special occasions as people draw one another out with questions, share experiences and search the scriptures. The person who raises the question finds it very helpful and encouraging – and we all learn a lot and strengthen our ability to help one another.

In any case, isn't this the way people like Paul actually learned and taught? His letters mostly start from problems, then draw in the scriptures. They don't expound scripture line by line, then look around for situations to which it can be applied. It may be useful to do that kind of study at times, but not every week.

Ruth: We've also learnt not to be bashful as your Jenny was because, although it may be my problem today, it will be yours on another occasion.

Pat: Something you said once before, Ruth, gave me the impression that you don't always plan a study, anyway. Is that so?

Ruth: I'm almost afraid to admit it in front of Alan for fear of being branded a heretic! But no, we don't always have a study. For example, now and again we decide to devote a whole evening to prayer. Once a month we focus a whole meeting on the children, though that may include the telling or reading of a story.

Tim: I'm surprised to hear you say that you deliberately choose not to have 'teaching' each week.

Graham: It's not so surprising if you consider what we said before about 'learning'. We're not locked up to viewing 'teaching' as the only means by which the Spirit can teach us. We look to God to teach us through our singing, prayers, the Bible, the Lord's Supper, conversation, the lives of others and his world. We also try to approach 'teaching' in a number of ways.

Tim: For example?

Graham: Well, there are the usual Bible studies and talks. Then sometimes we try to put ourselves in the position of the characters in the Bible account: ask ourselves how we'd feel or react if we were, for example, the prodigal son, the elder brother, a servant, or the father. It's amazing how such a familiar passage comes to life when approached this way.

Ruth: And how much the children from, say, eight years old are able to enter in and contribute to such a discussion.

Graham: Then, we occasionally use a book as a guide – say Jacques Ellul's *Prayer and Modern Man*.[2] We don't actually study the book, but rather use it as a resource for our own exploration of the subject.

Ruth: Sometimes people volunteer to share something that God's been teaching them. Like when Mary shared what she'd learnt about suffering during those long months of her illness; or when Mike came to a deeper appreciation of why Jesus had to die.

Graham: Then there are meditations, and we mustn't forget Joe's parables. Joe, one of our members, is a great observer of nature and God often reveals some important aspect of himself and his ways to him through the simplest observations.

---

2 J. Ellul, *Prayer and Modern Man*, Eerdmans: Grand Rapids, 1972

Remember the time Joe developed a five or ten-minute talk out of his realisation that there are no 'straight lines' with God? The few that do exist in nature (like a cliff or a desert) are dangerous places for people to be and yet we persist in wanting God to act in a straight-line manner.

Ruth: People found that so helpful. 'No straight lines with God' has become a catch-phrase in our group!

Graham: The beauty of it is that it's such a simple picture to remember and yet it says so much: like 'I am the Good Shepherd', or 'you are the salt of the world'.

Ruth: What continually surprises me is the extent of God's imagination: the multitude of different ways he uses to teach us what we need to learn. It is fantastic!

Tim: I can see I need to give this area a lot more thought. Perhaps I'll have a look in the local Christian bookshop and see if they have something on it.

Graham: Oh, Tim — there you go again wanting more instruction, more teaching, but this time from a book! Not that I'm against books — heaven knows, I read enough myself. However, what I'd like to encourage you to do is sit down quietly for an hour or two, think back over your life and make a list of how God taught you the various things that mean most to you. I'll bet you're surprised by the end product!

Tim: Actually, now that I think of it, people in the Bible learned God's message in all sorts of ways. It has history, poems, prayers, stories, sermons, parables, letters, dreams, visions and direct life experiences. So why shouldn't we?

Communion

Alan: Maybe I'm getting ahead of things, but your views on teaching are so different from what I've understood by it, that I'm wondering what you think about the Eucharist.

Tim: Before Graham and Ruth answer that, Alan, can I ask you whether you celebrate the Lord's Supper in the home church you belong to?

Alan: Yes, we do.

Carol: How often?

Alan: What do you think, Pat? About every five or six weeks?

Pat: Roughly. It depends how available Eric and Ron are.

Carol: They're your minister and his assistant, aren't they?

Pat: That's right.

Tim: So you can only have the Lord's Supper when one of them is present?

Alan: Yes. Both Eric and Ron wish that wasn't the case. But the bishop in our diocese has made it quite clear that the Eucharist should only take place when someone authorised is leading it.

Graham: Does that mean you have to follow one of the forms of service in the Prayer Book?

Alan: Not necessarily. When Eric leads it we have a fairly liturgical service, but Ron includes a number of extempore elements.

Pat: He'd like to do away with the Prayer Book for home church use. I overheard him saying to the bishop once that the services in the Prayer Book were designed for public worship, not small groups meeting in homes.

Ruth: And what did the bishop make of that?

Pat: He didn't seem all that impressed.

Alan: I'm not all that convinced myself!

Pat: But Alan, think how much more freedom it would give us.

Alan: Perhaps. I do wish we didn't have to depend on the ministers in order to celebrate Communion. What's to stop one of us standing in when they can't make it? That's what we do at work when the managing director isn't available for certain functions.

Tim: Our situation is different, but we still have a problem in this area. Some of the ministers in the churches we attend are a little suspicious of our home church, especially when it comes to our holding the Lord's Supper. We're anxious to keep as good relations with them as we can, so we've tried to find another way of approaching the issue.

We have a common meal each week which we call an 'agape'. At some point during the meal, we break bread and drink wine, giving thanks and linking them with the death and resurrection of Christ. We don't call it a Lord's Supper – probably the ministers I mentioned wouldn't regard it as valid even if we did. We have no authorised person to officiate at it and we don't always use Jesus' words of institution. But for many of the members in our group it is the Lord's Supper and those who have doubts about that can still benefit from it.

Pat: I must say, I like the sound of that. What do you think, Alan?

Alan: I'm not sure.

Graham: As a way of dealing with a specific situation, I think it has a lot going for it. But I guess I'd hope that in time you could be more open about the whole matter.

Carol: That's what I tell Tim. I think we bend over backwards too much not to offend at times. Coming from a non-church background, I find it all rather unimportant.

Tim: Maybe so. But tell me, Graham, why do you think we should eventually go further than we do at present?

Graham: For the simple reason that scripturally the Lord's Supper belongs as much in the home church meeting as in the meeting of the whole church. But there's another reason as well. Until people acknowledge this to be the case, they will never see such gatherings in the home as being just as much an expression of church as the Sunday service.

Ruth: I find some ministers' reactions quite contradictory here. They are happy to let people gather to study the Bible in their homes, with a non-theologically trained person leading, yet they refuse to allow the Lord's Supper to be celebrated in homes by church members. I could understand an old-style Catholic having this attitude, but I just can't understand a Protestant minister thinking this way. I'd have thought there was more danger in letting people interpret the Bible in their homes than allowing them to celebrate the Lord's Supper there.

Alan: I'd never thought of it from that angle. I must ask Eric about it next time I see him. He's always on about the Reformation freeing the church from over-emphasising the sacraments at the expense of the Word.

Ruth: Mind you, even when we began to have the Lord's Supper regularly in our home, we had some difficulties knowing how to approach it.

Pat: What kinds of difficulties?

Ruth: We were convinced that the Lord's Supper should be

an actual meal and that the experience of real fellowship with one another was a vital part of it. Originally we introduced bread and wine, as distinct from the other food, at some point during the meal. But we found that doing this altered both the atmosphere of the meeting and the way people related. Instead of bringing us into greater contact with the reality of God and leading us into a deeper fellowship with one another, it tended to make both more stilted and artificial.

Pat: What did you do?

Ruth: We concluded that, even though we all believed the bread and wine to be quite ordinary – *extra*ordinary only because of the significance Jesus attached to them – that we were somehow regarding them as sacred in the wrong way. So we decided to use whatever food and drink made up the meal on a particular evening, since that would be more natural to us.

Graham: In fact, for a while we found we had to forego 'communion-type' prayers over the food and drink altogether, apart from saying a general grace.

Alan: Does that mean you don't use bread and wine any more?

Ruth: No. Sometimes these are an ordinary part of the meal itself, anyway. Occasionally we have them in addition to the other food and drink, since we find now that introducing them doesn't have the same effect as it used to.

Pat: And do you have Communion every week?

Ruth: Since we always have a meal together, we always treat that as the Lord's meal.

Pat: And do the children take part?

Ruth: Yes. We reason that just as they come to know the word of God by listening to it from their earliest days, so they come to know the meaning of the Lord's Supper by participating in it.

Tim: And I presume there's no one person who presides over the meal?

Ruth: Either the host family or different members of the group in turn take responsibility for it.

Pat: Always following a similar pattern?

Ruth: No. Sometimes the host or hostess introduces it with scripture and prayer; sometimes with a reading, hymn or personal statement and prayer; sometimes we all pray or sing, perhaps holding on to one another in some way to demonstrate our unity.

One of the things we appreciate is the real vitality it brings to the meal. For example, once or twice we've structured a whole evening around the meal, interleaving the entrees, main course, dessert and coffee, with singing, then some teaching, fellowship and finally praying, concluding with a blessing over the port. It has been a quite remarkable and profound experience.

Gifts

Carol: The way Graham and Ruth have talked about their group intrigues me. Do you mind if I ask if your group is charismatic?

Ruth: It depends what you mean by charismatic. I wouldn't say we were charismatic in the way that word is sometimes associated with a certain way of exercising spiritual gifts. . .

Graham: And with some gifts more than others – usually the more exotic ones, like prophesying or speaking in tongues!

Carol: Well, what did you mean by 'gifts' then, if you weren't referring to those?

Graham: We'd define 'gifts' more broadly than that. It seems to us that when Paul talks about Christians gathering together as church, he is stressing that everyone has a contribution to bring and that the range of gifts people have is broader than the lists in his writings.

Ruth: So not just 'teaching', 'organisational ability', or for that matter 'prophecy' and 'speaking in tongues', but gifts like 'welcoming' and 'hospitality', 'listening' and 'asking the appropriate question', 'wonder' and 'laughter'.

Pat: Don't you think the best gift that any of us brings to the church is ourselves, in all our complexity?

Ruth: I couldn't agree more. And it follows that sometimes our greatest contribution to the church is admitting our weakness and need.

Pat: It never ceases to amaze me to see God at work in such a situation. Just a couple of weeks ago one of our teenagers broke down in a flood of tears. She's under a lot of pressure one way or another at the moment. She's worried about final exams coming up at school; she doesn't know what she wants to do in the future; and, as if these weren't enough, she's just broken off a romance that has been going for eighteen months!

Alan: Who'd be young again!

Pat: It was really encouraging, Alan, wasn't it, to see the way various people in the group sought to calm her, draw her out and then pray with her.

Alan: Even Colin, who's more renowned for putting his foot in it, went over and gave her a bit of a hug.

Pat: But especially Edith. She's our group 'grandmother'. Having someone like that is a tremendous boon – one of the most wonderful gifts God can give to a church.

Carol: Well, I can see that lots of gifts were involved in dealing with that situation. But do you experience what you called the more exotic gifts in your group as well?

Ruth: Yes, we do. They're a regular feature of our life together, though you could come on any given night and not witness any.

Graham: Let me hasten to add that they are exercised in a very matter-of-fact manner, springing naturally out of the life of the group.

Tim: What do you mean by that?

Graham: Well, no one uses a special tone of voice or words if they feel they have some direct word from God to someone in the group or the group as a whole. Prophecy can be quite conversational, and come up indirectly in someone's prayer, praise or sharing.

Take 'laying on of hands'. Hardly anyone in our group has ever asked in one of our meetings if anyone wants hands laid on them, as I've heard done elsewhere. We touch a person, or put our arms around them, whatever seems appropriate – for healing, yes, but also when we want to identify with someone in their need, like that teenage girl you spoke of, Pat. Or maybe when it's someone's birthday and we want to especially commend them to God.

Ruth: The group also did that for us before we took that weekend for St Bede's on the importance of home churching.

Graham: That was the whole group. Sometimes it may only be one member who does it for another, or several. It varies.

Carol: Has there been any tension in the group here? You know, someone who doesn't believe in this approach or whatever?

Ruth: Not lately. However about seven or eight years ago we had considerable tension in the group between the 'haves' and the 'have nots'.

Graham: It was very sad, really. One couple had a charismatic experience outside the home church and began to speak in tongues and prophesy. They also started to attend a 'charismatic' group. As the weeks went by, they became more convinced about the centrality of these gifts and tried to persuade the rest of us as well.

Ruth: That was quite understandable. They'd discovered something new and wanted to share it.

Graham: All would have been well if it had stopped there, but they began to demand that *everyone* in the group move in a 'charismatic' direction. A few of our people needed time and exposure to the gifts to come to that conclusion. So when we wouldn't all move as quickly as they desired, it became increasingly obvious that we were considered second-rate. Eventually they left us.

Ruth: That caused us a lot of pain and heart-searching. It took the group months to recover and even a couple of years later certain people felt very vulnerable about it.

Tim: Can you say a little more about how someone in the group can come to understand what gifts they have?

Graham: As I understand Paul's letters, it's not a matter of searching around for a gift to exercise or role to play in the church. You do see people approaching it that way, but that seems to be putting the cart before the horse. I like that verse – 1 Corinthians 14:12 I think it is – where Paul says 'if you're eager to see the Spirit manifesting himself among you, then strive to build up the church'. I understand that to mean: 'Don't concentrate on the gifts, but concentrate on the needs and potential of people in the church and seek to help them in any way that you can'. In doing so, you'll gradually discover what you have to give.

Pat: The other thing, surely, is people in the church telling

one another what they have found helpful in others' words or actions. That way we let each other know what is benefiting us most among all the things they say and do.
Graham: Exactly.
Carol: I find that very helpful, actually. I think I've always tended to look at this matter the other way round. Also, Graham's earlier point about gifts like prophecy not necessarily being something out of the ordinary so far as tone of voice, language or content is concerned. That made me wonder whether even our group doesn't experience more of the gifts than we realise.

Leadership

Tim: Talking about 'gifts' prompts me to ask you what you do about leadership in your groups? It's about a year since Alison and Richard started our group and I think it's about time we appointed a couple of elders.
Carol: It's Tim really who wants elders appointed; the others seem quite content to carry on democratically as we've been doing.
Tim: Richard's an obvious choice if you ask me, since he started the group. But he says he doesn't want the job.
Alan: I'd have thought Richard would make an excellent elder. He's a good teacher, isn't he?
Carol: Yes, he is, but he's reluctant to have anyone appointed to a position which might cause the rest of us to think that he'll take most of the responsibility.
Graham: A sort of ministerial role?
Tim and *Carol*: Yes.
Graham: How real a danger do you think that is?
Tim: I don't think it's a danger at all.
Carol: It's hard to tell, isn't it? At the moment everyone is keen to share the load, but if a leader were chosen...
Ruth: Pat, do you have a leader or elder in your home church?
Pat: Yes – George!
Tim: On what basis did you choose him?
Alan: Well, we didn't actually choose him. He was appointed by the minister when St Margaret's decided to have home churches.

Pat: All the leaders were chosen by the minister and assistant pastor.

Carol: Were they all men?

Pat: What do you think?

Alan: Go on, that's a bit tough. You can't have women exercising authority over men!

Carol: Why not?

Ruth: Did it never occur to anyone that a husband and wife could do the job together?

Pat: That's more or less how it works out in practice. Josie is just as much a leader as George. He may play a more prominent role, hosting the meetings and doing most of the teaching, but she is the one with the pastoral concerns and skills.

Alan: It's true. I can't deny it. I often think Josie has a better idea of where the group is at than George, but is it any wonder when you realise how much contact she has with the individual members?

Pat: They do complement each other well.

Alan: You're the leader of your group, aren't you, Graham?

Graham: Ruth and I are certainly the oldest members, but we're not the leaders. The others would be very upset if they thought anyone regarded us in that way.

Pat: Does your group operate like Tim and Carol's, then?

Graham: Yes and no. When we first started we were, I think, more like what I understand Tim and Carol to be saying. We tried to be egalitarian: everyone took it in turns to lead the studies, the meetings and the prayer times and to look after the children. No one was more prominent than anyone else.

Ruth: But it didn't work.

Tim: Why not?

Graham: After a while we began to see that in our zeal to get away from the mono-minister model, we'd fallen into an equally undesirable trap of thinking that we were all the same.

Tim: I'm lost. If you don't have a leader and yet you're not all leaders, what do you do?

Graham: I didn't say we weren't all leaders. I said we weren't all *equal*. If everyone is regarded as equal that can lead to a certain amount of confusion. On the other hand if you have a single leader, there is a danger of too much routine. Recognising that we are all leaders but not all equally leaders has brought both order and balance.

Ruth: It's a matter of discerning what gifts and maturity each person has and then being prepared to listen and submit to one another accordingly.

Graham: Say we are meeting at the Smith's place – Mary is busy with the children and Bruce is talking to someone, not realising that we should have started the meeting. We don't all just continue talking and waiting. Someone will suggest we ought to get under way – and that could be anyone in the group.

Ruth: And we are all free to shape the meeting with a song, a prayer, a reading, a question or a suggestion whenever we feel it's appropriate, even if a few people have a greater sensitivity to the overall direction of the gathering.

Alan: Do you equate what's appropriate with the Spirit's leading?

Ruth: Most of the time. That follows, doesn't it, if people are seeking to do what pleases God when they come together? Occasionally someone is prompted to do or say something which, on the surface, doesn't appear to be appropriate.

Tim: What happens then?

Ruth: We have to test it, weigh it. That's happening informally and almost unconsciously all the time and there are occasions when the rest of the group questions what someone says or does.

Graham: It all gets back to this business of discernment. It's not enough to assume that, since Ruth here has a great deal of wisdom, that she'll always be wise. Sometimes God chooses to give it to a teenager. And it's not enough to assume that if someone has a special gift of prayer, he'll always be the one who prays the 'right' prayer. Sometimes it will be Joan, Mary, or even Graham.

Ruth: I suppose the nearest thing we have to a leader or elders is what we call the pastoral centre of a group.

Graham: In some respects; but they're still not leaders, are they?

Carol: What's a pastoral centre?

Ruth: We've come to see that each group, whether it's recognised formally or not, needs what we call a pastoral centre. It's usually made up of a small number of people who have a total commitment to the group, people who are able to 'see' the group as an identity in its own right rather than as a collection of individuals. They're able to keep their eyes fixed on the fundamental aims of the community and the main principles that should govern its life.

Graham: The people who form the pastoral centre also manage to give confidence to the group when it's going through a rough patch. They are able to mediate between people in the group who are at odds with one another. They have the capacity to draw out the quieter members and keep the more dominant in place. But they don't have to be formally appointed or specially trained for the purpose. It's less a case of natural talent or theological education than, as with parenthood, a developing love and wisdom gained through experience.

Growth

Carol: Tim, I've just glanced at the time. I had no idea it was almost twelve. I'll have to go soon.

Graham: Reminds me of our home church meetings. We start at 6.00 p.m. after work on a Friday and, even though we finish the more organised part of the meeting around 10.00 p.m. or 10.30 p.m., there always seem to be some of us still there at midnight.

Tim: Yes, we've had some marathons ourselves now and again. But look, before I take Carol home, there's one last issue I'd like to raise.

Ruth: How about another cup of coffee to keep us going?

Graham: Let me get it, Ruth. You spent enough time in the kitchen earlier.

Ruth: I won't argue!

Tim: It's actually a practical issue for our own group. We've slowly grown in numbers since we started and some of us are wondering whether we're beginning to get too large.

Alan: How many are there in the group?

Tim: We've got ten adults, three teenagers who are there throughout the whole meeting – and how many children, Carol?

Carol: Eight. Three at school and the rest still at home.

Tim: But there are also one or two other people enquiring about joining.

Ruth: Yes, you wouldn't want to get too much larger.

Pat: We have a rule that, when there are fifteen adults attending regularly, we divide automatically into two groups.

Ruth: How does that work?

Pat: To be honest, it hasn't worked out too well. Last time it took our half of the group quite a while to recover and the other half lost members after a few months and eventually folded.

Ruth: That doesn't surprise me. I know of a number of cases where something similar has happened. My own view iş that a wrong model is being followed when you multiply a group that way.

Alan: But surely the model of cell division is the most appropriate.

Tim: The few books I've read which talk about this all seem to promote it.

Ruth: But the Bible compares the church to other things than a cell, for example a vine, a body or a family. You don't just slice a vine in two and expect it to reproduce itself. You have to take a small branch and plant it separately with considerable care.

Pat: That makes much more sense to me. I've always felt the other way of dividing was too severe. It caused a lot of upset when we went through it.

Alan: But surely it's good for a group to be shaken up a bit every now and again. Otherwise it becomes too in-centred and complacent.

Ruth: That sometimes happens, but it doesn't have to work out that way. We find that we get enough surprises in the normal course of events, with people having to move inter-state, problems and difficulties that arise or new members joining. So we appreciate the stability of long-term relationships with at least a few in the group.

Tim: I can understand that. I've belonged to other small groups where you could only stay together for six months or had to divide regularly. As a result, we had to keep on starting all over again. We never really developed much depth in our fellowship.

Graham: Here's the coffee. Just help yourself to milk and sugar from the tray.

Tim: But even if you follow a different model from the 'cell' one, how do you know who ought to be the nucleus of a new group?

Ruth: Our cluster of home churches had to learn the hard way, I'm afraid. In fact, some of our early experiments weren't too successful. The first time our groups multiplied, we did it along purely geographical lines. But that proved too drastic: it separated a number of people who had much to give one another, including a few who had strong prior relationships. The second time round the groups tried to avoid this, except where they felt God gave them the encouragement to do so, and allowed people to choose which group they would join. The problem that then arose was an imbalance of certain gifts between the two, making it difficult for one of the groups to establish itself properly.

Carol: So what did you do the next time you had to divide?

Ruth: Take over, Graham, so I can drink my coffee.

Graham: We gave careful consideration to the question of gifts and ensured that the newer group had a fair representation. We even asked whether there were any people in the original group who were prepared to act as the pastoral centre of the newer group. A married couple volunteered, saying that they had always felt they would like to do that. So we gave them our blessing to begin.

Tim: And did everything work out OK that time?

Graham: Unfortunately, no. That couple never really delivered what they'd promised. Although the group did manage to survive for a number of years, eventually it realised it didn't have enough resources to continue. But we learned something important from the experience. We should never have taken the couple's word in the first place. If they really did have a pastoral concern, it would have come out to some extent in the initial group, even though there were others who were operating in a pastoral way. We wouldn't make that mistake again, however sincerely people put themselves forward.

Pat: So the next time you took that into account?

Ruth: We did, but things took a quite different course. There were two couples whom the rest of us felt could form the pastoral nucleus of a new church. They talked and prayed about it, but felt that circumstances prevented them from taking on this responsibility at the time. On reflection, we all felt that they had come to the right decision.

Tim: What did you do then?

Graham: First of all, we had to cope with having an over-large group. So once a month we met in two homes and once a month divided into two groups in the same home for part of the evening. We also had to ask God to provide some other answer to the problem of size. What eventually happened was that several of our members had to move elsewhere in the country and a couple of others went overseas for a year. God simply reduced the size of the group to manageable proportions again.

Ruth: On another occasion so many people wanted to join at the same time that our group and another group loaned out two couples to help the newcomers find their feet as a church. That had never occurred to us as a possibility before. Six months later, one of the couples who were helping the new group joined them permanently.

Carol: I get the impression from what you're saying that, although we should find an appropriate model for dividing and also build certain resources into a new group, we must remain open to a variety of possibilities in this area.

Ruth: Yes. While there are principles to keep in mind, there are no simple formulae. God is very versatile when it comes to dealing with some of these problems.

Tim: Would that also be true for the size a group reaches before it divides?

Ruth: There's no magical number. It varies from group to group. But there's a point where the quality of relationships begins to lessen, people aren't able to contribute as freely as they did before, and practical difficulties arise in connection with seating, meals and children.

Carol: When we have visitors in the group we're aware of some of these things now. But I hate the thought of losing fellowship with the people I've come to love and value.

Graham: But you'll start to lose that anyway if you just keep growing larger and larger. That's the first thing people complain about when they move out of a home and start meeting in a hall or a church.

Carol: I suppose so.

Tim: Do you think it's ever right to say 'no' to someone who wants to join your home church?

Ruth: We've certainly felt it right to pray at times that God would not add anyone to our group for the time being, particularly when we've been going through a time of self-examination or are dealing with some crisis. We've also occasionally recommended people to another group, feeling that for some reason it would be more helpful to them or because, quite literally, we had no room. Once I encouraged another group to redirect someone in our direction. The group concerned was very fragile at the time and the person enquiring was a dominant and rather insensitive person who had been a key factor in a previous group coming to an end.

Graham: We find it helpful always to invite people who indicate interest in our church to a meal with another couple from the group – not to screen them, but to find out if our kind of group is really what they are after. But the main thing as I see it, is that we don't say 'no' to people simply because they're different from us or will introduce problems into our group.

Alan: One last question before we finish. I notice, Ruth, that you never refer to groups dividing, but only to them multiplying.

Ruth: We came to feel that to talk about 'dividing' had too many negative connotations – although it's a lot better than talking about 'splitting' – whereas multiplying is a far more positive way of looking at the situation.

Graham: It also reminds us that the 'problems' we're talking about are problems of *growth*, not decline – far and away the best problems to have!

While much more could be said about all these aspects of home church life, something of the range of approaches and quality of experience has come through in the exchanges between our conversation partners. In the end, each home church has to work through its own dilemmas and develop its individual character. That is why we have avoided giving prescriptions and preferred to give descriptions instead. In reacting to these, and seeking the guidance God promises, each home church can begin to chart its own distinctive course.

While there will be recognisable similarities between home churches, there will also be some of that delightful diversity that we find in God's creation and the people around us. Visiting another home church, therefore, is always something of an adventure.

8

Growing pains in the family:

Tensions in home church life

WHILE SOME HOME CHURCHES HAVE no difficulty in getting under way, in others minor problems arise near the beginning. These usually take the form of slight disagreements that appear in early discussions between members of the group. Often these disagreements spring from differing views about the nature of the Christian faith. Others concern the importance of various long-standing Christian practices. Some have more to do with the behaviour appropriate to Christians in certain circumstances. Happily, none of these differences is fundamental. The more serious difficulties tend to emerge later in a group's life. We shall examine them further on in this chapter.

Differing views

1. Disagreements over doctrine
Many home churches contain people from different denominational backgrounds. Even where a home church is part of a local congregation, not all members will share the same denominational upbringing.

Though doctrinal differences may arise at the start of a group's life, mostly they take a little while to come to the forefront. The reason is that initially the more personal, daily needs of people in the group take precedence. Mostly people have joined the group specifically to discuss these needs and find help on them. In any case, most churchgoers are less preoccupied with traditional doctrinal disputes. Only where doctrines bear directly upon everyday problems do most church members take a serious interest in them.

One of the early home church clusters, made up of people from different backgrounds, found a creative way of dealing with this difficulty:

> There is little dispute about the general way of operating in our household groups since that is why people are coming together. But what about doctrine? For example, we had Baptists who believed in believers' baptism and Anglicans who believed in infant baptism. What do you do when you have in the one church people with two such strongly held beliefs, both of which have clear and contrary practical outworkings? We had a friendly dispute at the beginning, but then gradually evolved a methodology applicable to 'historical areas of dispute'. This refers to those doctrinal areas within the historical churches that have been disputed for centuries and to which no final solution has been found.
>
> Take baptism for example, or such matters as predestination and free will, the time and character of the Second Coming, and the nature of the Lord's Supper. Christians have quoted scripture backwards and forwards at each other on these issues, still without coming to any conclusive solution. If this is the case in Christendom, it is only with some difficulty that we are all likely to come to one conclusion in our groups. Therefore, we recognised these as historical areas of dispute and endeavoured to respect one another's opinions.
>
> When we found this initial acceptance, there was much greater readiness to listen without prejudice to each other's point of view. This helped people to appreciate others and their different positions better. Quite often we were then able to sit down and discuss these questions afresh. On some we have come to a mutually agreeable decision, while on others we have agreed to disagree and have recognised that such differences of opinions are no barrier to fellowship. People are not really interested in arguing among themselves; the fellowship becomes more important to them. Part of Christian freedom is accepting those whom God has accepted, and accepting each other 'without disputes over opinion' or questions regarding their spirituality and

Christian orthodoxy. If Christ has received us, then we must receive one another. That is really the basis of our fellowship – a common experience and love of Jesus Christ.[1]

2. Disagreements over practices

On issues where a group as a whole has to make practical decisions, it can accept a plurality of approaches rather than alienating people by insisting on one. Take baptism, for instance. If a baby is born into one of the families, members ask the parents how they would like their new child to be accepted into the church. If the parents prefer the baby to be baptised, the home church can arrange this. If some form of dedication is preferred, then this can be organised. Where the parents are uncertain, others in the group can go through the relevant biblical passages and help them reach a clear decision on the matter.

On the question of the Lord's Supper, members of some house churches have a more symbolic, others a more dynamic, view of its operation. Some members desire a quite informal, others a more liturgical celebration. One group decided that as their meetings were held in various homes, the family hosting the gathering should have freedom to organise the meal as it saw fit. This enabled different ways of celebrating the communion meal to take place. Gradually, people came to see how enriching this was to their own understanding of Communion. This custom prevented it from becoming a repetitive ritual.

This principle can be applied to a whole range of views on which people differ. For example, some Christians prefer traditional hymns and others scripture choruses, some charismatic songs and others Christian folk music. There is a place for all in church – as well as compositions written by members of the group. We do not have to even like songs to enter into them with a brother or sister who does.

This is also true of various translations of the Bible or of study material. Indeed, so long as the bulk of the members regard the Bible as inspired and authoritative, they do not

1 G.N. Moon, 'Household Churches in Canberra 1968-71', *Interchange*, Vol.3, No.2, 1971, p.113

all need to adopt the same interpretation of what that means to study it profitably together and hear the voice of God in it.

Neither need all members of a home church agree on the value of certain gifts of the Spirit for them to be exercised in church. There is room for those who speak in tongues and those who do not, for those who pray for healing by laying on of hands and for those who just pray, for those who are given some direct prophetic message and for those who share their experiences.

Other matters that tend to divide Christians today can be treated in the same manner. Differing views, such as on the role of women in the church, may be aired at the beginning — though it might be impossible to resolve these to everyone's satisfaction at the outset. It is preferable for a home church to begin operating in a way that reflects the various attitudes within it. Then the members can explore together not only what the Bible says about the issue, but what they have learned from their experience in the group. If all are open to the truth, the Spirit will bring sufficient agreement for all to continue in unity. If not, some may withdraw and search for a more doctrinally homogeneous study group.

A more difficult area is counselling people in the area of interrelationships — someone whose marriage is breaking down or who is unsure of his/her sexual orientation. We are not necessarily thinking of people who are committing adultery or engaging in promiscuous gay activity. Such people are unlikely to want to join such a group anyway. We are thinking of the many people who are experiencing dislocation in their inner lives and substantial emotional stress. A group does well to open its arms to such people, accepting them as they are and helping them to work through their problem. In time God will clarify for one and all how the individuals in difficulty can best proceed.

Diverging perceptions
New groups usually go through a 'honeymoon' period. The length of time for this varies, though it is generally around nine months. But it might be as short as six months or as long as a year.

During this period the freshness of home church life – its freedom and relevance, opportunity and intimacy – tends to carry the group along. But when some of the novelty wears off, problems start to surface. These may emerge slowly, with few noticing anything wrong, or they may come out in a rush when everyone is least expecting them.

The 'problems' as such arise from the underlying perceptions people have of their role in the group rather than with particular doctrinal or practical matters, with what goes on in their imaginations and feelings rather than in their thoughts. The chief hindrances to our becoming a genuine Christian community lie within us: in our basic attitudes, expectations and motives. These are so intrinsic to our way of looking at others that we are often unaware of them. Yet they govern our relationships with each other, the way in which we seek to serve our fellow members and our view of what our home church should become.

1. An unaccepting attitude towards others

When you first join a small community of Christians, the chances are that you won't know many of the people very well. This can make you feel a bit of a stranger for a while, uncertain of yourself in their company and not always sure how to take what others say or do. But time passes. You settle into the group and begin to feel more relaxed. Your feeling of strangeness recedes as you become more familiar with the other members.

More time passes. Now you begin to know people a little too well. You become aware of the way they like to dress and of the look they get on their face when they're feeling upset or on top of life. You come to recognise their mannerisms – the way they twitch an eyebrow, or turn down a corner of the mouth – as well as some of their other habits. You become familiar with their attitudes, prejudices and hobby-horses. Sometimes you can predict exactly what they are going to say about a certain issue before they have spoken a word!

In particular, you begin to notice the ways in which people respond to certain others in the group. This will become more obvious where members have different class back-

174/Growing pains in the family

grounds, lifestyles, outlook on society, temperament or tastes and attitudes to childrearing.

Other potential sources of conflict are differing views about how the Christian life is to be lived and how growth to spiritual maturity takes place. It is all too easy in such circumstances to begin to look down on others, to begin to compare yourself with others and feel superior to them. When that happens, you may be tempted to give them less time during the meetings and spend more time with those who are like-minded. You may even find yourself passing sentence upon them because they don't match up to your requirements. In that moment the basis for developing a stronger bond is lost and, with it, the hope of the whole group becoming a genuine community.

There is an important distinction here. It is permissible to *discern* the differences between ourselves and others, even their weaknesses and failings. The apostle Paul constantly urges his readers to exercise discernment in all their dealings: with God, one another and the wider society. Some members of the church will have a gift in this direction — they will see more quickly than the rest the weaker points in others and in the church as a whole. Such people are in a way the conscience of a group. But this discernment should include knowledge of the factors that sometimes give rise to other people's differences, such as family background, disappointing experiences, present difficulties, as well as a recognition of our own weaknesses and failings.

It is not discerning the truth about people that creates problems, but yielding to the temptation to *judge* others in the light of such differences. We have no right to do that. We have too many failings ourselves. We do not have sufficient knowledge to come to a proper decision. Only God has the knowledge to pass sentence in this way. In any case, has he not created us differently — in looks and temperament, in interests and abilities — and called us to complement and help one another? Equally, his creation demonstrates how much he loves and appreciates diversity. And does he not in Christ accept us as we are, with all our weaknesses and failings, indicating how we are also to accept and forgive, rather than reject and condemn, one another?

But members of a group sometimes find this hard to do. Compare the following letter from a home church that was facing this problem:

The difficulty we seem to be battling with is the different ways we all have of relating to God. Stephen once said to me it was as if he and Jenny had two different Gods so differently did they approach him.

In church, this is magnified ten times over... Those whose relationship with God has much in common tend to gravitate towards one another, with an accompanying sense of enthusiasm in their sharing of the benefits they find. Then come various forms of judgment on those not so like-minded...

This has time and again provided a problem for the institutional church. How much more is it felt in a home church? We cannot underestimate how deeply threatened people become by those whose approach is different and how desperately they seek the security of those who think the same way. Because we are not sure how to go about tackling this problem, we are inclined to avoid it by finding the 'lowest' common denominator of agreement and sticking with that. This seems to entail just meeting together, sharing our concerns and interests, and trying to be involved in one another's lives as far as we are able.

I write 'lowest' in inverted commas because I don't really consider this 'low'. In fact, it has the potential to be the 'highest' – if anyone sees the possibility contained in it. But at present people feel without anchor, insecure, with vague feelings of 'there should be something more', 'is this enough?'... The answer I'm gradually finding for myself (not without considerable difficulty and heartsearching) is that God does not have to be approached in only *one* way. We can delight in all the various ways people find God working in their lives.

Whilst we know something of the power of a group of like-minded Christians praying in agreement, we have yet to experience the greater glory of *un*like-minded people genuinely loving, respecting and encouraging one another in their differences until God brings about an undreamt-of unity in spirit. Our home church sits on the brink of this possibility because of the unique opportunity it offers for this unity to develop.

Acceptance of differences, then, and forgiveness of others' failings are crucial if more than a limited or superficial community life is to be experienced.

2. Unrealistic expectations of the group

When you join a home church, you're bound to have some image of what the group should be like. This may have come from a number of sources: sermons or books on the nature of Christian community, actual experience in a small group beforehand, projections of your own needs and aspirations.

It's quite natural that you should have some picture in your mind of how a group should function. Though people occasionally join groups without any preconceptions, usually they will have some. It's rare for us to go into any new situation with a completely open attitude as to what is involved. It's what we do with these dreams of community that matters. If they are not handled properly, they can jeopardise the very venture they seek to launch.

First, our picture of the ideal Christian community is bound to be one-sided. No one person can have the whole truth about God's will. The Spirit distributes insights into the nature of community life to different people. That is why only *together*, as all share their understanding, can a fully rounded portrait of community emerge.

Second, our picture of community is bound to be partly wrong. We are still too affected by self – and therefore still too vulnerable to creating a community in our own image – for any of us to have an undistorted view. We need each other not only to fill out our one-sided views, but also to correct our false ones.

Third, if our home church doesn't develop in the direction of our ideal picture, it is all too easy to find the group wanting. Then we begin to distance ourselves from it and start blaming it for not living up to our expectations. In doing this, we undermine even further any chance the group has of deepening its communal life.

As Bonhoeffer points out, God wants us to recognise and work with the actual situation before us, not be preoccupied with the ideal, purely hypothetical one. The home church is made up of people who are imperfect, imbalanced and, maybe, immature. Whatever changes God brings about within them, they will go on being this way for a long time to come. As he says:

> Just as surely as God desires to lead us to a knowledge of genuine Christian fellowship, so surely must we be overwhelmed by a great disillusionment with others, with Christians in general and, if we are fortunate, with ourselves. By sheer grace, God will not permit us to live even for a brief period in a dream world. He does not abandon us to those rapturous experiences and lofty moods that come over us like a dream. God is not a God of the emotions, but the God of truth. Only that fellowship which faces such disillusionment, with all its unhappy and ugly aspects, begins to be what it should be in God's sight – begins to grasp in faith the promise that is given to it. The sooner this shock of disillusionment comes to an individual and to a community, the better for both. A community which cannot bear and cannot survive such a crisis, which insists upon keeping its illusion when it should be shattered, permanently loses in that moment the promise of Christian community. Sooner or later it will collapse.
>
> Every human dream that is injected into the Christian community is a hindrance to genuine community and must be banished if genuine community is to survive. He who loves his dream of a community more than the Christian community itself becomes a destroyer of the latter, even though his personal intentions may be ever so honest and earnest and sacrificial.[2]

What are some of the false expectations we can have about community? One is the feeling that the community is primarily there for us: to encircle us, support us, love us. Now community involves all of these, but it also calls for each of us to encircle, support and love others as well. It's true that some people in a home church may have to be carried for a time by the remainder, receiving rather than giving. But eventually there comes a point where each of us

---

2 D. Bonhoeffer, *Life Together*, SCM: London, 1954, pp.16-17

has, in Jean Vanier's words, to move 'from community for myself to myself for the community'.[3]

Another false expectation is the belief that the home church is there to solve our problems. These problems may arise from serious personal, family or vocational difficulties we are experiencing. The community is certainly there to listen to us, talk with us, pray for us and practically help us when we are in difficulties. But it is not primarily a therapeutic or welfare group to solve all our problems for us. As one of the members of our home church cluster put it: 'We are here not primarily to solve each other's problems, but to provide the supportive context within which each with God's help can begin to work through their own problems.'

A further false expectation is that everyone will become friends in the home church or that it is there our closest friendships will develop. Now we may make one or two friends in the group to which we belong. But sometimes those whom God places us amongst will be people with whom we have little in common. There may even be some whom we have great difficulty in liking. The genius of a home church is the way in which it brings the most unlikely people together and calls upon them to form a community. This means that, normally speaking, you should not expect the group to meet your basic friendship needs. If it does, God has given you a bonus; if it doesn't, don't judge the group for it.

Refusing to hold on to expectations does not mean that it is wrong for people in a home church to have some sense of where they would like to go and how they can best arrive there. But this goal should not stem from some ideal that you bring to the community. It should arise out of the actual life of the community, the gifts of the members, their level of maturity and the particular mission your group may have.

We are not talking about an ideal imposed upon the community from outside, but about a sense of direction derived from what is happening in the community itself. It is only as we forsake our idolatrous absorption with an ideal

---

3 J. Vanier, *Community and Growth*, St. Paul: Sydney, 1979, p.26

and seek to serve and enhance the community as it is, that real advance takes place. It's the old gospel principle in new dress: only if you are prepared to lose your ideal do you have any hope of finding it.

At this point another distinction becomes useful: the distinction between expectations and hopes. It's one thing to have *expectations* about the progress of a group. Such an attitude places demands upon the group and upon the individuals within it. It fashions a kind of law for others and only produces disappointment and frustration for the one who does this when it is not fulfilled. It's another thing altogether to have *hopes*. These do not insist on their own way, but recognise that people at times are bound to fail. Indeed, the one who has hopes rather than expectations realises that to go one step forward it is sometimes necessary for a group to take one step to the side – or even two steps back. Of course, when individuals criticise a community for failing to meet their ideal requirements, it is often because they are unwilling to face up to their own flaws and weaknesses.

3. The danger of failing to affirm others' value and encourage their potential

When you come into a home church, you tend to come with a relatively low estimate of your own gifts and status as a person. There are various reasons for this. It could partly stem from the kind of Christianity in which you were nurtured. Certain forms of Christianity make both positive rules (read the Bible every day, witness at every opportunity, pray at all times) and negative rules (don't drink or dance, don't mix with certain people, don't listen to certain kinds of music) for their adherents. Your failure to live up to these may have only demonstrated to you what a second-rate Christian you are.

But low self-esteem also comes from the wider cultural ethos in which you were raised. Anglo-Saxon males in general – and Australian males in particular – are very poor at praising their children, except for certain 'masculine' endeavours such as sport. Females fare better at the hands of their mothers, but often only for fulfilling certain 'female' roles or functions. They are generally encouraged to feel they are inferior to males and that they make a less useful contribution to society. The messages of the advertising industry, peer group pressure and the structures of our society mostly serve to reinforce these attitudes.

As a result, most people who join a group come with a relatively low self-esteem and with a corresponding inability to encourage others to have a higher estimate of themselves. This leads to a 'catch-22' situation. Almost everyone is looking for affirmation, but almost no one is able to give it. Indeed, when you have low self-esteem, you not only tend to withhold gratitude and praise from others, but often put others down. This reaction may not always be obvious: it comes through more in the tone of voice, the raised eyebrow or the knowing exchange of smiles with another. But its effect is still felt. After a while this inability to show appreciation of each other and encourage the development of each others' gifts can produce a state of stagnation, a sense of 'going nowhere' in the group as a whole. It can even lead to those who had the courage to express their needs withdrawing even more into their shells.

The irony of this situation is that every single Christian is inestimably valuable. You yourself are a son or daughter of God. What higher status can you have? However unworthy you may feel at times or however much you may fail to reflect your Father's character, he only ever sees you in and through Christ – sinless, fully mature, perfect in him, as the person you will one day be. Also, through the Spirit, you have been given certain gifts to share with others. What higher qualifications could you possess? However little you may understand what these are and however unsure you may be about the way you exercise them, God has made a present of them to you. In time, you will be able to make full use of them.

Once again, there is an important distinction to bear in mind. We have to learn the art of focusing on the *strengths* of others, not their faults, seeing potential strengths in even their *weaknesses*. For God does not so much take away our shortcomings as transform them into advantages. So we have to ask God to help us see others from his perspective rather than our own. While we can still be aware of others' faults, we will discern the potential in even their most fragile qualities.

What a difference it would make if people saw each other this way and then treated each other accordingly! Instead of concentrating on each other's inadequacies, we'd be thanking God for the privilege of knowing one another. We'd also be building one another up through praise and encouragement of one another's efforts and good points.

C.S. Lewis captures the essence of this attitude in one of his most eloquent passages. Although it deals with people in general rather than Christians in particular, it is relevant here:

> It is a serious thing to live in a society of possible gods and goddesses, to remember that the dullest and most uninteresting person you can talk to may one day be a creature which, if you saw it now, you would be strongly tempted to worship, or else a horror and a corruption such as you now meet, if at all, only in a nightmare. All day long we are, in some degree, helping each other to one or other of these destinations. It is in the light of these overwhelming possibilities, it is with the awe and the circumspection proper to them, that we should conduct all our dealings with one another, all friendships, all loves, all play, all politics. There are no *ordinary* people. You have never talked to a mere mortal. Nations, cultures, arts, civilisations – these are mortal, and their life is to ours as the life of a gnat. But it is immortals whom we joke with, work with, marry, snub, and exploit – immortal horrors or everlasting splendours. This does not mean that we are to be perpetually solemn. We must play. But our merriment must be of that kind (and it is, in fact, the merriest kind) which exists between people who have, from the outset, taken each other seriously – no flippancy, no superiority, no presumption. And our charity must be a real and costly love, with deep feeling for the sins in spite of which we love the sinner – no mere tolerance, or indulgence which parodies love as flippancy parodies merriment.[4]

---

4 C.S. Lewis, 'The Weight of Glory', *Screwtape Proposes a Toast*, Collins: London, 1965, p.109

When a group puts this into practice, it finds that the more each person values the other, the more all grow into the sorts of people God wants them to be. And the more gratitude and encouragement we express, the more everyone's gifts are identified, developed and appreciated.[5]

4. The danger of settling for lower standards

When people first link up with a home church, most are enthusiastic for this new way of meeting and want to make it work. Others, for various reasons, are more tentative.

As with entering any new situation, after a while some of the novelty wears off. There are many reasons for this, such as outside pressures that indirectly affect people's involvement, difficulties encountered in the course of the new enterprise, or some problem unresolved lying within. Any of these can sap the initial optimism and vitality that attends the beginning of a home church. The group often downgrades its standards. While this may be necessary for a time, it raises serious problems when it becomes the norm.

You may be the kind of person who has the tendency to take on too many responsibilities. If so, the chances are that your home church will gradually come to fit in after everything else. You won't have the time to pray for others in the group or make any significant contact during the week. You rarely get round to asking yourself whether there is a particular contribution you could bring or whether there is someone in the group to whom you should give special attention. You will come weary to the group because you have not preserved sufficient energy for it. You may regularly arrive late and doze off at some point during the evening.

On occasions there are understandable reasons for acting this way. Think of young mothers with pre-school children, men experiencing intermittent periods of intense busyness at work, or those suffering personal dislocation due to circumstances outside their control. In such situations other

5 On the importance of encouragement generally, see the helpful book by L.J. Crabb, Jnr, *Encouragement: The Key to Caring*, S. John Bacon: Melbourne, 1984.

members of the home church should take some of the burden. But where the problem stems from habitual busyness and long-term overcommitment, for your sake and for the sake of the group as a whole it is important that they challenge your priorities.

But this is not the only course. The drift towards lower-level functioning in a group may come less from outside pressures than from the dynamics of the group itself. If one or two strong personalities tend to be sceptical about their faith, over-critical of others or lackadaisical in manner, others may feel inhibited. The problem can also arise from a positive feature: the genuine concern of members for one another. People may be so preoccupied with sharing their problems that they never move from concentration on the negative to celebration of the positive.

What can be done about this? There is a key role for certain people, especially those who form part of the pastoral centre of a group. They can act as a counterweight to these tendencies and create the climate in which others feel less inhibited. This may mean cutting across the dominant atmosphere in the group.

But one factor more than any other will cause a group to settle for a lower common denominator: us. In the last analysis, the quality of a home church's life will reflect the quality of the lives of its individual members. If we allow the values and pressures of surrounding society to grip us more than they should, then this will affect the vitality of the groups to which we belong. If we do not carry any given task out to the utmost of our ability, then all lose out in the process. If in coming together we are more intent on what others can contribute to us than on what we can contribute to them, then all will be the poorer.

The attitude called for is captured by Francis of Assisi's prayer: 'Lord make me an instrument of thy peace'. We should gather together:

> not so much to be consoled as to console;
> not so much to be loved as to love;
> not so much to be understood as to understand
> for it is in giving that one receives;

> it is in self-forgetfulness that one finds;
> it is in pardoning that one is pardoned.

If only two or three come to a group in this spirit, the remainder will reach out for something more. To come in this spirit is to come in the spirit of Christ, reflecting in our attitude towards others his commitment to us.

Here, we need to keep a final distinction in mind: that between the general *calling* of Christ and the specific *stage* we are at in our personal pilgrimage. All of us are at different levels of maturity and at different points in our life-cycle. Some are young in faith, some are older; some are free of family and work demands, some are not. Further, some want to fully identify themselves with the group, others are newcomers or are in transit; some find that life is going smoothly for them at the moment, some are passing through a crisis of identity, vocation or relationship. Given these differences, we should have a realistic understanding of what each is capable of attaining.

This concept of stages applies to the group as a whole. For example, where a home church is made up mostly of young marrieds with children, the group will not have much energy and the meetings will reflect this. During the meetings themselves, children will be more distracting and demanding, further affecting the quality of the gatherings. If other members of the group retain some ideal of a quiet, spiritually charged church in their minds, they will feel frustrated. If the young marrieds come expecting others to take the burden of their children, they will be constantly disappointed. Both must adapt to the situation in which they find themselves, creatively making the most of it and looking for ways to minimise its difficulties. They might pray that God will bring a few others into the group who can help share the overall responsibility. But they may simply have to grit their teeth and carry on, appreciating the good things that come out of their being together despite the difficulties.

The key is to be content with what you have. This was the attitude Paul adopted to the varying circumstances in which he found himself:

I have learnt to manage on whatever I have. I know how to
cope with having little and having much. I have been very
thoroughly initiated into the human lot with all its ups and
downs. . . and have strength for anything through him who
gives me power (Philippians 4:12-13).

But this spirit of contentment – like the spirit of acceptance,
service, encouragement and responsibility already
mentioned – cannot be manufactured and does not reside
fully in any one individual. Ultimately, it is a fruit of the
Spirit. And only as we come together, making up for each
other's lack and immaturity, can we exhibit a peaceful
attitude in any comprehensive way.

Conflicting personalities

The most difficult problems for a group arise not from the
views or perceptions of its members, but from who they are.
In a larger organisation, people are able to hide part of
themselves from one another, or only reveal it in a forma-
lised way. Generally, the basic conflicts between people,
such as disagreements at annual general meetings, are not
honestly dealt with in such settings, or in times of worship,
Bible study and prayer. As a result, many parts of people's
lives lie unchallenged, remaining at an immature or self-
centred level.

In a home church, where people cannot help coming into
closer contact with one another, hidden tensions will
eventually emerge and have to be resolved. Anyone joining
a home church who does not realise this is in for a shock.
Christian fellowship does not result in problems being
ignored; it brings them out into the open, intensifies them
and creates the possibility of their resolution.

1. Points of tension

A key area for personality clashes is punctuality. Some
people regularly fail to turn up on time! Such seem to find
it constitutionally impossible to arrive at the appointed
hour: it is part of their make-up. They are likely to be late
for *any* type of meeting or appointment.

This tends to be a touchy subject and no one likes to offend
others. Eventually, when the matter is raised, the offending

person may apologise for their habitual lateness. For two or three weeks everything is fine, then the old behaviour pattern reasserts itself. Even giving helpful hints to the latecomer, such as preparing their contribution to the meal the night before or setting their clock early, rarely seems to have the desired effect. The problem is so deeply rooted that only prayer will produce the necessary character change.

Another area of conflict is the discipline of children. Families have quite different attitudes to this matter. Sometimes these arise out of their different class or ethnic backgrounds, sometimes out of different approaches to child-rearing. It is not uncommon to find one family in a group exercising a very tight rein over their children, while another largely lets theirs do as they please. Some parents believe in physical discipline of their children, others do not.

The potential for tension and conflict over this issue is considerable, especially when there are a number of children in the group. At first, members of a home church tend to let each family handle problem situations their own way. They do not wish to intrude on what is a very delicate, highly vulnerable area. Today many parents feel insecure about their ability to raise children. They also have a good deal of their own ego invested in them. Thus parents can become touchy when they suspect someone is criticising their children.

How does a group come to terms with this situation?

Nothing positive can happen until trust is built between the parents and a relationship established between children and other members of the group. An older couple in the group may be able to step in even before general trust is created. Their experience and age will generally enable them to get away with calling an unruly child into line or freeing an over-protected one from its parents. Those who form the pastoral nucleus of a group, even if not much older than the others, can sometimes help at this stage. Once other parents have got to know the children in the group, they can begin to overcome some difficulties by creating positive alternatives, e.g. directing their attention, placing them on their laps, or occasionally taking them out to play.

Gradually all the parents in a group need to reach the point where they can allow others to discipline their children in the way most natural to those parents. This takes time and may only come after some heart-stopping moments. To some extent, the problem will always remain, only changing in form as children grow up. However, the whole exercise is enormously educational for parents with a one-sided view of child-rearing and beneficial in the long-term for all the children involved.

2. Problems with people
If a home church contains someone who is particularly demanding, this can also create difficulties. We are not thinking here of those with a specific need, whether long-term (e.g. a chronic illness) or short-term (e.g. a personal crisis). We have in mind people who are fairly obsessive or insecure within themselves.

These will attempt to manipulate or test the group to see whether it will accept them. They will tend to make continuous, intrusive, at times overwhelming, demands upon particular people, even the group as a whole. They will expect people to listen to them at length, to be involved in all sorts of activities for them, perhaps to revolve whole meetings frequently around their particular needs.

Others will tend to make intermittent attacks upon the group or periodically withdraw from it in a desperate attempt to provoke the acceptance they desire. In such cases, the problem is generally compounded by the difficulty the group has in fully accepting such a person, something that is very quickly sensed by the individual concerned. It is always easier to accept those who accept you, always harder to accept those who don't.

When a problem of this kind arises, a home church can only bear with the unwarranted demands or criticisms, carefully scrutinising its own attitudes, and seek to demonstrate a practical love for these people. Unfortunately, this will not always solve the problem. The sense of insecurity runs so deep in some that it takes many years of patient prayer for them and attention to them to change their self-perception. As this begins to happen, it may become possible for other members to speak honestly with the persons concerned about their over-demanding or over-critical attitude. Not everyone can do this: there are some from whom such people would never take such frank comments. Those who form the pastoral nucleus of a group, or who have some psychological expertise, have the best chance of doing so.

It is not only those who draw the energies of a group toward them who can create difficulties. There are also those who are very generous in their help to others. Appearances can be deceptive. What is happening on the surface may disguise something quite different. The service of others can spring from a variety of motives. A person may give time to people, listen to their concerns and sincerely pray for them. But this may be motivated by a search *for* love rather than be an expression of love. In this case, the compulsion to love is mixed with a genuine compassion for others. By such means some apparently selfless people convince themselves that they are needed and valued, lovable and loved.

One of the indications of this kind of self-interested love is its tendency to control others, to mould them rather than free them to find their own individual destiny. Firmness is essential here: sometimes in private, occasionally in the meeting itself. However gentle and respectful this is, it may still be viewed by the person concerned as a challenge to their sense of selfhood. Only if they learn how to receive the love of the group will they begin to lose their compulsion to dominate.

Again, sometimes the unselfish service of others springs from a real love for them, but one with a limit around it. Someone may long to help others, doing so from genuinely Christian motives, but will find it extremely difficult to *receive* any help in return. Such a person needs to be always in the position of the helper, never the helped. This leads to a very one-sided relationship with others, who come to feel they are more the objects of mission than part of a reciprocal relationship. Even where the helper does open himself or herself to others, in the end they tend to define God's will for themselves quite independently of others.

The attitude inherent in this helping mentality will sometimes carry over into the person's approach to the church as a whole. They may treat it as an object of mission too, sometimes betraying this by talking about 'it' rather than 'us', 'you' rather than 'we'. Only through patient encouragement to see themselves as members of a common body, not as directors of a particular enterprise, can this be overcome. Once again, there may be a special role here for the pastoral nucleus.

Conclusion

The road to community is not an easy one. It is fraught with difficulties and tensions. While at times it can be exhilarating, at other times it can be harrowing. While it undoubtedly includes 'high' moments, it also encompasses 'low' ones. While there are times when you feel you could not survive without the home church, there are times when you wonder whether it is really worth the trouble.

A helpful analogy here is the wider family into which we are born. We did not choose our relatives; neither do we choose those with whom we are involved in church. We do not necessarily have a great deal in common with our relatives, except the natural bond that unites us; nor, except spiritually, may we have much in common with others in the church. We have occasional tensions and contretemps with our relatives, just as we do with people from time to time in the church. To expect a trouble-free passage, a succession of pious experiences, or constant in-depth relationships is to have an unrealistic and romantic view of the church.

These difficulties and tensions are heightened by the fact that, since there are still relatively few home churches, those who tend to join them include a high proportion of independently minded or rather needy people. For it takes a certain degree of independence or desperation to take the step into community. The high percentage of such people in home churches generally results in sharper-edged relationships.

Such problems can only be tackled in a spirit of thankfulness and patience. Dietrich Bonhoeffer speaks about the importance of gratefulness. He reminds us that only if we give thanks for the 'little things' for which we can be grateful, even in the midst of problems, will the 'big things' we desire from God come our way:

We think we dare not be satisfied with the small measure of spiritual knowledge, experience and love that has been given us, and that we must constantly be looking forward eagerly to the higher ground... We pray for the big things and forget to give thanks for the ordinary, small (and yet really not small) gifts. How can God entrust great things to one who will not thankfully receive from Him the little things? If we do not give thanks daily for the Christian fellowship in which we have been placed, even where there is no great experience, no discoverable riches, but much weakness, small faith and difficulty; if, on the contrary, we only keep complaining that everything is so paltry and petty, so far from what we expected, then we hinder God from letting our fellowship grow according to the measure and riches which are there for us all in Jesus Christ.[6]

Not only individuals but the community as a whole should find ways of regularly giving thanks and not only in prayer. There are many things to celebrate, e.g. birthdays, special events in people's lives, moving into a new home, reunions etc.

Jean Vanier says about the spirit of patience:

We shouldn't get discouraged when things go badly and there are tensions. Each of us has to grow, each of us has the right to a bad patch and to weariness, to months of doubt and confusion. We have to know how to hold on through these difficult times and wait for happier ones.[7]

If we have come to terms with the fact that our individual Christian lives will be full of ups and downs, advances and retreats, delights and difficulties, why should we expect communal Christian life to be any different? This being so, during times of tension we have to discover how to defuse the situation. Someone needs to know the moment to produce a bottle of champagne or a chocolate cake.

There is an important role for the visionary in a group to

---

6 D. Bonhoeffer, op. cit., p.19

7 J. Vanier, op. cit., p.220

help it lift its eyes to its high calling in Christ. The central place occupied by thanksgiving and patience in the New Testament therefore becomes very understandable. Paul tells us that he learned to be content in all circumstances, whether he was receiving much or little (Philippians 4:12). He also lists patience as the first characteristic of Christian love (1 Corinthians 13:4). Without thanksgiving and patience as its constant companions, a home church – or any other form of Christian community – has no chance of survival.

9

On the importance of inreach:

Ministering to children and adults

IN TURNING TO THE WIDER INFLUENCE of home churches, we have to be careful where to begin. Just as the experience of belonging to a home church inverts many attitudes that we held previously, ideas of mission and outreach are also likely to be affected.

Throughout the previous chapters, we have regularly referred to the wider ministry of home churches to local churches, their neighbourhood and the society around them. In looking more closely at this important aspect of home church life, however, we need to begin with their potential for having a greater impact on those whom local churches tend to disadvantage. We have in mind people on the edges of a congregation, not fully at home in it.

In many cases, home churches, without any effort on their part, attract such people and give them a home. In other words, to some extent they are involved in 'outreach' without being aware of it. It simply happens. People come to them instead of their having to go to the people. Even when the people are already there, home churches are involved in what may be called 'inreach' to them. This concept is as important as outreach – as we now hope to show.

Despite the fact that there are many interest groups in churches, certain people in a congregation still miss out. Consider, for example, the drift from Sunday schools and fellowship groups. Whatever value these may have, they fragment the family and fail to integrate younger people into the total community of the church. This is one of the reasons why the majority of Sunday school pupils never join a youth fellowship and why the majority of teenagers never successfully bridge the gap between youth fellowship and adult church.

Single people also tend to be at a disadvantage. So are those married to a non-believing spouse, those who are separated or divorced and those who are widowed. Even where a senior fellowship exists for unmarried people, where divorcees are fully accepted and where the bereaved receive comfort and support from individuals in the church, the outreach generally takes place within the context of a peer group or pastoral visit. A broader, inter-generational setting does not exist.

People with physical or psychological disadvantages, though they may have access to special facilities, counselling and healing services, tend to be related to as individuals or as a crowd, not in a small group which can minister to them in a more effective way. Despite certain gains over the last decade, women in Christian circles continue to occupy a disadvantaged position. And for all the existence of senior citizens' meetings or services for the aged, there is an under-provision for older members of the church.

Inreach among children

The place of children in a home church has always been a matter for considerable discussion. No one we know claims to have all the answers. In the middle of such a discussion some years ago, one of the women declared, 'What we do for our children in a home church will be as different from Sunday school as is worship in a home church from a typical Sunday morning service.'

We all recognised the truth of her words, but what did they mean in practice? Most people did not want a repetition of the school-type activity children experience during the week, but what to put in its place? We began to realise that whatever shape this took, it would give flesh to two basic principles on which we were unanimous. First, that the responsibility for the Christian education of our children lay primarily with the parents. In this respect, Lawrence O.

Richards' *You the Parent* was a great encouragement.[1] Second, that as a small church we could really become God's family and make the children as much a part of all that we did as everyone else. Both these principles are as valid for members of a home church based in a congregation whose children may attend Sunday school, as for people in a more independent home church setting. It is important in both to find new ways of integrating children into the meeting. But to do that requires a new way of looking at Christian education.

□ THEORY

Every child is a unique individual, created in the image of God, with a capacity to choose whether he/she will respond to God's love or not. Because of this, God relates to each child individually. There is no blueprint of the course of that relationship for us to follow, either with respect to the manner in which it develops or the period of time involved.

In practice, as parents and as churches, this means that we endeavour to introduce our children to God as the creator and sustainer of the universe and the Father of our Lord Jesus Christ – someone whom we love and seek to honour with our whole lives, someone who loves them more than we do. While we encourage the relationship between the child and God to grow, we do not force it, but seek to discern where the relationship is at at that point. We then actively encourage its development by prayer and 'specific input'.

We are not surprised when our children begin to question and doubt, since we recognise this as a necessary precursor to new growth and understanding. Of course, it is our earnest desire that our children grow into a mature relationship with God. For some this will be relatively easy, for others exceedingly difficult. For some it will come early in life, for some later – and for some, maybe not at all. In our searching of the scriptures, we have not found any evidence to support the belief that all the children of believing parents will themselves in turn become Christians. Distressing though this would be, we recognise that God

1   L.O. Richards, *You The Parent*, Chicago: Moody, 1974

does not coerce anyone into a relationship with himself and that we should not attempt to do this, either. Our responsibility as parents or the church is to be faithful: to do and become all that God asks of us. The rest is between God and the child.

A second theoretical aspect has to do with the character of the Christian life. The Christian life has at its heart a trinitarian relationship: with God, through Jesus Christ, in the power of the Spirit. Though this involves beliefs, it is not *primarily* an acceptance of certain doctrines. Jesus commanded us to 'love the Lord your God with all your heart... and your neighbour as yourself'. The danger with too great an emphasis on doctrines is that they tend to become all-important. Not only do they lower our eyes from God himself to man-made formulae; they create divisions between people who are brothers and sisters in Christ. Putting the emphasis where Jesus does reminds us of our need of God's forgiveness (even of our doctrinal errors) and that we are all at different stages in our relationship with him.

This relationship with God is not just occasional. It permeates the whole of our lives, leaving no aspect of our personalities, work contacts, circle of friends, leisure or church life untouched. This relationship is a dynamic one, constantly changing, constantly growing. But the character of that growth is not a straight line from one growth experience to another. It is often a case of one step forward and two steps backward before we surge forward into new understanding and a deeper level of commitment. The times of these periods of growth are not in our hands, but God's.

(a) Young children

For the child, this relationship with God begins at the moment of birth. This is precisely why God lays the responsibility of introducing children to him on the shoulders of the parents. For it is they who are closest to their children during those important formative years till seven or eight.

How can a little child actually learn to relate to God? An illustration may help. When our children were babies, we lived for several years in England. Their grandmothers, uncles, aunts and cousins were in Australia. However, the boys did not have to wait until we returned to Australia to get to know and love some of their relatives. This had happened over previous years through stories we had told them of our childhood, through the sending and receiving of letters, parcels, tapes and photographs, and through listening to us talk about these people as we related to them in the present. When we did eventually return and the boys 'saw' the relatives for themselves, the bonds formed were all the stronger for the way in which they had learned to love their relatives through us. So it is with children and God. They first learn to relate to him through us, their parents.

Surely this is what God had in mind in Deuteronomy 6:20ff where he talks of the responsibility parents have to explain the law to children. Unfortunately, very few of us are sufficiently mature as Christians when we become parents to be confident in our capacity to do this. We are also much too aware of our shortcomings as models, as 'living epistles' read by our children.[2] Yet we tend to set extra-ordinarily high standards for ourselves, regarding ourselves as failures when we do not reach them.

One of the questions we have asked in the home church is whether that is what God asks of us? Slowly, we have come to appreciate that he doesn't. What God asks of us is not to be people who have 'arrived', who have all the answers, but to be people who are learning to love him with all our hearts, minds and strength. We will be people who make mistakes and are not afraid to ask for forgiveness; people whose understanding is not perfect, but who seek to grow in knowledge and wisdom; people who are learning to love themselves and their fellow creatures; people who find it hard to trust, but are gradually gaining confidence in a God who is totally dependable. Can we really ask more of ourselves than this? Our children are then allowed to share our pilgrimage: to learn that the Christian life is not necessarily a straight line affair, lived on an even keel, but very

---

2 The fullest development of a theory of Christian education along these lines may be found in another book by L.O. Richards, *A Theology of Children's Ministry*, Grand Rapids: Zondervan, 1983. See especially the section on the importance and character of the modelling process (pp.78-79).

much an up-and-down matter, full of doubt, despair and uncertainty as well as confidence, joy and assurance.

Fortunately, although the responsibility for children lies 'primarily' with the parents, it does not lie 'solely' with them. This is where the church comes in. Home churches should take their responsibilities to children very seriously.

A home church begins its ministry to the children through ministering to their parents. It encourages their growth to maturity in all areas of their lives, including parenting. The latter happens naturally through observation, shared anecdotes, questions, reading, or by searching the scriptures together on issues like discipline. Of course, sometimes we learn from others what *not* to do more than what to do! This ministry of the home church to parents actually begins before children are born, indeed even before people are married.

A home church also ministers to children, prior to their birth, through its prayers for each child from the moment it hears of its conception. After his/her birth, it is important to welcome the child into the church in some tangible way. In those home churches attached to denominations, it is usual for this to take place at a regular service. Whether it has the form of child dedication or infant baptism depends on the tradition of that denomination. This should not prevent the home church from also welcoming the child as well. In independent home churches, this welcome can take the form of a baptism or a dedication and, as illustrated earlier, can involve the whole membership in a creative and moving way. In our home church, we all accept the responsibility of becoming godparents to the child.

Since the children are a regular part of home churches, they have other models before them than those provided by their parents. From a very early age they learn that there is no one set way of relating to God. They learn that there are different styles of being Christian: middle-class, working-class, intellectual, practical, activist or counter-culture. They also learn the dynamics of what being God's family means: its responsibilities, its tensions and its struggles; the costs as well as the rewards. The rewards for children can be great. Apart from those already mentioned, there are the benefits of many 'uncles', 'aunts', 'cousins', 'sisters', 'brothers', 'grandmothers' and 'grandfathers' in the Lord with whom to celebrate Christmas, Easter and birthdays, play and have special outings, chat on the telephone and exchange letters.

Of course, some rewards are not always perceived as such by the child. It can be very trying to find oneself with people, be they adults or children, with whom you have little in common. Sometimes a child finds it difficult to take others as they are and to begin to love them. Yet that is what being part of a home church means – for children as well as adults. As such, it is a unique social laboratory for children coming to understand the central meaning of the gospel.

(b) The teenagers

During teenage years, the quality of relationships between children and adults becomes increasingly important. As young people begin to separate themselves from their parents, there are others to whom they can turn for advice about career, friendships and romance. There are also people with whom they can discuss politics, sport, music, literature and faith. There are people to whom they can turn if they sometimes feel misunderstood at home. Because there is no definite separation of age-groups in a home church, it is potentially easy for a teenager to move to being an adult member of the group. This transition is but one of a series of transitions already made.

When very young, children join in only some parts of the meeting, in the singing, playing, storytelling and eating. As they enter primary years, they remain longer in the group, entering more into the praying, study and discussion. When they reach mid-teenage years, they begin to want to join in all that happens in the meeting, as part and parcel of their desire to join the adult world.

Naturally, some teenagers find it easier to make this adjustment than others. This depends on how much the group seeks to include them, their relationship with the parents and their own developing convictions. But even if one of them decides to 'drop out' of the group, that is not the end of the matter. The relationship they have established with other members ensures a continuing link with the home church and all that it stands for.

The peer group issue is a difficult one, resolved by home churches in different ways. Those attached to denominational churches usually have fellowship or youth groups that teenagers can attend. Some independent home churches run similar groups which cater for the needs of their own teenagers as well as others in the community. Other home churches have attempted to bring teenagers from a number of groups together for joint activities. In our own home church cluster, we have had more success in gathering together such groups around a common interest. We are also experimenting with inviting isolated teenagers over fifteen years of age to join another group which has teenagers in it.

But our experience with teenagers in the home churches makes us wonder if a specifically Christian peer group is as important as some parents tend to think. Whenever the question of the peer group is raised by people outside the home church, we are tempted to ask: 'Isn't the average Christian teenager more deprived of quality relationships with adults than with peers? Aren't those relationships ultimately more significant?' We too easily forget that for nineteen centuries young people in Christian families matured in faith without the benefit of Christian peer group organisations.

□ PRACTICE

How do children participate in an actual home church gathering? This depends on the number of children in a particular group, the age range, and the imagination and skill of the adults.

To begin with, children love to sing. It is not difficult to include special songs which children like: 'Away in a manger', 'All things bright and beautiful', 'He's got the whole world in his hands', 'Bananas in pyjamas' or 'Humpty Dumpty'. Even when the songs are more suitable for adults, percussion instruments, clapping or dancing makes it possible for younger members to participate. Some children will be confident enough to provide items like a song, a dance or a mime – or play an instrument, read a story or recite a poem. It is good to spend time specifically with children at some point in a home church gathering. This may take the form of a story (either told or read, biblical or other), a flannel-graph presentation, a mime or a play. It can include games and a time of prayer in which the children participate.

It is also important for children to have fellowship with one another at their own level. Most often this means playing somewhere together, with one or more adults present. As the children get older, it is possible to include them more with the adults, for example when biblical material is approached in an imaginative manner. This can be done by asking people to identify with the characters in a given story or event, or by role playing, followed by adults and children discussing together.[3]

Some groups allocate one day a month as 'children's day'. This provides the extended time necessary to picnic and play games, or to engage in some creative activity like making a frieze or a set of puppets. A picnic should not be seen as a soft option. Approached rightly, it is an important way of getting to know God, the creator of the universe, celebrating his world and celebrating the life and energy he gives us.

But ministry to the children does not stop here. Outside home church meetings, there are occasional outings with adults, opportunities to play with other children, group visits to the cinema, museums or concerts as well as overnight (or weekend) stays with adults and other children.[4]

Whether or not the children participate in the Lord's Supper again varies from group to group. Those home churches attached to denominational churches have difficulty celebrating the Lord's Supper together with children. In independent home churches it is different. The meeting usually revolves around a meal to which everyone brings a

---

3 For other suggestions, see for example R. Trudinger, *Home Groups: God's Strategy for Church Growth*, Logos International: 1979, pp.94-98.

4 See further M. & M. Frances, *A Patchwork Family*, Nashville: Broadman, 1978, pp.78ff.

contribution and which, as mentioned earlier, most people regard as the Lord's Supper. Children take part in this quite naturally, gradually learning as they do so what is involved in Jesus' death for them and the way we should share our lives with one another.

Some people may feel that, where bread and wine are separated from the other food and drink, the children should only take part in the actual meal. There is room for considerable variety here. It goes without saying, we hope, that adults talk and relate to children and young people in the context of the meal in the same way as adults chat with one another.

So far as baptism is concerned, enough has been said already about the options open to parents when a new child comes into the family. A dedication or infant baptism in a home church setting is normally a moving and challenging occasion for all concerned and particularly encouraging for the parents. In later years, opportunity will arise, depending on the denominational allegiance or otherwise of the group, for young people to declare their full consciousness of God's commitment to them and of their commitment to him through baptism. Once again, the home church setting gives special significance to such an occasion. The atmosphere of an extended Christian family, plus the freedom to construct a form of service appropriate to the individual, adds much to what happens. The recent baptism of an eighteen-year-old at a favourite fishing spot on the edge of a quiet mountain stream, encircled on the sandy shore by the members of our home church cluster, was a very special event.

So far we have been concentrating on a home church's ministry to children. It would not be right to leave it there, for children themselves contribute a great deal to the life of a home church. Just as the adults provide 'uncles', 'aunts' and so on for children, so children become 'grandchildren', 'nephews', 'nieces', younger 'brothers' and 'sisters' to others. It is a marvellous thing to have a baby come into a home church: to watch him/her grow, developing his/her own personality, forming relationships, enjoying the world God made for us, and learning to be part of our Christian family. The simplicity of children's prayers, questions, observations and loving can be a profound experience and encouragement. The searching questions – and provocative arguments – of teenagers may cause us to think afresh or remind us of our own struggles of faith. There is also the joy of seeing them make real strides in their relationship with God as they find their niche in the church.

Children also help us learn – one of the reasons, no doubt, why Jesus used them as a model to his disciples. They also show us how to unbend, play, give of ourselves emotionally and celebrate more freely. Their direct, unreflective responses encourage us to be more direct and spontaneous. They teach us patience. But perhaps the most important contribution children can make is just being there, helping create a genuine family atmosphere, stretching our feelings, imaginations and ideas to the limit as they demand our consideration and love.

The first child in any family is disadvantaged in that the parents have to learn their parenting skills as they go. Happily, the second child gets the benefit of parents who are more confident and competent. So, too, in a home church. The first generation of children in home churches are, in a sense, the guinea pigs. The second generation will receive the benefits of all we have learnt. We would rather it had been otherwise, but unfortunately there have been no models to follow.

Finally, we would be remiss in not acknowledging the important part prayer plays in our ministry to the children. We pray for the children in all facets of their lives. We also pray for their parents, and for ourselves as a church in relation to the children so that they may come to know and love the same Father as we ourselves do.

Inreach among adults
(a) Single people
Most single people want to meet someone of the opposite sex, settle down and have children. No church, be it large or small, can guarantee the right match for a single person, even a match of any kind. It is possible that God will answer the desires of some in the context of the gathering of the whole church: in services on Sunday at a denominational

church or the combined activities of a cluster of home churches. It is not, however, the church's responsibility to solve the problem of being single any more than it is the church's responsibility to solve any member's particular problem. The church is there to provide support and encouragement while *God* helps people to solve their own problems. God may or may not involve other members of the church in this process.

Not all single people want to marry. Some have made a conscious choice to remain single – to care for aged parents, to pursue a vocation unhindered by family ties, or as a response to problems in relating to the opposite sex. Whatever the reason, single people need to find a home somewhere: they need a place to belong. This is necessary for all of us if we are to have equilibrium in our lives and develop into mature persons.

Friendships are one form of attachment, but they are not sufficient. They are too homogeneous, too similar in respect to age, interests and personal compatibility, to bring people into touch with all of life. But a home church is well equipped to provide the secure, accepting environment in which the single person can resolve, with God's help, the question of being single.

First, it provides a set of family relationships which many singles in our society lack. There is not only the emotional support which such relationships offer, but also the physical contact. The hugs, kisses, knowing looks and nudges which are a genuine expression of life together are vital to the single person.

Second, within the context of these relationships it should be possible to discuss the issues raised by being single, such as how much to travel, whom to holiday with, where to buy a home or not, whether to look for a vocational-type job, how to cope when most of one's friends become married, not having children of one's own, coming to terms with sexual desires.

Third, precisely because they are single, without spouse and children, some single people have time and energy to give to a home church which marrieds lack. Some are able to contribute through talks, Bible studies, readings from the scriptures, a book or a poem, or contributing a song or musical item. Some singles relate particularly well to children and teenagers. Outside the gathering, singles may contribute to the welfare of a family by taking the children on outings, being a guest in the home, or babysitting while housebound parents play sport or pursue some cultural interest. The very fact that singles are not preoccupied permanently with children introduces a different perspective into their conversation, helping marrieds maintain a broader interest in the world around them.

(b) Lone attenders

Not all lone adults are in fact 'singles'. Some leave non-believing spouses at home, while others are either separated, divorced or widowed. These people are usually accompanied by a number of children. The needs of such family units are great, especially those trying to come to terms with a divorce or separation. Because they are especially in need of love and acceptance, a small group is better able to provide these than a larger, amorphous gathering.

Just as a church cannot solve all the problems related to being single, neither can it meet all the needs of its lone attendees. The church can certainly lighten their burdens, but it is only God who can ultimately sustain them. How does a home church lighten the load of such people?

Those with unbelieving partners frequently find their spouses are more open to attending a home church than a traditional service. Friendships can develop between the spouse and other members of the home church as they meet socially for dinner parties, picnics or birthday celebrations. More than one unsympathetic spouse has eventually joined a home church because of the barriers being broken down in this way. But this does not always happen. The church has to help the Christian partner accept their spouse as he or she is, while still actively praying that God will draw the other person to himself eventually.

What about those who are separated or divorced? It is important to accept them just as they are, taking a real interest in them and their problems – a costly and time-consuming exercise. Some families bring with them many hurts and unresolved conflicts. Some are so vulnerable that their very attitude dares the church to love them, warts and all. Others quite unconsciously demand of members of the church that they make up the lack left by the absent spouse and parent. It is not uncommon for a deserted husband or wife, widow or widower, to expect the church to satisfy their need of affection and to give the same attention to the children. The children may also require of the church the affection and attention that they crave from the missing mother or father. Some of these have additional expectations. Some can be fulfilled by the church, but it cannot fully compensate for the relationship with the absent family member. Only by the grace of God will its members be sufficient for the task.

But the benefit is not all 'one way'. Precisely because the need of such families draws out the concern and prayer of the church, they are a gift from God. Naturally, it is hard for the people in need to see their situation this way, especially when they feel so weak. Yet that is the deeper reality.

Happily, not all such families are demanding. Many contribute actively to the life of a home church. In fact, the lessons from their particular circumstances and struggles can be of enormous help to others. Given the almost total lack of separations or divorces among couples attending home churches, there must be something about this kind of group which enables them to overcome the problems that cause so many marriage breakdowns today.

Volumes have been written about the importance of a caring group of people to those who are grieving. Nor does the need for a supportive and loving family diminish as the grieving process recedes. Rather it is crucial that the bereaved be able to discover their new identity and role in just such a setting.

In each of these situations the home church can give practical as well as emotional and spiritual assistance, e.g. providing meals, minding children, supporting financially, mowing lawns, handing on children's clothing and so on. The amount and nature of the pastoral care depends on the church's particular resources of personnel — and the number of needy families already within its ranks.

We know of one home church that seems to have been called by God to have a special ministry to such people. Over the years, it has catered for many needy people. At the time of writing, this home church has at its centre two stable nuclear families, around whom cluster five single or divorced people and eight children. While there are obvious limits to the practical help that two families can give, we would like to pay tribute to the wealth of love and the richness of relationships that exist among them.

(c) The disadvantaged

The word 'disadvantaged' is not one we particularly like to use. As Jean Vanier tirelessly points out, 'we are all disadvantaged these days', even if the disabilities of some are a little more physically or psychologically obvious. In the church, not only are sexual, class and ethnic differentiations overcome (cf. Galatians 3:28), but others as well. Handicapped and physically whole, retarded and fully developed, unemployed and affluent – we meet as equals in the sight of God, each with our distinctive gift to share.

For a variety of reasons, home churches tend to attract a disproportionate number of 'disadvantaged' people. Perhaps such churches have a flexibility which makes it easier for such people to fit in without drawing attention to themselves. For example, if someone suffers from a chronically bad back, it is more acceptable to lie on the floor in a lounge-room than in the aisle of a church! If someone is hard of hearing, it is easier to ask people to look at them as they talk so that they can lip-read. If someone is virtually blind or has a serious learning disability, it is easier for the home church to adjust some of its activities to their particular requirements.

We have also found that a home church has an informality – in dress as well as manner – which low-income and unemployed people find more conducive. This is even more the case when, as often happens, members in the home church are themselves pursuing a simpler lifestyle. Being in touch with the circumstances of those in need, they can also extend financial assistance to low-income or unemployed people.

We can think of a number of cases where this has happened. One couple paid the rent of another couple who were branching out into a new venture, till the latter became financially established. One home church supported an unemployed father whose particular situation meant that his family could not survive on the dole alone. Another group met the unexpected large bills of a deserted mother and children, as well as occasionally tidying up the garden, providing vegetables, or paying for a family outing to the cinema or a restaurant. In these days of growing unemployment and single-parent families, there is much that a small, committed group can do to supplement financial assistance that comes from other quarters. More importantly, such acts of generosity reinforce the diminishing self-confidence people in these situations tend to have. In the long term, it is the loss of self-esteem that is more difficult to endure and more damaging to the person than living close to the poverty line.

Of course, belonging to a home church does not automatically solve the problems of the handicapped, the retarded or the unemployed. Members of a home church have their own disabilities to overcome. At times they can ignore those less well off, can say something insensitive or out of place, or can conduct their meetings as if other people's problems don't exist. As Jean Vanier points out:

> When a community welcomes people who have been on the margins of society, things usually go quite well to begin with. Then, for many reasons, these people start to become marginal to the society of the community as well. They throw crises which can be very painful for the community and cause it considerable confusion, because it feels so powerless. The community is then caught in a trap from which it is hard to escape. But if the crises bring it to a sense of its own poverty, they can also be a grace.
>
> There is something prophetic in people who seem marginal and difficult; they force the community to become alert, because what they are demanding is authenticity. Too many communities are founded on dreams and fine words: there is so much talk about love, truth and peace. Marginal people are demanding. Their cries are cries of truth because they sense the emptiness of many of our words... But some-

times marginal people can become a focus for unity, because they . . . can force the community to pull itself together.[5]

(d) The aged

Unfortunately, there are not as yet many aged people within the ranks of home churches, whether within independent groups or within the orbit of a local church. The reasons for this can only be guessed at. One might be that, as we get older, we cling to what is familiar. We don't like changes. Another reason might lie in the social attitudes of older people: for many of them religion is a private matter between the individual and God.

When older people have been encouraged to attend a home church, they have often declined to do so. As the oldest in the group by some years, they felt they would be lonely. Despite assurances that they would be treated as one of the family, until *another* older person joined the group they would not attend. Someone else had to be first.

One unmarried older person felt out of place because all the members of the group were married couples. When in New Zealand a couple of years ago, we asked someone in an intentional community if they had any older members. He smiled and replied: 'Unfortunately no. We're going to have to grow our own!' The one consolation we have is that we are fifteen years nearer to its realisation than we were at the beginning.

When there *are* older people in home churches, they have much to contribute. There is the wealth of wisdom they have accumulated over the years, the model that they provide for all those who are younger, their different perspective on life, and the sense of continuity with the past that they create. Many children, deprived of regular contact with their grandparents, come to gain substitute grandmothers or grandfathers. It is crucial for children to have this kind of relationship with older people – and vice versa. Being less absorbed with activities, older people have time to visit and be visited, to talk and to listen, to reflect and to

5 J. Vanier, *Community and Growth*, Sydney: St Paul, 1979, pp.204-205

pray. They often have more patience. In these and other ways older people add much to the life of a home church and gain much from it themselves.

As with us all, older people have their failings. They can be hard of hearing, forgetful, repetitive, overbearing or demanding. The older they get, the more difficult they can become. They tend to become set in their ideas and find alterations in the way things are done hard to handle. They also become more dependent upon others for transport and for help. But it is important to live with the tension that such relationships bring. For it is there that we learn what it means to be a genuinely extended family, spanning several generations – what it means to accept other people, with all their offputting idiosyncrasies.

(e) Women generally

When people ask, in relation to home church gatherings, 'What about the women?' we are tempted to reply '*What* about the women?' However much the New Testament differentiated between the activities of men and women in the church – and there is far less than many people make out – and whatever biological and psychological differences exist between them, we cannot find any cultural or theological backing for a male-dominated church.[6] Both women and men ought to be able to participate in the gatherings according to the gifts which God has given them. Both men and women should be able to give talks, lead discussions, exercise pastoral gifts, introduce the Lord's Supper and baptise – as well as pray, read the Bible, choose hymns, mind children, prepare meals and wash up afterwards. We are one body and individually members of it. Although we do not all have exactly the same functions, one half of the body cannot say to the other 'We have no need of you' or 'You have less to offer than we have.'

That's the ideal. However much we seek to offload it, we still carry some cultural and theological baggage with us into the church. So, while all we have said in the previous paragraph is true, there is still a tendency at times for men

---

6 On the grounds for this, see R. Banks, 'Paul and Women's Liberation,' *Interchange*, No.18, 1976, pp.81-105.

in home churches to be a little more upfront than women.

To balance this, women are generally more pastorally aware and active than men, and better able to share in the meetings. In fact, in the early days of one home church, women dominated the group. With hindsight it became clear that there were two main causes. First, it was the women who were used to participating in small groups, whether informal coffee mornings or more formal Bible studies. The men had not had the opportunity to develop similar skills and were unused to sharing their walk with God. Second, the women were rejoicing in their newfound freedom to participate fully. This meant that they did most of the talking, even to telling others what their husbands thought! Was this what lay behind Paul's request to the women in his first letter to the Corinthians?

In general, however, a home church not only encourages women to minister in ways so often denied them in the church, but provides the best setting for both men and women to discover their individual gifts and to work out their divine complementarity.

Before leaving this subject, we should mention one special group of women, viz: those who have a number of young children and are largely housebound. In our society, such women often live a long way from their parents, perhaps in another city. With so many women in the workforce today, they frequently have few daytime neighbours to call on as well. The kind of help a home church can give is typified by the offer of one middle-aged woman to take first one, then two and finally three off the hands of their mother for a few hours each week. This gave the mother some time to herself and continued for some years. Now the mother looks for opportunities to do the same herself for someone else in a similar position.

Unfortunately, the scattering of members in a home church can make this difficult. But sometimes there are several couples with young children in the same home church who can band together to look after each other's children. Now and again they may even be able to give each other weekends without any children at all.

Conclusion

There is one extra kind of 'inreach' worth mentioning, applying only to some situations, not others. Just occasionally the need of a particular person or marginal group is so great that it comes to dominate most of what takes place in a home church. For example, there may be so many children that very little happens that is not child-oriented. Again, the desperate plight of one or more lonely, deserted or bereaved people – or of one or more people in acute physical, psychological or economic distress – may be so overwhelming that meetings tend to continually revolve around their concerns. Or there may be one or more women who so constantly feel the need to raise 'the women's issue' that both it and they tend to dominate discussions.

For a time, some over-emphasis in each of these directions is understandable, even healthy. It is a form of 'reverse discrimination' which is quite legitimate. Also, the occasional centring of a group on a particular person or issue has its proper place. We should always be aware of those who are most needy in our midst – that is one of the things which a home church, because of its flexibility, can do easily.

But where a person or an issue becomes the major preoccupation of a group, that group is doomed to fail. Other members will begin to look elsewhere to make up for the fellowship, celebration, learning, praise and support they are lacking.

In saying this, we do not wish to detract from the basic thesis. While the home church may not meet all the needs of these various groups, it does provide something fundamental to each. For this reason, it is a pity that Christians working in the educational, welfare or feminist field do not see home churches as an important part of the church's contribution to solving the problems of marginal people in society.[7]

---

7 For example, there are many excellent suggestions about what congregations and denominations can do for socially disadvantaged members of society in A. Nichols, *Reluctant Conscience: Closing the Gap Between Gospel and Reality in Australia*, Melbourne: Dove, 1984, but home churches do not come into view.

Those who are already in home churches should be especially conscious of their obligations to those marginalised by society in some way. They also have the opportunity to reach out and draw in 'the poor, the maimed, the lame and the blind' (Luke 14:13). It is for such people that the church also exists and can provide a home.

———10———
Agents of transformation:
Reaching out to the community at large

TO WHAT EXTENT SHOULD A HOME CHURCH involve itself in outreach? Some people would answer: 'To the fullest stretch of its capacities. The church exists primarily for mission and we are compelled to take up every opportunity that presents itself to us.' Others would go even further: 'The main reason for setting up home churches is to evangelise those who are outside the church, and to engage in social action in the surrounding community.'

It is extremely important for people involved in a home church to know what is its basic purpose. Is it to engage in mission of some kind, whether evangelism, social action, or some combination of the two? Or is it the development of the personal maturity and gifts of its individual members?

The relationship between church and mission
In fact, neither mission nor the development of gifts is the ultimate purpose of a home church. Its chief end is to nurture a genuine community life as a 'signpost' to the coming kingdom of God, a visible 'bridge' between the present and future. It is to create an alternative society in the midst of the different beliefs, values and standards of our prevailing culture. It is to show what life is all about and what human relationships can really be like in this world of ours.

There is nothing more important than fulfilling these objectives. What could take pre-eminence over planting a little colony of heaven, however imperfect, in a neighbourhood, suburb or city? What could be more important than developing a divine counter-culture in the heart of secular society? What is more fundamental than demonstrating to all who are round about the real meaning of life? These are the very things of which our world is in the greatest need.

What, then, of those two well-known definitions of the purpose of the church: 'the church exists primarily for others and for mission to them'; 'the church exists primarily for the glorification and enjoyment of God'? Both statements say something that is crucial, but both contain an element of confusion. Let us rephrase them to clarify what we mean: '*Christians* exist primarily for others and for mission to them'; 'the chief end of humankind is to glorify God and to enjoy him for ever'. The first statement is our own way of making this point. The second, of course, is from the opening declaration of the Westminster Confession.

The confusion arises because the word 'church' is used in such a loose way today. It does not only refer to the *gathering* of local Christians, to sing, pray, learn and share. 'Church' is used to describe the cluster of *organisations* around them, many of which are designed to reach the outsider. It also describes the scattered members of the community, even when they are not meeting together, but going about their daily activities.

It is quite appropriate for organisations attached to the church to have mission as their main purpose, though we should not restrict that only to evangelism. Individuals who attend a church should also seek to glorify God and enjoy him in everything that they do. But when Christians gather together, they should not turn every service into an evangelistic meeting or a social action committee. Nor do they only focus on God, allowing nothing else but thoughts directed to him to take place in their gathering. Instead of concentrating mainly on outsiders, the sermon, prayers and celebration of the Lord's meal should concentrate mostly on Christians' own responsibilities, desires and privileges. While attention is specifically directed to God, people should be aware that glorifying him does not primarily consist of making statements to him or singing his praises, but actually *doing* what he asks. The first request God makes is that his children reflect in their own relationships the same quality of life and character he himself possesses.

It is for these reasons that Paul insists that the chief end of the church is neither mission nor worship, as we understand these terms, but the building up of one another into the likeness of God in Christ – through fellowship with God and with one another.

Where does this leave us with respect to mission? We need to keep clear in our minds two different kinds of structure: the 'church' gathering, whose main purpose is to have fellowship with God and one another and to build ourselves up into Christ, and the organisation for 'mission' whose primary task is to take the message and compassion of God to those outside the church.

There is a direct link between these two. In 'church' we should help one another to identify our personal responsibility in mission. We should encourage every member to enter into that (perhaps in conjunction with some organisation designed for mission). We should also pray for each other as we carry out our responsibilities in this area (possibly supporting some financially so they can do this full-time). In organisations for 'mission', we will aim to win people to the gospel. We will seek to demonstrate the compassion and just dealings of God. We will also attempt to draw people into the fellowship of a church.

The more we build one another up in church, the more effective we are in mission. The more we engage in mission, the more we broaden the vision and deepen the fellowship of those in our church. The moment we begin to confuse these two divinely ordered structures, turning church – as we have defined it – into a mission or a mission into the church, we start to lose both.[1] The twin concepts of mission and church can co-exist but only in a *community*, whether

---

1 Further to the distinction between 'church' and 'mission', see D.W.B. Robinson, 'The Doctrine of the Church and its Implications for Evangelism', *Interchange*, No.15, 1974, pp.156-162 and R. Banks, *Paul's Idea of Community: The Early House Churches in their Historical Setting*, Sydney: Anzea, 1979, pp.182-192 (Exeter: Paternoster; Grand Rapids: Eerdmans, 1980, pp.161-170).

itinerant or residential – such as the original Orders of the Catholic Church, the Moravians after the Reformation, or the radical Protestant communities of today.

Home churches and mission: possibilities
To understand mission properly, it is necessary to define the concept in the broadest possible terms. To engage in it effectively, we must be sensitive to the needs of particular groups.

Mission is directed not only to people but to *structures* – otherwise we leave a central and pervasive aspect of our society out of range. To assume that changing individuals will change structure only leaves structures to go their own way, becoming ever more totalitarian and intrusive.

Mission involves not only evangelism, but also social action. The whole of life is to be brought in contact with the gospel. Both evangelism and social action are part and parcel of the one reality, just as were Jesus' preaching and healing. While individuals and evangelism are at the core of mission, they can only artificially be separated from structures and social action. Individuals exist in various structures; spiritual needs are inextricably connected with human needs in general.

We must also be sensitive to particular groups who are most in need of help. Of course, in one sense *all* people and structures are in need. We can never opt for a selective approach which includes some, but excludes others. But throughout the history of Israel, God displayed a special concern for the underprivileged, the disadvantaged and the oppressed – for the 'losers' in society. This was not decided in purely economic or political terms. There were religious losers (those who stood for God against his detractors), social losers (the orphans and widows) and legal losers (the small landowners and so on).

Throughout the Gospels we see how Jesus displayed a special concern for those marginalised by society. Although alert to those deprived economically or politically, Jesus gave special attention to the physically unwell (the deaf, blind and paralysed), the social outcasts (the leper and tax-gatherer), ethnic groups (Samaritans and Gentiles) and reli-

gious nonconformists (those who did not belong to
established religious parties).

While our concern should be for all people and structures,
we should be especially concerned to reach out to those who
are particularly vulnerable. Home churches have a special
responsibility and opportunity in this respect.

Who, in our increasingly middle-class, predominantly
affluent and democratically governed society, are the marginalised groups? David Prior comments:

> It is clear, therefore, that after the example of Jesus we
> should be seeking out the needy and the marginalised, while
> being sensitive and straight with those who cross our path
> who are not so clearly in need. Here it is right to say that
> in Africa and Latin America, the needs of the under-
> privileged are blatant and overwhelming... But who are the
> needy and the marginalised in Europe and North America?
> Whom should the church, and in particular our home
> churches, be seeking out? Because the majority of people
> who cross our paths do not have such blatant needs, in what
> direction should we deliberately move in order 'to seek and
> to save the lost'? Of course, the needy are not exclusively
> the materially impoverished. The marginalised are not only
> those in slums... but all whose background or occupation
> pushes them to the margins of society... For example...
> single-parent families are often deprived of the opportunity
> to be full and accepted members of the community...
> single people can easily be marginalised...in most situa-
> tions the elderly or incapacitated are pushed off to the
> margins... in many cultures, there is still a tendency to
> marginalise women and highlight men... we need also to
> put question marks against the way we treat children...
> There is a ministry of Christian support and service which
> home churches can give to unmarried mothers and to
> homosexuals... Two particular groups of people are
> manifestly marginalised in most Western countries today –
> the unemployed and immigrants.[2]

In other words, many of the most needy are the *same* people
identified in chapter 9 as the ones *already* in home

2 D. Prior, *The Church in the Home*, London: Marshall, Morgan &
   Scott, 1983, pp.117-121

churches. Precisely because home churches provide whatever other needs these people may have – a close-knit, practically oriented support-system – they have a special opportunity to minister to such people.

Home churches could complement the ministry of various Christian organisations and local churches to other needy people. David Prior himself lists alcoholics, drug addicts, and ex-prisoners. There are also many who cannot cope with the pace of modern life and are breaking down physically or psychologically. There are also isolated, nonconformist or alternative members of our society: those in politics, the arts or counter-culture; those wounded by their experience of various exotic sects; the increasing number of young and middle-aged people who have had absolutely no connection with the institutional church. These are all valid areas for ministry.

Some examples
(a) Evangelism

In most cases, home churches tend to place evangelism to one side for a time. There are two reasons for this. First, people need to develop their relationships with one another and establish the foundation of their common life. Second, they often realise that their previous activities have been so church-oriented that they no longer have any significant relationships with non-Christians.

Eventually, however, the subject of evangelism begins to move to the forefront of their concern. This involves the recognition that God gives some people a greater capacity and boldness to share the gospel with others. It is the group's responsibility to endorse anyone in their midst who has the gift and to encourage them to exercise it. All gradually find, however, that there is a flow-on from their home church experience into their daily contacts with neighbours, colleagues and relatives. They have a greater ease in their company. They feel less awkward referring to the church and to God. They discover more relevant ways of linking up their convictions and values with everyday life. Their skills in the area of sharing hospitality also grow.

If, sometimes, members of home churches hesitate to

express their faith as much as they could, it is because they are uncertain about how best to do this and what effect it will have. They are inclined to be cautious about traditional evangelistic methods, venues and appeals, because they have become aware of their weaknesses and limits. They also find that certain people react negatively to any approach along these lines. While those in a home church tend to become clear about what they do not want to do, they generally remain unsure for a time about what to put in its place. However, this becomes less of a dilemma as people grow in confidence and various experiments are attempted.

What are some of these experiments?

* A married couple in one group decided to open up their home on the same Saturday every month, extending an invitation to all the people they knew, Christian and other, to come along. It began with a meal, had as its centrepiece a discussion (introduced by a talk) on some problematic aspect of modern life, and concluded with a leisurely, mostly home-made supper that allowed people to mix and talk late into the evening. This 'open night' drew a wide variety of people, depending upon the topic for discussion. Among those who came were a number of lapsed or non-Christians.

* Another (older) person decided to give a significant amount of her time to getting to know the people in her immediate neighbourhood. Over the years, her genuine interest, ready availability, sympathetic listening and wise advice resulted in many people seeking her out, particularly at times of crisis. This often led to discussion about the spiritual dimension of life and prayer over the problem.

* Several members of another home church established a pre-school group in an area where few support facilities or social activities for parents existed. Their willingness to give freely of their time to the pre-school group, and their general concern for the problems of those who brought their children, led to requests for further understanding of what motivated them. This resulted in the formation of a weekday Bible study. Eventually a number of these people joined the home church itself.

* The majority of members in another group asked friends and acquaintances, and one or two others who appeared open, if they would be interested in coming to an afternoon to discuss the claims of Christianity – and their objections to it. A number were willing to do so.

* One of us has run a group over several months each year under the title 'Between Belief and Unbelief'. Advertised in the leading daily paper and limited to around fifteen adults, this forum has centred on the doubts of those who have come along. These people include confused Christians, those who are uncertain whether they are Christian or not, and those weighing up whether they wish to become Christians.

* A small group of people belonging to different home churches has begun to invite friends and colleagues to a series of informal discussions in a park or restaurant to consider the truth claims and relevance of Christianity.

These are only some of the possibilities for creative evangelism. There are other approaches which could be attempted. In the USA, one pastor working with home churches considers what he terms '*Oikos*-evangelism' as the most relevant way people may be reached with the gospel today. Drawing on Michael Green's reference to the significant place of the extended household or *oikos* in the early Christian movement, Thomas Wolf argues:

> The basic thrust of New Testament evangelism was not individual evangelism, not mass evangelism, and was definitely not child evangelism. The normative pattern of evangelism in the early church was *oikos* evangelism... sharing the astoundingly good news about Jesus in one's sphere of influence, the interlocking social systems composed of family, friends and associates.[3]

The first churches were built on the same basis, with the home as their focus. A return to the same close nexus between home church and *oikos* evangelism, as is beginning

---

3 Thomas A. Wolf, 'Oikos Evangelism: Key to the Future', *Future Church*, ed. R.W. Neighbour Jnr, Nashville: Broadman, 1980, p.166

to happen in some places, could be just as effective a combination today.

One of the most provocative pleas for a closer association between evangelism and the home church comes from a leading Uniting Church evangelist in South Australia. Out of his experiences with house groups in the hard-bitten mining town of Broken Hill – plus reflection on the evangelism in the early church and the character of Australian society – Deane Meatheringham came to the following conclusions. Although what he has to say comes out of a special concern for the 'working-class', it would also apply to 'alternative lifestyle' and what Alex Buzo refers to as 'new class' people as well:

While I was at Broken Hill, we had very few men in the churches I pastored. Through a friendship with the husbands of some women in one of the churches, I went with them to a bar in a local club. Before entering the ministry, I had been a carpenter and mixed with men, but at the bar I was in a cultural situation where I was self-conscious and struggled with the 'liturgy'. As I reflected on the experience, I thought what it would be like for one of those fellows to step into our row of wooden pews on Sunday morning and be surrounded by a ritual and feeling which had no relationship with anything he knew. Does he have to become more feminine, learn our hymns and like them, understand a way of expression which is fairly middle-class, and accept the overload of all the Uniting Church machinery if he obeyed a call to minister in the parish?

Our churches have a culture. Some people talk of the 'Uniting Church ethos'. We grow best in middle-class areas, where people have a lifestyle that readily relates. Our progress amongst blue-collar workers is limited at best and, even where we have churches in working-class areas, they are usually attended by a remnant of middle-class people, or working-class people who live middle-class lives.

In the past when the church has considered beginning a work in a new area we became concerned about erecting a building. Does the church suffer from an 'edifice complex'? Our buildings witness to our inflexibility. 'As soon as we erect a building, we cut down on our options by at least seventy-five per cent. Once the building is up and in use, the church program and budget are largely determined... Architecture petrifies the program' (Howard Snyder, *The Problem with Wine Skins*, p.70). Snyder argues that a fine church building may only attract the people who identify with its culture, but repel the poor.

For the first 150 years of the church's fastest growth, there were very few, if any, special church buildings. They could not have large assemblies. It was 'the church in your house' (Philemon 2).

It has been shown that the majority of people who are unbelievers will not cross a cultural line in order to become Christians. We could add to this another observation: that the vast numbers of people who are not Christians will not come into our churches... What we are seeking to convey is that a church under the Holy Spirit should be looking to grow by extending more churches in its community.

One possibility which we could consider is the idea of working out from a 'hot centre'. This was usually Paul's approach. This would mean an evangelist moving into an area and setting up a home. He would work from that centre. Through contact and a holistic ministry, he may find people who are willing to meet with him in either his home or theirs. This would be a teaching, caring community time.

As people become believers, then this would become the church in so-and-so's house. In time these people would reach the people in their own culture, remembering that experience has shown that peoples often become Christians in groups. More groups or churches would begin in time, and people would not have to be pushed through a denominational structural qualifier...

I am not arguing for autonomous, independent churches, but [for] a connecting, interdependent fellowship of churches.[4]

There are a number of such experiments in progress in newer areas of our large cities, such as the western suburbs of Sydney.

4   D. Meatheringham, 'Evangelising those outside the Church Culture through House Churches', *House Churches: A Discussion Booklet*, ed. D. Brookes, Adelaide: Uniting Church, 1983, pp.7-11. On the issue of evangelism generally, see his *Gospel Incandescent*, Adelaide: New Creation Publications, 1981.

(b) Social responsibility

Here, the term 'social responsibility' covers not just issue-oriented activities but also the responsibilities Christians have at work and in their neighbourhood. As with evangelism, there is a direct overflow from the experience of a home church into these areas.

As people begin to learn about what is involved in real caring, they become aware of what can be done *practically* for others. The extent of such help depends upon the time and energy they have and the particular gifts God has given them.

As people in a home church begin to talk about their work situations, and the problems or opportunities arising from them, they gain a clearer appreciation of how to think and act Christianly on the job. Admittedly, conversation about their work dilemmas in a home church situation will only take them so far. In-depth discussion with a group of Christian colleagues is necessary if they are to come to grips with their fundamental dilemmas.

As members of a home church share with one another some of their specific social concerns, others become sensitised to various needs and challenged to do something about them. In each of these ways, experience in a home church tends to develop a greater awareness of our personal social responsibility.

In the area of neighbourhood involvement, one Baptist congregation in Melbourne has designed home churches to have a special ministry in their immediate vicinity. The people involved in these home churches are all encouraged to live in the same or adjacent street, often renting accommodation together. That way the home church is well placed to identify the particular needs of people in the street and alleviate them. This particular home church model probably works best with predominantly single, younger and childless married people in a local church setting, though it is one towards which some independent home churches would like to move. Already certain members of these buy homes near other members with that end partly in view.

Another home church, on the fringe of a large city, has had considerable outreach into the neighbourhood. As a result of personal contacts of its members and the reputation the church itself enjoys among many people in the community, this group has had an influence out of all proportion to its actual size. Financial assistance to needy families, practical help to single parents, emotional support to people psychologically or even mentally disturbed, accommodation for homeless young people, an 'open home' for lonely people wanting a chat – all this has been undertaken by a small group of fewer than a dozen people.

In the vocational area, many people involved in home churches tend to move into occupations that are meeting social needs. In one cluster of home churches, comprising only around thirty adults, the following occupations and positions were represented: regional director for several institutions for psychologically disturbed youngsters, two high-school counsellors and a third in training, principal of a special school for children with intellectual disabilities (now chairperson of the local group of L'Arche communities for the handicapped), director of a federal government aged-care programme, administrator of a resource centre for the study of Christianity and Australian society, two house-wives involved in part-time counselling, an advisor in the Commonwealth Employment Scheme, a talented musician who had a far-reaching influence on the city's cultural life, a young single woman who was a social worker. This is a very high proportion of involvement in the social, educational and cultural welfare field for a relatively small group of people.

Members of another home church were involved in a working-group of senior public servants in Canberra. Meeting over four years, it gradually developed seminars for other public servants in all Australian cities, helped organise the first-ever National Conference of Christian Public Servants in Australia, and contributed to a book arising out of the conference.[5] Three of the five key people involved came from one home church; another member of

---

5 See R. Banks (ed.), *Private Values and Public Policy: The Ethics of Decision-Making in Government Administration*, Sydney: Anzea, 1983.

the home church helped lead sessions at the conference itself. Once again, this was a concentrated and wide-reaching effort from a small group of people.

Other possibilities lie before people in home churches to express their social responsibility.

On learning of the desertion of a middle-aged mother and her two primary school-age children, one home church invited her to come with no obligations or expectations being placed upon her. The aim was simply to give her a secure environment in which to work through her pain and doubts – and to give her children a surrogate family. The family accepted the invitation, becoming vital members of the group and staying over two years until moving to another city.

Another group accepted an ex-clergyman who had left the ministry to work through his homosexual orientation. He stayed with the group because it was the only Christian community he had found in which he felt he could be honest about his situation, and yet feel accepted and loved.

One group became the home for a couple emerging from a hierarchical, quasi-Christian sect which had excommunicated them. So hurt were they and wary of any institutional church, that they lived without organised fellowship for two years. Finally, they were invited to join the nucleus of a new group. They agreed and are still members.

A person who had belonged to a Sydney-based home church wrote of the diverse, but related, efforts of all the members of his group:

The group did not have one major focus for ministry, but tended to try and support its members in whatever practical ministry they were involved in.

A lot of these ministries tended to focus around disadvantaged young people through unemployment or accommodation programmes, counselling, tutoring or teaching. Members of the community were either youth workers or committee members of management bodies for youth welfare programmes. Others participated in play groups or school-based activities.

Some served on advisory bodies to state and federal government on youth and community affairs and others taught at a nearby College of Advanced Education in welfare and teaching courses.

The vegetable co-operative (still functioning) enabled the distribution of small amounts of food to disadvantaged families. Two local youth accommodation projects also benefited from participation in the co-operative.

There are many other ways in which home churches can alleviate or creatively deal with the social problems that exist in our society. Take, for example, the vexed area of social work.

When functioning properly, church is intended to promote genuine care by the members for one another. This covers all aspects of their life. People's bodily and material needs, along with their personal and social welfare, are comprehensively catered for. This does not mean that all such needs will be met in this way. There may be exceptional circumstances or difficulties which require help from specialist agencies or skilled personnel. But many of the problems with which social workers frequently have to deal should never arise in such a community.

Paul once upbraided the Corinthian Christians for taking legal disputes between members to court, instead of searching out people from their own group who could judge them. By analogy, there are many situations ordinarily requiring professional assistance which Christians should be able to handle in their own churches. There are two sides to this. The reality of Christian community life should prevent many ordinary social problems arising. It should also support people in such a way that they can cope with more serious difficulties, such as those arising from bereavement, desertion, divorce, unemployment and disability.

The problem is that this so seldom happens and that churches have developed structures and attitudes that hinder its taking place. This failure of the church to be the church actually contributes to the present demand for expanded social services. In some cases, where church life is particularly legalistic, divisive or poverty-stricken, it even generates problems in people who did not previously possess them. The proper fulfilment of the church's role could decrease substantially the call upon social welfare agencies. When Christians belonging to such a community are also helpful to people outside, other sectors of the population are affected as well.

The early Christian understanding of care is relevant to those outside the local Christian community in another way. Its principles, suitably modified for different frameworks and cast in a secular rather than religious key, can be implemented in the everyday world of business and leisure. They can be formulated in ways which provide models for the establishment or revitalisation of other institutions in society. Although such associations would have their own particular objects, such as the production and sale of goods or the provision of leisure facilities, they can benefit from certain features of early church life.

Co-operatives for one purpose or another are a good example. Here, all members can participate in formulating the association's ground rules, in making decisions affecting important aspects of its operation and in the actual running of its day-to-day business. Here, too, limits can be set on its size so that the personal dimension is retained and constraints placed on its aspirations. It should reflect actual skills and interests of its members, rather than search for maximum profit on the one hand, or competitive glory on the other.

We think particularly of a local co-operative craft shop, numbering some sixty members and consciously set up on modified 'early church' principles. All voluntarily share in the production and evaluation of items for sale, in decisions about policy and the association's daily operations and in manning the shop they have rented and other outside exhibitions. The co-operative aims at providing an outlet for its members' skills and a community within which they can develop their craft. Any profit made by the shop is given to charity and the size of the association is restricted so that unnecessary duplication of interests or overproduction of items is avoided.

The point we wish to make about this is not that the endeavour has been successful – itself quite an achievement in our increasingly large-scale and profit-maximising business world – but rather the way it has drawn both women and men out of their aimless suburbia- or retirement-induced existence. A number have commented on the fact that they no longer need to reach for the Valium tablets or call on professional help to cope with loss of personal identity or loneliness. Genuine relationships with others have been established and a greater sense of self-worth developed. The co-operative has also practically helped those members undergoing severe strains. Indirectly, therefore, the co-operative has made a significant contribution to the lives of many of its members at all the levels about which we have been talking.[6]

(c) Cultural dimensions

According to Jacques Ellul, it is not primarily evangelism or social action which should occupy Christians today, but the creation of a distinctively Christian style of life – one that does not so much deny the world, as confront and transform it. Out of such a witness may come the germs of the new social order which we so desperately need. The ancient world, catalysed by Christianity, and the medieval world, stimulated by the Reformation, led to the emergence of new social conditions, a new type of culture and a new form of civilisation. Today, something similar needs to happen.

The quest for a distinctively Christian way of life, both individual and corporate, would ultimately give a greater impetus to our evangelistic efforts and our attempts to bring social change. Arguing that contemporary Christians are more influenced in their style of life by their social environment than their spiritual convictions, Ellul says that the search for a new style of life should embrace every aspect of life:

> our way of practising hospitality... the way we dress and the food we eat... the way we manage our financial affairs... being accessible to one's neighbour... the posi-

6 R. Banks, 'The Early Church as a Caring Community and Its Implications for Social Work Today', *Interchange*, No.30, 1982, pp.40-43

tion one ought to take on current social and political questions... the decisions which relate to the personal employment of our time.[7]

It is precisely these sorts of questions which come up and are best worked through in a home church setting. Here they are not just subjects for study, but matters which people must do something about. Concrete examples, lived joyfully and enthusiastically before one's eyes, are worth a thousand words. As Ellul stresses:

> This is necessarily a corporate act. It is impossible for the isolated Christian to follow this path. In order to undertake this search for a 'new style of life', every Christian ought to feel that he is supported by others, not only for spiritual... but also for purely material reasons.[8]

Ronald Sider picks up a similar thread in *Rich Christians in an Age of Hunger*:

> The God of the Bible is calling Christians today to live in fundamental nonconformity to existing society... The overwhelming majority of churches, however, do not provide the context in which brothers and sisters can encourage, admonish and disciple each other. We desperately need new settings and structures... What are some of the promising models of Christian community for our time? House churches within larger congregations, individual house churches and very small traditional churches.... It is in that kind of setting – and perhaps only in that kind of setting – that the church today will be able to forge a faithful lifestyle for Christians in an Age of Hunger. In small house church settings brothers and sisters can challenge each other's affluent lifestyles... discuss finances... share tips for simple living etc.[9]

---

7 J. Ellul, *The Presence of the Kingdom*, London: SCM, 1951, p.148

8 *Op. cit.*, p.149

9 R. Sider, *Rich Christians in an Age of Hunger*, London: Hodder & Stoughton, 1978, pp.163-168

Naturally, such financial commitment is easier to talk about than do. Most of us are defensive about the way we spend our money or the amount we give away. But Sider's point holds true: money should be a normal component of home church discussion.

Home churches have another contribution to make. They show how lightly the church can travel through this expensive, large-scale institutional world. They do not need costly buildings, whether churches or halls, in which to meet. They do not require complex organisational structures, with salaried officers to sustain them. They are a pilgrim church on its way to God's future society.

Other aspects of home church life help counter those tendencies in our society which lead to greater fragmentation. For example, the rediscovery of the extended family has brought people across the generations into touch with one another again. The support system provided by a home church improves communication between parents and their children, strengthens marriages and fosters healthy friendships. Given the increasing incidence of divorce, including divorce between Christians, this is a real contribution to a current social malaise.

The anthropologist Margaret Mead has raised another problematic aspect of Western society. This is what she calls the 'sexualising' of all encounter between the sexes, even at the most everyday level. The sexual dimension unconsciously intrudes, she says, in an unhelpful way, into most encounters between men and women, even if they are married, but especially if they are single. People either react by being overly reserved with one another or overly physical. A home church is one environment where relationships can be both desexualised yet, at the same time, given appropriate physical expression – through hugs, kisses and embraces.

Another way in which home churches can make a contribution is through the creation of new rituals to celebrate such events as birthdays, settling into a new house or moving away, change of seasons, special occasions in people's lives, specific city or national celebrations. These help to renew ways of celebrating with others in a culture where old rituals are quietly fading away and new ones are usually artificially programmed spectator events.

One cluster of home churches meets in a local park, aptly named 'Corroboree Park', every Australia Day to celebrate what it means to be Australian Christians. Everyone is encouraged to bring a poem, story, song, anecdote, hymn, joke, psalm, reading or meditation which has an Australian emphasis. Children take part as well as adults. Someone may speak briefly about being a Christian in our particular society or describe the plight of its more needy members. We close the meeting with thanksgiving to God, praying for our city and its people, various aspects of national life, the flora, fauna and landscape which people appreciate so much, the Aboriginal inhabitants of the land who have been so poorly treated, and for the discernment and strength to make a vital Christian contribution to our nation's life.

There are other possibilities beside these. In an article entitled 'A Biblical View of Education', Bill Andersen seeks to develop a model for education derived from the early Christian understanding of home church life, with its strong holistic, participatory and family-type character.[10] The experiences of contemporary home groups could help fill out the provocative and exciting suggestions he makes.

In another article entitled 'Politics, Vision and the Common Good', ethicist Stanley Hauerwas points out that the democratic society in which we live did not begin primarily from abstract doctrines, but from the living experience of the Puritan congregations as a fellowship of equals. As a consequence, he says, the most lasting contribution the church can make to politics is not statements about particular issues, but to 'be itself', a genuine community.[11] Here are new insights about the nature and structure of a participatory style of democracy, to offset the creeping centralisation and bureaucratisation of modern government.

10 W.E. Andersen, 'A Biblical View of Education', *Journal of Christian Education*, Papers 77, 1983, pp.15-30

11 S. Hauerwas, 'Politics, Vision and the Common Good', *Vision and Virtue: Essays in Christian Ethical Reflection*, Notre Dame: Uni. of Notre Dame, 1981, pp.239-240

Although it may sound pretentious to talk about the potential influence of home churches for the wider educational and political world, we need only remember the contribution made by the fragile, scattered early Christian communities – or later Anabaptist, Quaker and Puritan groups – to existing forms of educational and political life.

Beyond our own Western culture we have to look to the global village, particularly the Two-thirds World. Here, too, home churches can make a small but crucial contribution. As Jean Vanier points out:

> Communities which live simply and without waste help people to discover a whole new way of life, which demands fewer financial resources but more commitment to relationships. Is there a better way to bridge the gulf which widens daily between rich and poor countries?[12]

A corporate embodiment of a simpler lifestyle takes pressure off the resources of Two-thirds World countries and is more likely to awaken the consciences of people in the affluent West than occasional hand-outs, weekends of fasting or appeals to governments to increase the proportion of foreign aid. Also, by improving the quality of relationships, helping people integrate their private and public roles, we learn how to live in, without becoming overwhelmed by, a technological society. Developing countries need such concrete models, learning from our mistakes as they work their way through their own industrial and technological revolution.

Conclusion

We began this chapter with a discussion of the distinction between 'church' and 'mission'. Paradoxically, while still separate concepts, the two can be combined. First, with respect to evangelism.

In his prophetic book *A Theology of the Laity*, Hendrik Kraemer argued that by developing new forms of fellowship and community in the church:

---

12 J. Vanier, *Community and Growth*, Sydney: St Paul, 1979, p.234

...a greater act of evangelism would be done than all evangelistic campaigns together... The direct approach has no great promise, because the de-religionising of vast sectors of people in modern society has deep-seated and long-range historical causes. The indirect approach, by really being communities of mutual upbuilding, of witness and service, by building in the desert of modern life genuine Christian cells, is the one indicated... For the world wants to *see* redemption. It is not interested in its being talked about.[13]

Second, with respect to social action. Art Gish writes in his *Living in Christian Community*:

Our primary work in social change goes beyond changing the hearts of individuals or transforming power structures, for it comes from the understanding that the main social structure through which God's redeeming work is effected in the world is the Christian community. Our energies for world betterment are channeled through the church, for our hope for a new social order is found more in the church than in the world. Our best efforts at 'saving the world' are directed toward building up the body of Christ, the first-fruits of the new order.

The creation of Christian community is the most radical political action one can ever experience, especially if it involves breaking down social barriers, proclaiming liberty to the captives and establishing justice. It is the coming to concrete reality of a new life that will not only show what is wrong with the old, but point so clearly to the new which is possible that the old can no longer command our loyalty and devotion... Our responsibility to the world is always first to be the church: to embody what God wants to say to the whole world, to live and demonstrate what salvation means.[14]

Third, with respect to cultural transformation. As the well-known historian, Herbert Butterfield, tirelessly insisted:

---

13 H. Kraemer, *A Theology of the Laity*, London: Lutterworth, 1958, pp.177-179

14 A. Gish, *Living in Christian Community*, Sydney: Albatross, 1979, p.293

... the strongest organisational unit in the world's history would appear to be that which we call a cell; for it is a remorseless self-multiplier; it is exceptionally difficult to destroy; it can preserve its intensity of local life while vast organisations quickly wither when they are weakened at the centre; it can defy the power of governments; and it is the appropriate lever for prising open any status quo. Whether we take early Christianity or sixteenth-century Calvinism or modern communism, this seems the appointed way by which a mere handful of people may open up a new chapter in the history of civilisation.[15]

Home churches are not the only form of church life which can fulfil this responsibility – or any of the other possibilities we have mentioned. Residential communities, for example, in certain respects can embody them more. But few of us are called to live in such a context, whereas belonging to a home church is an option open to us all.

---

15 H. Butterfield, 'The Role of the Individual in History', *Writings on Christianity and History*, ed. C.T. McIntire, New York, OUP, 1979, p.24

Conclusion

MANY PEOPLE ARE CONCERNED about the state of the Christian church today. They would like to see it develop a greater sense of community and a more effective approach to mission. As a result, we are being wooed by various suggestions about how best we can go about renewing the church and reaching out to others in society. This advice seems to fall into two main categories: either 'bringing the church up-to-date', or 'bringing the church back to basics'.

Bringing the church up-to-date

Some are convinced that the chief problem lies in our theology. It is argued that we need to trade in our old doctrinal models for new, more attractive and streamlined ones. So, out with the supernatural, out with anything that smacks of myth, out with all the traditional jargon that no one understands any more.

Others would point the finger at the church's lack of involvement in society. Its one-sided preoccupation with the private sphere and its reactionary attitudes to moral and political questions are regarded as the chief stumbling block to its wider effectiveness. It is thought that only a radical change in its social outlook can turn the tide of increasing public indifference.

A few would regard the church's organisation as its biggest liability. From top to bottom a more businesslike approach is required. This means helping clergy and lay-people to become more efficient in managing their time, to gain a clearer understanding of their target audience and to advertise their presence more effectively.

Lastly, some would identify the cultural gap between Christians and their surrounding society as the key problem. The crucial task is thus seen as that of indigenising the church so that its architecture, worship and beliefs become more accessible to the average citizen. The church needs to be 'more Australian', 'more working-class' or 'more relevant'.

Now each of these proposals has a real point, but they inevitably leave out a vital element. Without getting caught up in detail, let us quickly identify their respective strengths and weaknesses.

We do need a more contemporary theology. But this has less to do with jettisoning traditional formulations in favour of more transitory, up-to-date ones than with taking theology out of its professional, academic setting into the everyday world. If we did that, we would find a language for the enduring claims of the gospel: the language we use in daily life and conversation.

It is also true that we need to be more involved in society. However, this does not mean turning the Christian church into a social and political entity. Important though it is to grapple with such issues, the real forces which shape our society operate at a more subterranean and intimate level. Only the rebirth of a genuinely prophetic vision will identify these and tell us how to deal with them.

Again, we cannot deny that Christian institutions are generally far less effective than they should be. This is why we can learn something from that codified commonsense that marks much business thinking. But the gospel is fundamentally at odds with managerial approaches to church life. There is a danger of overlooking the slower, deeper, ultimately more efficient methods that the Holy Spirit generally uses.

As for indigenising our Christianity, by all means let us proceed as vigorously as we can. But at the level of attitudes – to time, property, organisation and money – people in churches are far too Australian and Western already! We need both a critique and a celebration of our Australianness if we are to execute this task successfully. All these changes will bring about renewal in only a limited way. They will certainly make the life that already exists in the church more understandable, relevant, effective and accessible. But of themselves they cannot generate new life. They may create the conditions by which this is made possible, but they do not bring it into being.

Getting back to basics

The Second Vatican Council encouraged Catholics to rediscover what it means to be the people of God and a pilgrim church. Ecumenical statements speak similarly of the need to become a servant church, involved in creating a responsible society. The emphasis here is upon recapturing certain basic Christian qualities in the life of the church.

Among Christians from predominantly Reformed and conservative circles, clarion calls have come for a new reformation of corporate Christian life. This entails a revival of expository preaching, the practice of baptismal discipline and a return to the office of eldership. It also involves a strong emphasis upon teaching the basic Reformed doctrines and creating a theologically informed laity.

Those influenced by the charismatic movement, or by the new interest in spirituality, stress the importance of personal renewal. The place of small fellowship groups, or of weekend retreats, in bringing about this renewal is emphasised. These are also intended to have implications for the corporate life of the congregation and for the general welfare of society.

The church growth movement, both in its older mission theology and newer mass-church forms, is also prompted by certain biblical impulses. However these also encourage it to take contemporary conditions seriously. In particular, the church growth movement stresses certain sociological factors involved in effective outreach and church planting.

Now, each of these proposals has a point but also some real inadequacies. Reminding people that they should have a pilgrim or servant mentality is no small thing. But if this is the churches' calling, why do they continue to carry such a heavy burden of physical plant, complex organisation and unnecessary tradition on their back? Where are the radical *structural* changes to accompany the stirring ecclesiastical rhetoric?

Proclamation of the word and a clear understanding of the church's role also have their place. It is also important to have a theologically articulate laity. But while preaching and teaching stimulate understanding, they do not necessarily touch other aspects of our personalities or bring a change in ethical behaviour. Nor do structural reforms in the church guarantee an enlarged experience of community and a wider sense of vision in the church.

The charismatic movement's emphasis upon the gifts and responsibilities of all church members certainly moves in this direction. But often it only marginally affects the dominant role of the church leader leaving unchanged traditional structures of congregational life. Personal renewal through meditation, other spiritual disciplines and retreats has certainly released much-needed life into the church. But such renewal is often contained by the old ecclesiastical wineskins and does not always spill over into a struggle for the structural transformation of the church or society.

The church growth movement, in both its older and new versions, does seek a real engagement with various subcultures in society, but only at an evangelistic, not structural level. Its attempts to revitalise church life tend to concentrate on particular aspects of corporate Christian activity, for example discipling and equipping believers, leaving out other aspects of spiritual and interpersonal development. Indeed, the church growth movement treats the church as an instrument, without value in itself.

These different types of biblical reforms do contain the promise of regenerating this or that aspect of church life. But each retains too narrow a vision of what is required, not always allowing even that to have its full force. Nor do they relate their vision to the actual conditions and broader needs of the society around them.

We conclude: all these proposals have something to offer, but all offer more than they can deliver. We should listen to each attentively, but should sift carefully what each has to say. Neither singly nor combined do they provide us with the resources we need to fulfil our hopes for renewal of the church or for a greater impact upon society. We need something more if a genuine movement towards either of these two goals is to be accomplished.

Locating the missing factor

We have argued that the vital contribution of the home church in congregational life, or among displaced Christians, is the missing factor in restructuring the church for community and mission today.

We are not claiming that the home church is a panacea for all the problems Christians face, or a vehicle for fulfilling all the opportunities that lie before them. Each of the proposals for church renewal considered above has something to contribute. However, both on biblical and contemporary grounds, we believe that the home church approach is fundamental to any quest for renewal. Also it is one of the key contexts for implementing those other proposals. The home church dimension is basic to any attempt at regrouping the people of God for community and mission. It is at once contemporary *and* biblical: there are persuasive sociological and theological reasons for proceeding in this direction. It is a way of 'getting back to basics' and 'bringing the church up to date' at the same time.

For the home church approach to have its proper effect, however, it must avoid three pitfalls. First, it must never be regarded as a halfway house, that is, it should not be merely an introductory step to more conventional congregational structures. Second, the home church approach must not be seen simply as a means to some end or as a technique to achieve some objective, for example a vehicle for evangelism or a sense of fellowship. Third, it must not be introduced as an appendix to the lives of individuals or a church. Only if it is the central activity in the lives of the majority of its members, becoming the basic unit of church life, will it fulfil the potential it possesses.

Appendix:

Questions and answers about home churches

MANY QUESTIONS ARE ASKED about home churches by those who are uncertain about them or disagree with them. Sometimes these stem from a lack of understanding as to what belonging to a home church involves. Sometimes, questions arise from a false or one-sided interpretation of what the Bible says about the church or reflect a particular tradition which is simply equated with a biblical outlook. However, sometimes questions spring from perceived weaknesses in home churches that members of home churches admit to experiencing from time to time.

This chapter deals with some of the commonest questions asked about home churches: first, about home churches of any kind, even in a congregational setting; second, about the more independent groups.

Questions about home churches generally

Question: Don't people in home churches have a tendency to be inward-looking and cliquish?
Response: In our experience this is a problem which exists in theory, but not in practice. It's true that people in home churches tend to give more time to one another than do others in a congregation. This results, however, in a growing self-confidence and maturity which frees them to give more of themselves to others in the congregation. They are able to give to others outside their own group *precisely because* they receive so much from the group itself. By learning the skills

of listening, caring, praying and commitment to others within the home church, they become better equipped to use these skills for the benefit of the church at large.

Within a small group people also become more aware of their own gifts and are therefore better able to exercise these gifts in the congregation to which they belong. That is why the most effective way of deepening community in a local church is to establish one or two home churches within it, not attempt some large-scale raising of churchgoers' consciousness of their obligations in this area. The home churches gradually provide the people who can set an example for others, showing them what is involved.

Where people belong to an independent home church, the developing maturity, relational skills and gifts that come out of their life in the group can be put to the service of the wider Christian constituency and to those completely outside the church. Rather than being inward-looking and cliquish, our experience is that a far greater proportion of people in home churches are involved in inter-denominational and ecumenical activities than in the typical congregation. In fact, most of them find it impossible to contain the benefits they derive from their participation in home church within their own circle. This also applies to their involvement in wider community groups and organisations.

Indeed, as J. Oswald Sanders observed, it is the larger institutional churches which are most in danger of being inward-looking and cliquish. It is very easy to become so involved in the activities of the local church that there is no time to be involved in the world. Sadly, in some places, those who choose to give their time to Rotary, Girl Guides, Boy Scouts or other outside groups instead of church organisations are regarded as failing the church.

Question: Don't home churches breed a 'hothouse' atmosphere where everyone is expected to share their inner selves? Not everyone can cope with this.
Response: Of course, we are all like this to some extent, afraid to entrust our real selves to others. But there are those who want to share inner hopes, fears, needs and

experiences. The home church can provide a warm, safe and compassionate environment for such a person to speak, and for others to listen, share the concern, pray and honour the confidence.

As God answers the prayers of the church for such a person, and more reserved members see this happening, more of them feel confident to share too, and experience the same benefits. Sometimes it may take people a long time before they can do this to a significant degree. There will inevitably be some matters which they can share only with one or two other people in a group. There will also be some which it would not be appropriate to share with a group at all – though we all tend to draw the line here too narrowly.

Genuine giving of the self is one of the hallmarks of being a Christian, one of the essentials of 'church'. Love builds trust not only with God, but with one another. Indeed, we gradually come to see 'the God and Father of us all' in other members of the family. Presumably, that's why the apostle John tells us that we love God only insofar as we love one another (1 John 4:20). There is no need for this concern for one another to have an artificially cultivated 'hothouse' atmosphere. It can quite easily happen in a natural way, just as plants in a garden gradually grow by opening up to the warmth of the sun.

Many people find the possibility of remaining anonymous in a church or playing the role of the good Christian in a congregation contrary to the spirit of Christ and the gospel. Did Jesus remain anonymous for our sake or reveal himself to us? Did he give himself in only a limited way on our behalf or – when the time was right – all of himself in a sacrificial way? We are encouraged to follow his example in this as in all things. Thus Paul could remind the Corinthians:

> Dear friends in Corinth I have spoken frankly to you; we have opened our hearts wide. It is not we who have closed our hearts to you; it is you who have closed your hearts to us. I speak now as though you were my children: show us the same feelings that we have for you. Open your hearts wide! (2 Corinthians 6:11-13).

Question: What range of people do home churches mainly attract?

Response: Although the middle-classes do predominate in home churches in the West (as they do in *most* churches), there is a significant proportion of members who do not fit that classification. Also, from our reading of the scene in the Two-thirds World, it's quite clear that it is among the poor and the underprivileged that grassroots churches have their greatest appeal.

The character and style of a home church meeting made up of people with less formal education tends to be rather different from that of a middle-class home church. The concerns of the members are more concrete and their gatherings tend to be more informal and down to earth.

Where a home group is mixed, there comes with time and the grace of God a growing appreciation of each other's culture and the recognition that one is not better than the other, just different. It is a situation which has the potential for considerable misunderstanding and conflict as the two cultures and sets of values clash. But it is also one which has the potential for growth, not just in cross-cultural understanding, but in love, joy, peace, patience, kindness, goodness, trustfulness, gentleness and self-control – the fruit of the Spirit.

Home churches, like most small groups, initially tend to place too much emphasis upon deductive study of the Bible and upon more academic discussion of issues. This has its value for some, but means that only those whose minds work that way can participate and benefit fully. Any group which contains people with little formal education will soon find that their approach to the Bible and to discussion, though no less valuable, is different. They have a more experiential, less deductive approach to the Bible and a more anecdotal, less academic style of discussing. (This is also true of many middle class people – perhaps the majority – and of most teenagers in the group.) As a group starts to operate along these lines, more educated members in groups begin to discover additional ways of studying the Bible and discussing issues. They also begin to recognise that generally they spend too much time in study and discussion and not enough in praying and doing things together. If the group includes an intellectually handicapped person, it will often *have* to operate in this way so that that person is not excluded.

Question: How do you prevent a home church becoming a place where people share their ignorance or prejudices rather than engage in any systematic learning? Aren't they vulnerable to heresies of various kinds, particularly if there is a dominant person in the group?

Response: In any situation where one person is expected or authorised to teach week by week, there is a danger of ignorance, prejudice, imbalance and irrelevance – even if the speaker is a clergyman. The sort of teaching/learning that takes place within a home church is precisely that best suited to guard against these problems arising. First, because it encourages the participation of all present in discussion and questioning. If someone does not understand, they are free to say so. If they think what is being said is contrary to scripture, they are able to express their views. If they disagree, they are free to speak up. If they have something to contribute from their own experience – or a book they've read, a talk heard elsewhere – they have the opportunity to join in.

Second, because each group decides together what they are going to study, they are able to choose something relevant to the needs of the group or, perhaps, to an individual within it. Because it is vital to them to learn something that is relevant to their inner concerns and daily responsibilities, they are not satisfied with the airing of ignorances or prejudices. Generally, people come to home churches because they are hungry – hungry for fellowship and hungry for knowledge. They will not be satisfied with a superficial understanding any more than with superficial relationships. People also generally come to home churches with an openness to new truth. They want to discover what authentic Christianity is all about and are willing to leave behind their ignorances and re-examine their prejudices in order to do this. In other words, they are teachable and responsive to the Spirit.

Occasionally a home church isn't able to answer its own questions, even when it has gone into a subject fairly deeply. On these occasions, groups usually invite someone from outside the group to help. But it isn't only when a home church is stumped that it invites others in. Sometimes they ask in people from outside because they have their own contribution to make to the life of the church.

Now and again there is a problem with someone 'holding the floor'. This is generally a newcomer who has so many questions and thoughts bottled up inside that, when they find themselves in a situation where they are free to express themselves, it is as if the floodgates had been opened. In such cases, allowing the person to speak on for a time may begin to solve their underlying problem by giving them a new experience of acceptance and love. This may gradually remove the fear and worries that lie at the root of their volubility.

Riding a hobby horse is a different problem. Only once in our seventeen years of home church life have we met with someone who was unresponsive to the group's concern and patience in this respect. This was a man in his mid-forties for whom setting the world straight on the issue of sabbath observance was a personal mission in life. Every discussion ended up being about sabbath observance. The group invited him to take a series of studies on the topic over two or three weeks. At the end of that time when he could not persuade others to his point of view, he left, presumably in search of another group on whom he could try out his views. Such people tend to be more interested in their own ideas than in the people around them.

Question: Don't you find that a home church is too small to have an adequate breadth of gifts and resources to draw on and that the few who have outstanding gifts don't have enough scope to practise them?
Response: It is important to remember that some things are more easily learned when a group is small than when the group is large. First, members can come to understand and appreciate each other more and to recognise each others' weaknesses and strengths. Second, with God's help they

can work through what they are looking for in a church and what the Bible has to say about it. Third, they can establish certain priorities of commitment in relation to God, themselves and the world. It is much easier to work these questions through in a smaller group. This approach has an analogy in the human family where husband and wife require time to build their own relationship before the children come along.

Of course, whether the home church has few members or many is irrelevant if they are earnestly seeking to live in the Spirit. God can be trusted to provide all that is essential for their welfare. Indeed, it is often a surprise to people what a range of gifts even the most ordinary Christians have. These may include everything members of the home church would *like* to see taking place among them.

Most groups are tempted to complain at some point that they don't have all the gifts they would like or to the degree that they would prefer. It takes time to become thankful for whatever God has given and to recognise that, only by encouraging what is already there, will more gifts come their way. Perhaps this will be through the addition of new people. The point about gifts is that they are given by God so that his people can work with him to fulfil his loving purposes. When he gives people work to do, he ensures that they have the tools, the gifts, with which to do it. After all, it is his work.

In saying that God provides for our essential needs, we are not excluding visits from people in other home churches, or from those with theological or specialist knowledge. The earliest home churches counted such visits among their God-given resources, even if they did not depend on them for their week-by-week requirements.

God can also be trusted to find an outlet for those with outstanding gifts, whether it be in the wider home churches, denominational circles or some ministry to society at large. Within a home church, it is easier to discern those special gifts and to encourage those who possess them to find expression in a broader context. It is, after all, just an extension of our normal ministry to one another.

What we have found is that people of real talent are often more open to pursuing some experimental ministry. Their involvement in a home church helps them to see that people have needs additional to the ones commonly identified.

Question: Since they are without a recognised minister, do home churches tend to lack discipline?

Response: Perhaps this can best be answered by glancing at what goes on in a typical local church. How often does discipline in the New Testament sense take place within the local church? Mostly the rebellious aspects of people's lives that might require discipline are so hidden from view that no one is aware of them. Nominal attendance is also tolerated beyond the point where it is legitimate as a stage in a person's pilgrimage to a full commitment.

In a small group, however, any serious breaches in people's relationship with God or with one another will eventually come to light. Sometimes, these breaches have their roots in terrible experiences people have undergone, either in the past or the present. The individuals concerned need love and counsel rather than criticism and condemnation. Many people in home churches have gone through a crisis of faith or a crisis in relationships yet, through the patient acceptance and guidance of a group, finally managed to come through.

On a few occasions a group has had to confront one of its members, not generally with some doctrinal or moral failure but with behaviour which is harmful to the group as a whole. In cases where this has happened, there have always been positive aspects to the confrontation, all being forced to examine their attitudes and conduct.

Note the distinction between what is damaging to the group and what is damaging to the individual. It is only the first which is, strictly speaking, the province of the group. The second may be the responsibility of certain people within the group, especially those who form part of the pastoral core. However, we do well to heed Dietrich Bonhoeffer's words about the attitude that should accompany such admonition:

It will not seek to move others by all too personal, direct influence, by impure interference in the life of another. It will not take pleasure in pious, human fervor and excitement. It will rather meet the other person with the clear word of God and be ready to leave him alone with this word for a long time, willing to release him again in order that Christ may deal with him. It will respect the line that has been drawn between him and us by Christ, and it will find full fellowship with him in the Christ who alone binds us together. Thus this spiritual love will speak to Christ about a brother more than a brother about Christ.[1]

This is not an escape from tackling a problem head-on. Rather, it ensures that we only do so when it is appropriate and in an appropriate way. Because home churches develop loving relationships between members, it becomes easier for someone to accept discipline when this becomes necessary than in a less personal organisation.

But, for the most part, discipline goes on in a home church in a quiet, unobtrusive, unspoken way. It takes place, often without anyone realising it, through the words of a hymn, the reading of a scripture, the message of a study and, most especially, the passing comment, thoughtful action or example of another. Indeed, it is the open acceptance and practical concern of others which continually strikes at our consciousness, calling us to a greater love of God, commitment to each other and change in behaviour. This often operates subliminally, much as the ethos of a family – its beliefs, relationships and values – educates the children within it. Every member of a home church has a role to play here and every member has something to gain.

Question: Aren't the sorts of people who want to join home churches too caught up in their own interests to engage in effective outreach?

Response: Part of this question has been already answered in the discussion about whether home churches are inward-looking and cliquish. Here we would only add Jean Vanier's remark that 'My community is a springboard to all

1 D. Bonhoeffer, *Life Together*, SCM: London, 1954, p.26

humanity. I cannot be a universal brother unless I first love my people.'[2]

The other part of the question begs the question 'what is effective outreach'. If this is defined in a narrow way – some organised evangelistic endeavour on an inter-denominational basis – there is very little 'effective out-reach' in most home churches, as also in most congregations.

However the home church meeting itself sometimes becomes the instrument of 'outreach'. Now and again someone who is not a Christian wishes to join a home church: because they are lonely, are needing company, are in crisis, are seeking help or answers, or even because they think they are genuine believers. Here they see and experience for themselves the reality of God in the lives of others – a *living* evangelistic address, if you like. They also receive the love of God in tangible ways – through the interest and care of the members of the church. It should not come as a surprise, therefore, that as in 1 Corinthians 14:23-25, people have actually been converted in such gatherings.

But outreach also takes place in other ways. In fact, many Christians come into a home churching looking for more effect-ive ways of making their faith relevant to the people, situa-tions and structures around them. They sense that there is a compartmentalisation of their lives between private and public, spiritual and everyday, church and work. They want to reflect Christ in all their activities and relationships, in a way that is natural to themselves and appropriate to others. This leads some to integrate witness with extending hospitality, friendship and assistance to others so that it is impossible to tell where one begins and the other ends. It leads others to experiment with new forms of evangelism: from morning coffee sessions and lunchtime discussions in the park, to open evenings at home. It leads some to look for those who are needy and lonely in the neighbourhood in which they live.

Many members find their way into people-oriented or

2 J. Vanier, *Community and Growth*, St Paul: Sydney, 1979, p.20

need-oriented jobs. Others become involved in some form of community help for the more disadvantaged members of our society: the poor, the illiterate, the handicapped or the disturbed. Some try to build a sense of neighbourliness among the people around them, initiating ways of bringing them naturally together and, at special seasons like Christmas or Easter, introducing them to some aspect of the Christian story. A number are actively engaged in organisations designed to help Christians think through their social, occupational and political responsibilities in the light of the gospel.

In these and other ways people in home churches demonstrate their desire to make a contribution to the world around them, finding that the support, encouragement and freshness of home church life provides the best basis to do this.

Question: Isn't there an inherent instability about home churches? The fact that most of them fold after a while is evidence of this.

Response: The fact is that most of them do not fold after a while. A few do come to an end for quite understandable reasons, e.g. families moving interstate, members dispersing too far etc. Other groups stop because they were built on an inadequate foundation. For example, the groups might be simply an extra in a congregation's programme, their members too busy to give them the priority they deserved. Or the groups might be too homogeneous in age, lacking any older, more mature Christians who could act as a stable centre and pastoral force within it.

Some groups have ceased to exist because they tried to go it alone, falling victims to the principle that the group which seeks to live by itself will eventually die by itself. Others have come to grief as a result of poor communication patterns and inadequate problem-solving approaches. A few groups no longer exist purely because the minister gave them no encouragement or because the groups could not agree on their accountability to the wider church.

But some people have belonged to one home church for twelve years or more. In that time the group may have multiplied a number of times and therefore changed its character. Other groups have continued for five, eight or more years and show no signs of dispersing. Certainly home churches are more fragile than bricks and mortar or highly-structured organisations. But who says that a certain amount of instability is a bad thing? The family unit itself, which is the basis of our whole society, is probably the most fragile yet most durable institution we have. Too often we feel secure because we place our trust in the *wrong* things: buildings, programmes, liturgies, ministers. As Anthony Gibbings says, 'So often we make structures that give a feeling of security, but do not bring safety. Security brings protection from fears: safety brings liberation from them.'[3]

In a home church, stability – desirable as it is – comes from our degree of trust in God's faithfulness. A small group, aware of its dependence on God's provision, can be remarkably resilient, offering strength and protection to its members, particularly to those in special need. The ability of a home church to disappear without trace, should it die, would also seem to be a major advantage. How many defunct organisations have continued, draining people's time, energy and resources, purely because the problems of dissolving them were too great?

Questions about independent home churches

Question: Isn't it the case that the more independent home churches draw on the established churches for resources but don't give anything back?

Response: It's true that members of such home churches generally feel free to make use of the resources of the established churches. From time to time they invite people from denominational churches to speak to them. They may attend some courses at a theological college and make use of its library. But then both speakers and educational institutions generally make themselves available to all Christians, whatever their ecclesiastical allegiance, so there is nothing improper in this.

---

3 A. Gibbings, 'Letters of L'Arche', No.27, March 1981, p.20

In any case, some members of home churches do contribute to the life of the established churches. For example, with their college's permission, a number of theological students have spent time with home churches as part of their preparation for ministry. In one cluster of home churches two members speak regularly to clergy, theological students and missionary groups. Up to a dozen others have participated in weekend conferences for local churches, helping them develop a greater sense of community and establish home groups. A few preach or teach in other churches; two have led a mission in a mainstream church. Quite a number have been actively involved in interdenominational or ecumenical organisations. Several have a personal ministry to people in need within denominations. Money is also given to a specific denominational work. This range of activities scarcely suggests a parasitic relationship with the established churches.

Question: Doesn't the existence of independent home churches weaken the mainstream churches by taking people away from them?

Response: Home churches have never sought to draw people away from mainstream churches. They seldom advertise, they do not put out propaganda or pressure other people to join them. Almost all the people who belong to them had already severed their connections with the mainstream churches or never had any association with them. Those who leave local congregations specifically to join a home church do so mostly as a last resort when spiritually at the end of their tether.

Many home churches see one function of their existence as providing emergency relief. They provide a home for four identifiable groups: those who are 'refugees' from mainline churches, those who have grown up in the Christian counter-culture and find the established churches completely foreign, those who have worked their way out of unorthodox sects and are still suspicious of institutional Christianity, and those who have grown up in a totally non-church background. Rather than reducing the numbers in mainstream churches, these home churches are creating a place for those who otherwise would probably not belong anywhere. If denominational churches were establishing this form of community life within their own framework, there would be no need for independent home churches at all. It is because the mainstream churches are not doing this to any great extent that independent home churches exist.

In any case, what is a 'mainstream church' and what isn't? Are small churches like the Quakers or Mennonites, who have made such a significant Christian contribution, part of the mainstream? Or are they, by their continued existence, still weakening it? If home churches see themselves as pioneering something which they hope other churches will adopt – and which they simultaneously are helping other churches to develop – are they not strengthening rather than weakening them?

Question: Shouldn't those who want to belong to a home church seek to start them within existing churches?
Response: We would like nothing more. In fact, when people who belong to local congregations enquire about joining a home church, we always advise them to try and develop something within the church they are attending. If they find this impossible – the minister is against it, there are no other people interested, there are others who would like to join them but they are over-committed in the church already – we can sometimes put them in touch with another congregation belonging to their denomination where home churches are emerging. Only if they have no alternative would we suggest that they meet with an independent group. Even then we ask them whether they would like to continue attending their local church as well, in case they can still gain from, or contribute something to it.

On a few occasions people who belonged to independent home churches in one city, when they had to move to another, found a congregation moving in a home church direction and have committed themselves to it. A number of others, as already mentioned, give their time to helping local churches deepen their experience of community and begin to establish home churches. The reason why we do not all belong to denominational churches and try to develop home churches within them is that there are still very few places where this is a possibility. Where it is permitted, often so rigid is the control of what develops and so fixed the limits of such groups, that they cannot really take off. Here and there people have tried to work within one of these two situations – sometimes for many years – but have ended up getting nowhere, becoming emotionally and spiritually exhausted by the frustrations they encountered.

It is interesting, by the way, that those who say it is possible to establish home churches within local congregations are not generally doing anything about it themselves. Either they are not as serious about this as they make out or there are real obstacles to their doing so which they do not admit.

Question: Don't the members of home churches miss out on the sense of worship that you experience in a large group and emphasise fellowship at the expense of worship?

Response: It's true that many home churches initially major more on what we may call the horizontal than the vertical. This is understandable in view of the lack of real fellowship in many institutional churches. People in home churches also tend to a more natural and down-to-earth expression of their relationship with God. Since this often takes time to discover, they may feel constrained for a while in certain aspects of their meeting together. But in due course home churches seek and find a more satisfactory balance between the horizontal and the vertical and start to find more appropriate ways of relating to God.

In any case, some home churches regularly meet together as a larger group – about every six weeks. While we don't always have a 'service', frequently we do, especially on occasions like Easter and Christmas. At other times we combine 'worship' with some other activity, e.g. hearing about a missionary opportunity, learning practical skills, having some teaching, or sharing in fellowship with members of home churches in a local congregation. Sometimes we just have a picnic, go on a walk or play games with the children. But we would not see even the latter as altogether lacking in 'worship'. After all, when we take a genuine interest in each other's concerns, and when we consciously appreciate the grandeur of God's world, are we not serving one another and glorifying God?

Of course, in the New Testament the word 'worship' is never applied to what Christians do when they meet together. Worship of God was something that was supposed to characterise their whole lives, wherever they were and whatever they were doing (cf. Romans 12:1-2). The key elements in their meetings were 'service' and 'edification', i.e. they were to minister to one another and God in all that they said so as to build one another up into a genuine community and into Christ himself (Ephesians 4:11ff). *That's* the way we 'worship' God when we meet together. You don't have to be in a large group to do that, nor meet in a special building. As Jesus explained to the Samaritan woman, such worship can happen anywhere, provided it is done 'in spirit and in truth' (John 4:24).

But even if we concentrate on that aspect of meeting together in which we become particularly aware of the reality, the magnificence and the power of God, surely that doesn't depend on the size or location of the group? Otherwise you would have to say that the early Christians, who mostly met in small groups in homes, lacked a proper sense of worship. Many of us have discovered that God seems more vividly, intimately and concretely present in such surroundings. The very ordinariness of the setting and naturalness of the people highlight the extraordinariness of God and supernatural character of his working among us.

Question: Because they lack a denominational connection, do not home churches also lack a sense of tradition?
Response: We agree that some home churches are in danger of doing this. While traditions can fossilise and stultify, a community that cuts itself off from them runs the risk of losing something important. It is important to recognise, however, that home churches are endeavouring to recapture certain traditions which the wider church is in danger of overlooking. The survey in chapter 3 of this book identifies some of these. Once a home church has existed for a time, members begin to realise their kinship with certain other

groups from the past, perhaps present in a denomination other than the one they come from (e.g. the interest in simplicity of life found in Catholic orders or the social concern characteristic of the Quakers). They begin to investigate these, adapting them to the circumstances of their group.

However, home churches already draw on the traditions of many Christian groups. In music they use a mixture of Catholic and Protestant hymns, evangelical choruses and charismatic scriptural songs, as well as Christian folk music. The books they study, apart from the Bible, come from a variety of authors representing a number of different backgrounds. They are not averse to using prayers, poems and statements from whatever source they find helpful.

If, despite this, home churches still have a tendency to pay less respect to tradition than others, they would respectfully remind others that they face the opposite danger of idolising certain traditions and being trapped within them.

Question: Doesn't the lack of a confession of faith make it difficult for others to know whether home churches are doctrinally sound or not?
Response: This issue is very much a two-edged sword. Denominations which possess a confession of faith have not found it a guarantee of orthodoxy within their ranks or of vitality in their spiritual life. Most denominations now embrace a wide range of views, some of them quite contradictory and unbiblical.

Home churches are not the only Christian entities which have decided to do without a written basis of faith. Other groups, like the Churches of Christ, have no doctrinal basis and this does not seem to have disadvantaged them more than other denominations. Occasionally a home church does loosely define itself in terms of a covenant of commitment rather than a confession of faith, though such a covenant generally implies certain traditional beliefs.

Most home churches see themselves in the tradition of the earliest creeds (particularly the less detailed ones), standing on scripture as their normative authority (without committing themselves to any particular interpretation of its inerrancy or infallibility). They also regard the Spirit, who inspired the Bible in the first place and helped Christians down through the centuries apply it to their times, as still able to guide people today. They tolerate a diversity of viewpoints on matters over which many Christians traditionally have differed, but are not alone in doing this. Indeed, they regard many of the doctrines and practices which divide Christians as insufficient reasons for erecting barriers to fellowship between them.

Home churches believe that the majority of denominations have placed a one-sided emphasis upon the correctness of their doctrine at the expense of the quality of their love. This is despite the New Testament's declaration that love is greater than knowledge or even faith — though not separable from either — and that it is the depth of our love for others that tells us how much we actually know God himself.

Question: Don't the teenagers in home churches need the kind of Christian peer group that only the local church can provide?

Response: There are groups for whom this is not a problem because they have a number of teenagers within the one group. It should be pointed out, however, that those teenagers can be of very diverse personalities and interests, let alone commitment to Christ. Being in the one Christian family does not necessarily mean that they are close friends. Like adult members, they have to learn to love people very different to themselves and to accept others as they are. The inflexibility of some teenagers makes this hard work and taxes the imagination, energy, wisdom and patience of adults as they seek to set an example and occasionally arbitrate.

Some groups provide 'fellowship style' activities not only for their own teenagers, but for others in the wider community. However the more usual pattern is to have two or three teenagers of various ages within the one home church. How big an effort is made to cater to their needs depends upon the adults. In some groups they become integrated into the church without any difficulty as young adults from around the age of fifteen or sixteen, participating along with everyone else. Other groups have not managed to do this as successfully.

Attempts have also been made by some groups to provide joint activities for teenagers. However, teenagers have often shown little or no interest in these activities, though more recent attempts at catering for sub-groups rather than all in this age-range have shown more promise. One group is also experimenting with inviting isolated teenagers from adjacent groups into their own so as to bring several young people together.

The biggest contribution a home church has to make to teenagers is the quality of relationships with adults and other children. These relationships are nurtured not only within a home church meeting but outside it, not only through what most people would think of as church activities but through simply spending time together. Operating as it does as an extended Christian family, the home church has much to offer teenagers — a breadth and depth of relationship which are lacking in society today.

In all centuries but this, young people have grown up and matured as Christians without any special groups for them in the congregation. Certainly belonging to a youth fellowship is no guarantee of Christian continuity: there is a large drop-off between participation in a fellowship and membership of the church, as those involved in youth work well know. Just as many Christian parents prefer their children to mix with a wide group of peers in a state rather than church school system, so most parents in home churches prefer their children to have a broader peer group than the more usual Christian-oriented one.

Because so many children of Christian parents don't establish friendships with non-Christian peers, when they are older they neither have nor know how to develop quality relationships with non-Christian people. This is a key reason why adult Christians today engage in so little personal evangelism with their friends, colleagues and neighbours.

Question: What do people in independent home churches do about baptisms, marriages and funerals?

Response: If parents desire their children to be baptised, this occurs. The parents decide who it is they would like to perform the baptism at church and the form they would like the meeting to have. Adult baptisms do not present any difficulty either. You do not need an official person or formal liturgy to carry out an effective baptism, even by general church standards.

Where a home church member has married someone from another denomination, the couple has arranged with a minister either to have an informal ceremony in a home or out-of-doors in which there was opportunity for others to participate. Those who are coming up to marriageable age seem to prefer a civil ceremony, followed by a celebration in the home which includes prayers, songs, teaching, pledges of support and fellowship around the Lord's table. Or it would be possible for someone in a group of home churches to get a celebrant's licence.

It is not necessary to have an officiating clergyman for a funeral (nor even someone from a funeral parlour). Instead, we would have a gathering in the home of the person who has died, with their family, friends and other home church members. There we would celebrate the life of the one whom God has taken to himself – in stories, song, prayer, testimony, scripture, exhortation – with everyone able to participate in some way. We would also work out what practical help we could give the bereaved. This could include arrangements for the burial – even the actual burial itself where people desired it.

Question: Since these home churches don't have a full-time minister to support or a special building to maintain, what do they do with the money they give away?

Response: Because home churches do not have pastors or own buildings, members of home churches are able to give more freely to other people or organisations whether evangelistic or humanitarian.

Occasionally, a member of a home church moves into 'full-time' work – not among home churches (they do not require this) but among non-Christians or to the wider church. Even then, such people are generally supported on an individual basis, not out of any corporate funds. Home churches mostly follow the Pauline injunction that each person or family should set money aside for God's work and distribute it at the appropriate time (1 Corinthians 16:2). Where money is set aside *corporately* for a particular project, members decide *together* who will receive it.

People in home churches quite often give financial help to a needy person in their own or in another group, jointly or individually, without everyone knowing.

Question: Isn't it a problem for independent home churches that they have no physical witness in the community and no minister whom people outside the church can recognise?
Response: Does a lack of buildings necessarily mean there is no physical witness in the community? Our neighbours have commented a number of times about the 'parties' we have on Friday nights (presumably the singing and laughter they heard led them to conclude this!). That enabled us to explain that we were, in fact, 'churching'. The mere fact that a number of cars are parked outside a given home regularly indicates to people that 'something' goes on there. It's amazing how quickly the word spreads that it is in fact a 'church'. The very novelty of the situation ensures this.

The individuals and families of a home church more than anything else provide the 'physical' presence of church in the community and see themselves as 'ministers'. Because they are scattered they provide a number of 'ministers' in a community rather than just one. Isn't that what Jesus had in mind when he talked about 'salt' and 'light' in Matthew 5:15-16 and what Peter meant when he talked about Christians as a 'holy priesthood' in 1 Peter 2:5?

Some would argue that they have an advantage by having a building. But buildings can deter as much as attract people – some look unwelcoming or irrelevant. Remember, too, that the period of greatest expansion of the Christian cause took place in the first few centuries after Christ's death *before* the church had special buildings or separate clergy. It was the quality of the lives of the early Christians which influenced the wider community, not the grandeur of the physical plant.

Conclusion: There is one final reservation about home churches that we ought to mention. It is this: will not home churches eventually join together and become just another denomination like so many other new groups in the past?

There is little evidence in the home churches themselves, even the most independent ones, of any desire to become a denomination. In fact, by deciding not to own property, have official leaders or develop interlocking structures, they have deliberately attempted to guard against it. While home churches see themselves as fulfilling a responsibility to the spiritually homeless, many people within them are endeavouring to persuade the mainline churches to see that this is what they should be doing themselves. In other words, the members of independent home churches are trying to work themselves out of existence.

If the mainline churches take up the challenge, there may not be a need for such independent groups – and no need for congregational or inter-denominational home churches to break away. But if the mainline churches do not take up the challenge (or do so in a half-hearted or over-regimented way), then the independent home churches will have no option but to continue. As long as they find people bleeding by the roadside while mainline churches offer no help, home churches will stop to bind their wounds and exercise hospitality to them.

So then, whether or not home churches continue as an independent entity depends partly on whether or not sufficient mainline congregations restructure themselves around home churches as the basic unit of their life. But there are also people in home churches who would not wish to join an institutional church which had developed home churches within it. Such people have profound objections to supporting an organisation which invests so much money in building, so much time in meetings and so much effort in maintaining a hierarchical ministry and structure. Only if changes were also made in these broader areas of church life could these people with good conscience think of returning to the institutional church.

*   *   *